AFRICAN VOICES

OF THE ATLANTIC SLAVE TRADE

African Voices
of the Atlantic
Slave Trade

Beyond the Silence and the Shame

ANNE C. BAILEY

BEACON
150

Beacon Press

BOSTON

Beacon Press
25 Beacon Street
Boston, Massachusetts 02108-2892
www.beacon.org

Beacon Press books
are published under the auspices of
the Unitarian Universalist Association of Congregations.

07 06 05 8 7 6 5 4 3 2 1

This book is printed on acid-free paper that meets the uncoated paper
ANSI/NISO specifications for permanence as revised in 1992.

Composition by Wilsted & Taylor Publishing Services

Library of Congress Cataloging-in-Publication Data

Bailey, Anne C. (Anne Caroline)
  African voices of the Atlantic slave trade : beyond the silence and the
  shame / Anne C. Bailey.
      p. cm.
  Includes bibliographical references and index.
  ISBN 0-8070-5512-3 (cloth : alk. paper)
  1. Slave trade—Africa, West—History. 2. Slave trade—America—
  History. 3. Slave trade—Ghana—History. 4. Anlo (African people)—
  Social conditions. I. Title.

  HT1331.B34 2004
  306.3'62'096—dc22   2004015082

By God's grace, this book is dedicated to my mother,
Daphne Isabella Bailey—teacher, educator, counselor, and
fountain of unending support—and to my son, Mickias Joseph.

CONTENTS

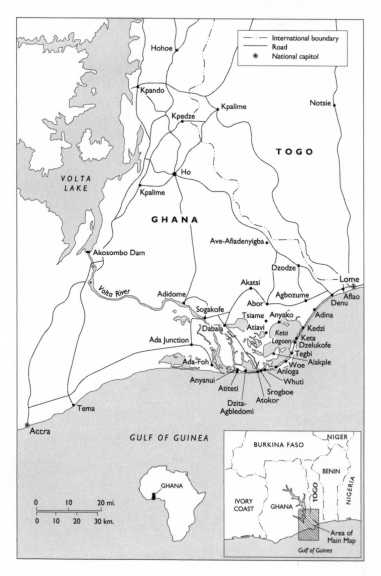

Southeastern Ghana

(From Guerts, Culture and the Senses
© 2002 The Regents of the University of California)

CHAPTER I

From the Middle Passage to Middle Quarters, Jamaica

The Transformation of a Personal Journey

In southern Ghana along the stretch of land off the Atlantic coast formerly known as the old Slave Coast, now known as Eweland, on many a night the striking rhythms of the drums can be heard from many miles away. They are so sure, so insistent in telling their story. With the Ewe talking drum leading the pack, stories of long ago are revealed one by one.

Yet we do not know the whole story. Here and on the other side of the Atlantic, in fact wherever people of African descent are to be found, there is a deafening silence on the subject of slavery and the Atlantic slave trade. All that remains are fragments which, like the scattered pieces of a broken vase, do not represent the whole. Under the silence are palpable sighs of regret, pain, sorrow, guilt, and shame.

Even before the publication in 1969 of Philip Curtin's seminal book, *The Atlantic Slave Trade: A Census,* historians and others have been engaged in debates and analyses of the effects of the trade on African societies. In *A Census,* Curtin attempted the first scientific study to determine the numbers of Africans who were taken from the shores of Africa and brought to the New World. W. E. B. DuBois was an early pioneer in this field, with *The Negro* in 1920 and later *The Suppression of the African Slave Trade, 1638–1870*. More recently, other authors, including the Nigerian Joseph Inikori in *Forced Migration: The Impact of the Export Slave Trade on African Societies* (London, 1982), have also participated in this debate. Also noteworthy are the works of Paul Lovejoy, Patrick Manning, Michael Gomez, and Boubacar Barry, who have made important contributions to the study of slavery and the transatlantic trade.[1]

The story of the trade, however, has rarely been told from the perspective of those who suffered the most. What remains to be done is the placing of *African* voices of this era at the center of any historical enterprise. No full and thorough analysis of African records—in particular oral records—has been attempted. Most historians have written about the trade using records of European traders and American planters, with only marginal references to oral history material. Yet European and American records, while important and critical to the study of the slave trade, do not sufficiently illuminate the African view of the trade as remembered by chiefs and others whose families were profoundly affected.

One possible reason that such a project has not been undertaken is because of the silence on the issue of slavery in Africa. With the exception of slave narratives such as those from the Federal Writers' Project of the Works Progress Administration (WPA), over 2,300 accounts of history as told by former slaves to mostly white interviewers from 1936 to 1938, this silence is mirrored in African American, Caribbean, and South American communities.[2] This book focuses on the few stories that *have* been remembered: the memories of the Anlo Ewe community, residents of an area in southeastern Ghana once famously called the old Slave Coast. Their memories of the slave trade—in particular of the nineteenth-century trade—are at the center of this work. These oral histories are also a starting point for bridging the gap between narratives in Africa and the Diaspora, in this way contributing to African Diaspora studies.[3] In sum, the underlying thesis of this project is the examination of the silence, memory, and fragments of the history of slavery and the slave trade as it pertains to both sides of the Atlantic.

Two key themes that emerge from this study are the questions of agency in the Atlantic slave trade and the impact of the trade on Anlo Ewe society and, by extension, other African societies. Starting with the assertion that the two themes are interrelated, I assess the impact of the trade in light of the various roles played by both European and African traders. I closely examine the *transformations* of the slave trade throughout the centuries, culminating in its last phase, 1850–90.[4] This period coincides with the revival of the trade precipitated by the tremendous demand of plantations in Cuba and Brazil. Moreover, 1850 marks the first serious attempt by the British, after years of resistance from the Ewe community, to extend their rule over Anlo territory by the purchase of slave forts from the Danes. Finally, this last phase of trade was characterized by an acute disruption in previous trading practices and operations—a change that had devastating effects on African social and political institutions.

Integral to this study is my own personal history or position vis-à-vis the silences in the history of slavery. As oral historian Alessandro Portelli says, in oral history "the narrator is now one of the characters, and the telling of the story is part of the story being told."[5] In other words, this kind of project requires a certain amount of personal involvement. Growing up in Jamaica, I was engulfed by this silence. Slavery and the slave trade were not exactly taboo subjects, but they were not subjects that many Jamaicans readily discussed. But in the midst of the prevailing silence, there were intriguing whispers of the stories of our past. In writing this book, I have been inspired by both personal and professional stories that linger along the contours of my own family history and our collective memory. Unlike Alex Haley in his groundbreaking *Roots,* however, I did not set out to trace a linear history from Africa to the Caribbean. Though there is great value in such research and much more of it needs to be done, my primary aim was an academic enterprise that would be a contribution to the study of the Atlantic slave trade much like those of the authors mentioned above, with a concentration on what could be learned from oral data.

At the same time, this enterprise admittedly comes from a very personal motivation. I found that my position—as a native of Jamaica, as a child of African descent whose history has been profoundly affected by slavery and the slave trade—was not something to hide under the false cover of "objective" research. To explain why the oral stories of the Anlo Ewe community in Ghana have consumed my efforts for almost fifteen years, I will have to start with the story of my own family and my own origins—that which is known and that which I still wish to know.

My origins, as is the case with far too many people of African descent in the Americas, are shrouded in mystery. Though my ancestors were likely slaves, I do not know their names. I do not know their port of embarkation in Africa, nor do I know their port of entry in Jamaica. My family history does not begin from the beginning as one would normally expect. Instead, it largely centers around my grandfather, David Cowan Barnaby (DCB) Ramsay. Born December 28, 1885, DCB Ramsay was a teacher's teacher and was said to have been a formidable man in his day. Born to a visionary mother named Bethsheba and David Sr., a farmer, in the rural village of Middle Quarters in the parish of St. Elizabeth, Jamaica, DCB Ramsay was destined from an early age to move beyond the confines of his little village. When he was just a boy—so the story goes in my family —Bethsheba looked beyond the small farms and the surrounding hills of Middle Quarters to a school on the hill called Full Neck and said, "You see that school? You will teach there one day."[6]

Without being literate herself, she had fashioned in her heart and mind a dream for her son that he would one day exceed. He eventually won a teaching scholarship to Mico College in Kingston under the mentorship of a teacher called Mr. Gushie, whose wisdom he was to quote much of his life. From Mico, DCB Ramsay went on to be a teacher and eventually a headmaster at schools in Porous, Nazareth, Magotty, and other areas around the island. Even now, in certain quarters of Jamaica, when people mention "Teacher Ramsay," they speak with a reverence and respect for the sound principles he represented, for he was not only a teacher in the classroom but also a lay preacher in the Moravian Church.[7]

Bethsheba, who was also called Miss Marma, the mother who had believed so much in her son, was by all accounts a fiery woman. She was a tempestuous lady with a strong spirit who, according to oral history, "used to ride a horse sidesaddle, in her gown and everything"—this in the days when women did not ride sidesaddle. People also said that "she had a mighty mouth and was proud of being black. She was like an African princess.... Everyone would just bow to her."[8] She was more often than not very nattily dressed, and it was from her that her son David was believed to have inherited his "boasiness," Jamaican for being dashing or flamboyant. She was a natural-born leader, the kind of woman who could have achieved much in another time—and indeed she was in her own way, with the dreams she nurtured for her children and her community. She was the spirit of Middle Quarters: a woman who is still remembered fondly and vividly by those who have lived long enough to pass on the tale.[9]

But who were the family ancestors and where did they hail from? Specifically, who were the last-known slave ancestors of this firebrand woman? Or of her quieter but no less self-assured husband? Were they, like Bethsheba, also firebrands? Were they brave-hearted maroons like those of Accompong, a maroon outpost not far from Middle Quarters in this area of St. Elizabeth? What language and what customs survived the dreaded Middle Passage and made it to Middle Quarters? Finally, what strategies did Bethsheba inherit from her African-born ancestors who had survived the cruel hand of slavery?

It appears that this knowledge died with my forebears. Today, only fragments remain. Stories of St. Elizabeth, the parish where Bethsheba and David Sr. were born, revolve around the history of the maroons or runaway slaves who fought the British at every turn to retain their freedom. "They say, most blacks were from the Koramantee strain—very difficult to handle. That's why they were able to have a revolution down in St. Elizabeth in Accompong—maroon country."[10] In fact, there is a particularly strong link between Ghana and Jamaica in terms of slave origins. Slaves from the then Gold Coast came to be known as "Cormantin" Negroes—a name from the coastal port Coramantin, where the English built their first port in 1631, said to be the "first slave prison on the coast." In almost two hundred years, nearly seven million slaves were exported through this port. In Jamaica, these slaves gained a reputation in the Jamaican Parliament for starting mutinies.[11]

For this reason, it was said in the days of my grandparents and great-grandparents, that people from St. Elizabeth were a proud people. The feats of the maroons reflected well on all the residents of the area even when, as in the case of my family, there was no direct evidence of a blood relationship to the maroons. Other major influences in the parish of St. Elizabeth included the Germans who, through the Moravian Church, were intensely involved in missionary and economic development efforts in the area. Stories abound of schools, churches, and factories set up by the German immigrant community. Full Neck—the school Bethsheba used as a focal point of her vision for her son—was in fact set up by the Moravian Church, which even now maintains deep ties in the community.

What is clear from my family history is that more is known about the relatively recent past than is known about the period when my family members were undoubtedly slaves. The details that do emerge from a largely silent past are important and revealing (and also a source of pride); but they also point to the fragmentary nature of the history of the African Diaspora.

In 2001 and 2002, I undertook an investigation into Jamaican public history to determine how Jamaicans remembered slavery in a contemporary context; this investigation did not bring up much more than my own sketchy past. Though there are several scholars, such as Kamau Braithwaite and others, who have written ably about the experience of slavery in Jamaica and the Caribbean in general, there is not much material at the level of public history.[12] Jamaica, where slavery was abolished in 1833, still has many physical reminders and relics of this past. Rose Hall Plantation is perhaps the most well-known historical site of the slavery period, but there are many other such plantations all over the island. Oral histories associated with some of these sites, in particular Rose Hall, have been fodder for tourists and fiction writers alike. The story of the great white witch of Rose Hall is still told to visitors to the site—complete with conjecture about her colorful personal life, with her male slave lovers and multiple husbands: all of whom she allegedly poisoned. Some of these sites have been transformed into guesthouses or inns, in this way masking their history. The Good Hope Estate in Falmouth, for example, was a 4,000-acre estate said to be home to more than 2,788 slaves. Its owner, John Harp, was known as a rich West Indian planter. Today it is an inn for tourists.[13]

This growing practice of silencing the past is also evident in the United States, much to the consternation of those who would rather the real knowledge of what took place on these plantations be readily available to the public. As John Michael Vlack, author of *Back of the Big House,* a book about slave plantation sites, says, "The problem here is that with slavery sites, if every slavery site gets fixed up, cleaned up, essentially sanitized then how can we ever hope to narrate and reconnect to that story if nothing is even close to the way it was?"[14]

This is a valid point. Furthermore, even when slave plantation sites are preserved as they were, the story of those who labored on the plantations, kept their masters in grand style, and enabled these very sites to be the living monuments that they are today is often left out. For example, the owner of the 1812 Caledonia Farm tells visitors that the slave quarters were in fact "servants'" quarters and says of the history of slavery, "Oh it is mentioned in passing but we don't dwell on it. We don't emphasize it."[15] From sanitation to omission, it is hard to say which is worse in terms of the preservation of the public memory of slavery and the implications this has for the heirs of that legacy today. It is here that we understand the distinction raised by Carole Boyce Davies and Molara Ogundipe-Leslie and other authors in their collection between the condition of silence versus being silenced.[16]

Other outlets for public history in Jamaica include conventional museums such as the National Gallery and the Institute of Jamaica's Museum Division. In a visit to the latter in December 2001, I witnessed a revival of sorts of images and events associated with this era, including an exhibit on the practice of Jonkanoo—once very popular and prevalent all over the island, particularly at Christmastime. This African-influenced masquerade of men and women, often on tall stilts dressed in caricature, was a means by which slaves mimicked their masters under the playful guise of music and colorful masks. The survival of this practice was all the more remarkable since African customs were not tolerated on plantations.

The exhibit began with a display of African masks and then traced the influence of this and other African traditions in today's Jonkanoo performances. Interesting to note, however, is the fact that these traditions are no longer as prevalent or widespread, save for the Jonkanoo performances of the well-known Goombeh House of St. Elizabeth. As a child, I remember running to our front gate with joy at the sound of the drums and the music that preceded these tall, tall men on stilts in bright colors that mirrored the most resplendent rainbow. Children up and down the block would follow them, dancing and swaying to the music. Their presence let everyone know that Christmas was around the corner. I have visited Jamaica virtually every Christmas for the last twenty years, but I cannot recall witnessing this once-familiar scene in the capital of Kingston. Whether this is necessarily a statement regarding the association of Jonkanoo with slavery or whether in an increasingly technological age such traditions are simply dying a natural death, it is hard to tell. One thing is fairly clear, however: Jamaicans are still somewhat uncomfortable with the subject of slavery and there exists, despite a number of excellent scholarly works on the subject by authors like Kamau Braithwaite, a general lack of specific information about the era.

An interview with David Brown and Hazel McCloun of the Jamaica Memory Bank regarding a recent exhibit in a newly opened museum in Montego Bay on slavery was very telling. News of the exhibit spread by word of mouth, and before long there were crowds of people standing in line to touch the implements of slavery. They were awestruck that in addition to chains and shackles, there were also mantraps used to literally break not only the physical but spiritual will of the slave. Reaction to the exhibit was varied but uniformly intense. Some chose not to deal with it, but others, according to Brown, responded with anger: "There is still an abhorrence to what happened." Others made comparisons with the economic disparities of today, "saying it is the same thing going on." In the end, 80–90 percent of the people chose to touch the implements of destruction and torture and became upset with museum officials when it was closing time and visitors had to leave.

The museum responded by extending its hours to accommodate the visitors.[17] The intense reaction to this exhibit may suggest that there is clearly renewed interest in slavery, but it also reveals that much of what was commonplace in this awful period is still not commonly known.

No, we do not know the whole story on our side, but as I was to find out in my travels and work in Ghana, we are not alone. There, too, is a silence on the issue of slavery—albeit for different reasons and different motivations. Fragments remain only slightly above the surface in an otherwise shallow well of memory. This was and is all the more surprising since in Ghana, as in many parts of the continent of Africa, family histories are greatly prized, and genealogies are lovingly passed down as precious family heirlooms.

As a preface to every interview I conducted in Eweland in southeastern Ghana, interviewees volunteered their family genealogy, often offering important details of the lives of clan members along the way. It was not uncommon for someone to go back eleven or so generations without having to consult a written document or record. They had also committed to memory details about important events in their history. For example, each year community members memorialize the last important exodus of the Anlo Ewes, which took place in the late seventeenth century. This migration brought them from an area called Notsie in modern-day Togo to where they live now by the coast of the Atlantic bordered by the Volta and Mona rivers.

Thus there is little question that the Anlos revere their history; yet on the subject of the slave trade, a subject they should doubtless know a great deal about, very few stories have been retained and retold, here as elsewhere in Ghana. What is behind this silence? How can a period of more than three hundred years in some areas on the continent (and for the Anlos from the seventeenth through the nineteenth centuries) be almost collectively forgotten even in light of the many slave castles and forts that still dot the landscape of Ghana and many other West and Central African countries?

On one level, there is a kind of shame associated with slavery that goes deeper than the Atlantic slave trade and its operations. Domestic slavery, which existed before its Atlantic counterpart, is a subject that most Ghanaians do not readily discuss. It is not considered proper to discuss or divulge someone's slave origin even if, by now, this origin has no practical or detrimental effect on the person's present life. As Ghanaian scholar Kofi Awoonor points out in his review of Ewe oral literature, "one of the most fearsome insults centers around slavery." Traditional griots such as Komi Ekpe used their awareness of this shame in performance of what is called halo poetry. Halo is the performance of poetry that includes insults of a particular person or a group. It was often used as a means of diffusing real-life conflicts since it was an opportunity to insult or criticize an offending party without resorting to violence. In fact, until it was banned by the British colonial authorities in the early twentieth century, halo was considered a useful social practice since it helped community members to express their grievances in a nonviolent manner.[18]

But even in halo, there were certain taboos and boundaries. To call someone a slave or his or her mother a slave was off-limits even within this kind of playful banter. The term was thought to be particularly offensive because before the intensified pursuits of the Atlantic slave trade, domestic slaves were usually criminals or debtors sold into slavery. Domestic slavery played the role prisons serve in industrialized societies. This stigma remained long after most of those who became slaves were taken from the general populace and suffered their new status through no fault of their own. The oral accounts I collected corroborated this view that the descendents of slaves do not take kindly to the mention of previous slave status in their families. Many, in fact, resorted to changing their names to bury this past. This shame has lingered even though there is now ample evidence that domestic slavery was a marginal economic and social force before Atlantic slavery took off in the fifteenth and sixteenth centuries. In fact, domestic slavery became a significant phenomenon in Africa only by the nineteenth century, when it was influenced by global forces and demand.[19]

In her thirteen-year investigation into the subject of slavery in all ten regions of Ghana, Dr. Akosua Perbi found that domestic slaves and servants were indispensable to chieftaincies in precolonial Ghana. She shows how slaves were vital not only to the maintenance of the political realm but to the economy, the military, traditional religious groups, and other social institutions. She goes so far as to suggest that the very concept of chieftaincy is deeply associated with the servitude of others, quoting an 1870 statement from the Okyenhene in Kyebi to support her claims: "Must I let my horn blowers, my drummers, my pipers, my sword bearers and executioners, my hammock carriers etc become Christians? If I do, then I can no longer carry out my ceremonies nor can I receive foreign embassies worthily. Whoever has an obligation to serve me, will never be allowed to become a Christian." This was his reply to Basel Missionaries at Kyebi regarding the possible conversion of those who attended to his needs.[20] It is, of course, not uncommon for regal authorities to have attendants who play a variety of roles. Certainly one of the things that distinguishes the Queen of England, for example, from a so-called commoner, would be the many people who attend her—from ladies-in-waiting to guards. The issue here is one of servitude and slavery, and the question is still open to debate: To what extent were Ghanaian societies dependent on different forms of servitude and how widespread was the practice?

Though there are varying views on this subject, it is fair to say that one impact of the history of servitude—whether it was marginal or widespread—is that there is now a shame attached to slave heritage. Much of this shame seems to be associated with the domestic forms of slavery, with reference to specific individuals in specific communities. There are recent stories, for example, of individuals who were in line for the position of chieftaincy in their home communities but who, at the point of decision, were disqualified because someone raised the issue of possible slave heritage.[21]

This shame regarding domestic slavery may very well have had an impact on the understanding and memorialization of Atlantic slavery, even though the forms of slavery were by definition quite different.[22] Chattel slavery in the Americas meant servitude in perpetuity. There were few ways out of such a system, which was codified in law. African slavery was much more varied and sometimes included ways in which slaves could rise above their station and even become chiefs. Still, it stands to reason that if there is a tacit taboo against divulging slave origins on the domestic level, such a taboo might be transferred to discussions of Atlantic slaves. This may be one reason for the silence on slavery.

Interestingly, for some groups that have an equally painful past, there has been an opposite reaction. Why, some have asked, do Jewish populations, for example, painstakingly remember while black populations largely forget?[23] One can speculate only that somehow Jews do not see their victimization as a kind of *permanent* powerlessness. In fact, they see the memorialization of their escape from slavery in Egypt and their survival of the Holocaust as opportunities to assert their agency. It is as if, in remembering, they are reclaiming their dignity and reclaiming their sense of pride while also solidifying bonds in and among members of the Jewish community worldwide.

Another reason for the silence may be connected to the history of the involvement of some Africans in the sale of others in the Atlantic slave trade. The question of African participation or agency in the trade, treated in detail in chapter 3, is a contro-

Author with tour group from Bono Manso and the Center for Savannah Civilization, touring old slave sites of downtown Accra.

Photo: Anne C. Bailey.

versial one that raises deep questions and problems on both sides of the Atlantic. Often this participation is examined in a vacuum outside of the context of the very real and dynamic external European and American forces that played a key role in the trade from demand to supply. The reality is that in the operations of the Atlantic slave trade, five of the six legs of the trade were exclusively controlled by external forces in America and Europe. The Harvard University Archive of over twenty-seven thousand slave ships, though it represents only a small fraction of the total number of slave ships that participated in slave traffic, attests to the depth and influence of such involvement. Furthermore, this issue of African agency is also often raised without much discussion of the ways in which some African societies resisted both internal and external forces and protected their communities from the trade. For these and other reasons, a natural defensiveness may arise when this subject is broached.

Finally, even though the colonial period in Africa lasted not longer than seventy years in some parts—a considerably shorter period than the Atlantic slave trade—it is the most recent and thus the effects and memories of this period are still fresh. New nations (the oldest of which is Ghana at forty-seven) are still struggling with "the burden of the past" of their colonial forebears; they are still grappling with institutional structures set up largely with Europe, not Africa, in mind as well as with the psychological legacy of having been occupied by a foreign force and forced to speak and operate in a foreign language. In such a context, the era of the Atlantic slave trade may seem very far away, if not unrelated to present, more pressing concerns. As one oral narrator, Kojo Jantuah, responded to the question of why the silence: "Firstly, it was a very painful past. Secondly, the intensity of colonialism prevented Africans from getting the necessary space needed to reflect on their own history. People are continually struggling to meet their basic needs."[24] Still, as will be shown in this study, the fact is that it was the era of the Atlantic slave trade that allowed for the slow but steady erosion of indigenous institutions, which in turn allowed European colonizers easier access and control over African societies.

Another possible reason for the silence on slavery may be discomfort with the issue of modern-day slavery in West Africa and other regions. The awful business of slave trafficking, according to those who have been tracking such efforts, is still alive in many parts of the world, including Asia, South America, and the African continent. The cases of slavery in southern Sudan and Mauritania are more well known, but according to one report, there are over 284,000 children at work in hazardous conditions in West Africa's cocoa industry. Many of these children are believed to be slaves. They end up on cocoa farms that contract with the major chocolate manufacturers in the West, such as Hershey.[25]

It must be said that there is no hard evidence of such slave activity taking place on cocoa farms in Ghana. In fact, the largest cocoa producing cooperative in Ghana, Kuapa Kokoo, has the distinction of being one of the few such operations in West Africa that bears the FAIRTRADE mark. This means that growers are assured of fair prices and a living wage.[26]

The practice of slavery in the form of *trokosi,* or female religious servitude, does, however, exist in southeastern Ghana, Togo, Benin, and Nigeria. Two centuries after the abolition of the slave trade, slavery continues in the form of "traditional" practices. Trokosi is a form of servitude in which a young woman is forced to serve a local religious order or shrine in atonement for some debt incurred or offense committed by her family. It is an institution left over from the eighteenth and nineteenth centuries that persists in spite of bills banning the practice passed in Ghana in 1998.[27] This is a very disturbing reality.

There is also the occasional report of foiled attempts at human trafficking. At the time of this writing, an article appeared in the Ghanaian newspaper, the *Chronicle,* with the following headline: "Couple Sell Child for 38 Million Cedis in Nkawanda Near Nkawkaw." In the end, the couple was arrested for conspiring to sell a three-year-old boy.[28] Notwithstanding the occasional article such as this, however, here as elsewhere around the world there are few spotlights on the issue of modern-day slavery. In spite of the fact that the UN and most European and African governments, for example, are on record as being vehemently opposed to slave traffic, aggressive efforts to eradicate slavery have largely been left to international advocacy organizations such as Anti-Slavery International in the United Kingdom.

I have outlined some of the reasons behind the silence on slavery on the African continent. Ironically, in the midst of this silence stand approximately fifty slave forts and castles, dotting the Atlantic coast of Ghana. Their presence so dominates the coast that one might think they would be very hard to ignore, much less forget. Historian Van Dantzig calls this coast "an ancient shopping street"; so much commercial activity in such a short stretch of coast is unparalleled in the world.[29] The overall purpose of such forts and castles was twofold: (1) to house up to one thousand slaves in holding pens on the Atlantic coast as they awaited European and American ships to take them on the dreaded Middle Passage to the Americas; and (2) to defend European interests on the coast by keeping competitors—internal and external—at bay. This was done with the help of up to one hundred guns and canons in the largest fortifications along the coast.[30]

It is, however, only in recent years that the history of these structures has been given attention. Many of them, such as Fort Prinzenstein in Keta in Eweland or Cape Coast Castle in Cape Coast, have been used for everything from schools to prisons. The male slave prison in Fort St. Sebastian in Shama, originally constructed by the Portuguese around 1520–26, is now used as a community tribunal. Christianborg Castle, in the capital of Accra, has been the seat of the government since colonial days; it performs the same function today for Ghana's postindependence government.

In 1979, the forts and castles were declared World Heritage monuments by UNESCO.[31] A decade ago, when I first came to Ghana, Cape Coast Castle and other slave forts enjoyed some

Cape Coast Castle, Ghana.

Photo: James O'Neill.

tourism but nothing compared to the immense tourist activity evident now. Ato Ashun, tour guide at Elmina Castle for the last five years, discusses this growth as well as the reaction of many of the tourists in an article in *West Africa*. All tourists, he says, are moved by the sight of the dungeons where slaves were kept for months before shipment as well as by the stories of how women were raped by their captors and other atrocities, but none more so than the many African Americans who come to visit the site, often on several occasions.[32]

Fort Prinzenstein, built by the Danes in the Anlo Ewe town of Keta in 1784 and eventually sold to the English in 1850, is now open to the public. In the year 2000, after substantial renovation work was done by the Ghana Museum Board and a local MP, Dan Abodakpi, tour guides and caretakers were hired to give visitors a glimpse of the era of the slave trade. Today Fort

Prinzenstein and other forts and castles are a routine stop on many a tourist itinerary, and there are greater resources being put into making these and other sites important destinations. African Americans and West Indians, in particular, are flocking to these historical sites in the hope of filling in some of the many gaps in information on their African origins.[33]

At the same time, though many in the Diaspora are generally glad that these historical monuments have recently been restored, Africans on the continent and Africans in the Diaspora sometimes seem to have different views about the purpose of their restoration. For Africans in the Diaspora, these monuments should not be treated as tourism "products." Though they welcome the fact that these sites will bring much-needed income to African nations, they are concerned that they should be treated in the same light as Jews and others perceive Auschwitz, Dachau, and other concentration camps.[34]

It should be said, however, that African Americans have not simply been visitors to these sites, they were also early pioneers in the effort to declare them historical monuments. As such, interest in the slave forts and castles did not begin with UNESCO's official historical declaration of these sites. Dr. Robert Lee, who came to Ghana in the 1950s at the invitation of Kwame Nkrumah, Ghana's first prime minister, spearheaded an effort to repair and restore Fort Abandze. In the 1970s, under the auspices of a new group called the African Descendants Association Foundation, Dr. Lee was given a fifty-year lease by the Ghana Museums Board to restore the slave fort with funds raised from communities in the African Diaspora.

"In those days," Lee said in an interview, "Maya Angelou and Tom Feelings were involved. We were going to use this example as a soul-searching rehabilitation exercise as it represented the relationship between Africa and its Diaspora. We felt if Africans and African Americans could get together, it would be a healing exercise. We could then deliver ourselves of [negative] mental images."[35] For a time this effort was supported quite vigorously by the Ghana Museum Board and visitors around the world.

African Americans and others who supported the African Descendents Association Foundation seemed to be once again attempting to fill in the gaps left by centuries of slavery and colonialism; even now, decades later, Diasporan communities are still drawn to the coast of Africa for these reasons, though some of are now perhaps less politically motivated than earlier visitors. African Americans in the fields of business, education, and the arts, for example, are seeking a way of life less encumbered by the realities of contemporary racism in America and are looking to bridge the cultural divide that slavery and slavery alone created. As such, it is not uncommon to find many African American and Caribbean nationals coming to Ghana at the end of the twentieth century and the beginning of the twenty-first to start cultural organizations with the aim of introducing the rich artistic cultures of Ghana and Africa in general to those in the Diaspora for whom the continent is still somewhat mysterious and distant.

Accra, the capital of Ghana, in particular, appears to be the new Paris for people of color in the Diaspora, just as Paris in the 1950s and beyond was a magnet for African American artists like Richard Wright and James Baldwin. Jazz clubs and reggae studios, including one founded by the late Bob Marley's wife, Rita Marley, are springing up.[36] In this way, those who came to break the silence of the past and to discover a part of an identity once lost are now adding to the mix their own rich cultural experience, with its unique American, Caribbean, and/or South American flavor. The silence is quietly being broken.

Black female literary giants in the Diaspora are also doing their part in to break the silence of the past. They do not hide from the ugliness but seek to probe it, analyze it, and mine from it meaning for the present and the future. In so doing, they courageously piece together the fragments of this history in their work. Thus the theme of a fragmented history that is the legacy of Africa and its Diaspora is recurrent and paramount in their works as it is in this volume. Toni Morrison with *Beloved,* Carol Boyce Davies and Molara Ogundipe-Leslie with the anthology *Moving beyond Boundaries,* Haitian Edwidge Danticat with *Krik? Krak!,* Jamaican Michelle Cliff with *No Telephone to Heaven,* and Antiguan Jamaica Kincaid with *A Small Place* all confront the "nightmare" that was slavery and colonialism, going even further to raise the question: Does a fragmented history lead to a fragmented identity? Even Cliff's use of language in *No Telephone to Heaven* indicates this sense of fragmentation. As she says in Nada Elia's *Trances, Dances, and Vociferations: Agency and Resistance in Africana's Women's Narratives,* "I alternate the King's English with patois not only to show the class background of characters, but to show that Jamaicans operate within a split consciousness."[37]

On the other side of the Atlantic, some though not many African authors have also dealt with slavery and the slave trade in the African past. Ayi Kwei Armah, Ghanaian novelist and poet, tackled the subject in his epic *Two Thousand Seasons.* His book *The Healers,* about the fall of the Asante empire and the traditional healers who see fragmentation as a lethal disease, also loosely relates to such themes. His book *Fragments* (1979), set in contemporary times, reflects on this idea of a fragmentary consciousness in the Diaspora in the story of Baako, a young man who, having traveled to the United States, returns to Ghana to make sense of his two worlds.

The main subject of this book—oral histories of the slave trade—reflects a marriage of history and literature and thus may be the perfect prism through which to explore this missing history. It could be said that this may very well be *Roots* in reverse —in the sense that instead of trying to plug all the gaps, the gaps, ironically, are the story. The fragments, the broken pieces of history and narrative that periodically, but not consistently, break the overwhelming silence on this period of slavery are at the center of this work. This silence—and, I hasten to add, the fragments of narrative—can be taken as texts of speech that when read, analyzed, and assessed with other historical sources add to our body of knowledge about the Atlantic slave trade.[38] These fragments reveal the impact of the slave trade on an African community, the complex reality of African involvement within the context of the predominant participation of European and American traders, and African resistance to the trade. Finally, these fragments of narrative in Africa correlate strongly with narratives of the African Diaspora in both concrete and metaphorical ways.

Chapter 2, "The Incident at Atorkor," brings us to the heart of my oral history collection. It is one of five main oral history tales that I examine in this text.[39] This incident, the 1856 kidnapping of famous drummers and traders by European or American slave traders off the Atlantic coast, is well known in the historical memory of the Ewe people yet is only a footnote in written historical accounts. It is what French historian Pierre Nora might call a "lieu de mémoire"—a site of memory imbued with great symbolic and/or political significance.[40] Coming as it did at the end of the slave-trade era, this incident represented an important turning point in the history of slave trading in this area and other areas in West Africa.

The significance of this watershed moment will be fully explored in this book. The story itself is a metaphor for the some of the major aspects of the slave-trade era—including African participation in the trade and the impact of the transatlantic slave trade on a particular region. It is thus a good starting point for greater discussion of such issues in the chapters that follow. Much attention will also be paid to the metaphorical elements within the narrative itself which, when analyzed, reveal what the Ewes find significant about this period. Finally, I will also consider these and other narratives within broader discussions of history and memory. Here, comparisons will be made to the history of the Holocaust and the Gulag of Russia.

In chapter 3 I will examine the complex issue of agency in the slave trade, using the Anlo Ewe example and the Atorkor incident as starting points for discussion. We look at the complex forces within and without Ewe society that drove the business of the trade. Finally, I will discuss the role of class in Africa. The idea that societies in Africa were classless before the advent of the European in the fifteenth century is a myth. In this chapter, we will see that one of the reasons some Africans participated in the slave trade has to do with their concepts of community at that time. There was a dichotomy not only between chiefs and others but also between kin and others. A complex system of kin networks determined in large part the way in which individuals interacted with others. Among the Anlo Ewe, kinship networks on the Atlantic coast were predominant in their understanding of community. Even other Ewes to the north were largely excluded from these networks, except in cases of intermarriage.

In chapter 4, we look at the other side of African agency in the slave trade—African resistance. We examine tales of resistance from both sides of the Atlantic, including the intriguing *The Slave Who Whipt her mistress and Ganed Her Fredom* by the fiesty ex-slave Sylvia Dubois. As Richard Rathbone points out, there are many examples on the continent of resistance to the slave trade.[41] In this volume, through the lens of oral narratives, we look at some of those examples within the Anlo Ewe community as well as within the communities of their African American and Caribbean counterparts.

In chapter 5, we look at the issue of European and American agency and the dominance of Europe and America in five of the six legs of the slave trade: (1) demand on plantations in the New World; (2) setup and organization in European ports; (3) setup and manning of slave forts and fortifications along the coast of Africa; (4) the Middle Passage journeys from the coast of Africa; (5) landing in the New World, including sales and auctions; and (6) industrialization of slave-made products in factories.

Chapters 6 and 7 ask readers to ponder the question: How can we measure the effects of a trade in human beings that lasted almost four hundred years? We learn from these narratives that there was a devastating effect on African societies, in particular on their social, political, and religious institutions. There was also a tremendous effect on their sense of identity and history. Like those who have suffered through a trauma of a very high degree, many Africans in West and Central Africa now experience a fragmented view of their past, which explains the blanket of silence and shame that covers the period of the slave trade for many African societies.

Finally, chapter 8 is unique in that I attempt here to connect the history of the slave trade to the history of the Diaspora through a review of the history of the reparations movement. In this chapter, we will look at how the conclusions drawn from this research on the slave trade impact historical and contemporary discussions of the issue of reparations. Two key themes emerge: reparations as redress and reparations as rememory.[42]

In sum, this volume attempts to break the silence on the issue of slavery and its modern-day implications. The purpose here is first an academic one: to add to the body of knowledge about the slave trade as well the study of the development of Western modernity. But this book has also been written in the spirit of the oral history material I collected. Just as for centuries Africans have been telling stories not simply for the sake of telling them but with a social function in mind, so do I, as a Caribbean American, hope to do the same. Bringing this subject of slavery and the slave trade to light may have the effect of freeing us from this past—thus creating a kind of catharsis, if you will, which in its best sense moves us to positive action. Beyond recriminations and accusations, may this period which, as Barnor Hesse says, is "forgotten like a bad dream," be remembered for the purpose of honoring those who did not survive it and addressing the problems and challenges faced by those who did.[43]

Still, though much will be revealed here, much remains shrouded in mystery. As said before, we do not know and may never know the whole story. Michel-Rolph Trouillot says, "Slavery is a ghost, both the past and a living presence; and the problem of historical representation is how to represent that ghost, something that is and yet is not."[44] Fragments of historical narratives point to gaps yet to be filled. For now, beyond the gaps, we look at one story from the era of the nineteenth-century slave trade that is still told along the Atlantic coast in Eweland: the incident at Atorkor.

CHAPTER 2

The Incident at Atorkor

A Break with the Past

This was the first time that people from this area were taken as slaves.
Chief Awusa Ndorkutsu of Atorkor

This chapter, in many ways the central chapter of the book, will look at the main oral historical account in this collection, which is also the one with the most documentary evidence. The incident at Atorkor took place in the 1850s and is the story of a group of drummers who were related to the chief of the area, Chief (Togbui) Ndorkutsu, the ancestor of the chief whom I interviewed in 1992 and 1993. This chief, who had enjoyed established trading relations with Europeans for decades, discovered in 1856 that slave traders had kidnapped members of his community, these respected drummers, in front of his very eyes. The incident caused storms within and without the Ewe community because it was an established norm that slaves came from the interior, not the coast. This is the primary reason that this single incident is still remembered today all over the Volta region and wherever Anlo Ewes of Ghana now reside, although so many others have been forgotten.

This is the one story that connects the university professor with the farmer and is viewed as synonymous with the era. It represents, above all, a watershed—a break with the past in terms of trading operations along the coast; a shift from organized structures and mutual agreements in the eighteenth century to disorder and chaos in the nineteenth. Furthermore, though it can be confirmed as an actual historical event, this story can and should also be read as a *metaphor* for the different phases of the Atlantic slave trade. Thus it is particularly pertinent to the themes of impact and agency. Finally, this story is significant because it represents *an independent mode of historical representation*: a unique understanding and conception of history and the process of history making consistent with important aspects of Ewe culture.

As such, this chapter presents through the retelling of this one important episode some of the larger issues regarding the impact of the slave trade on African communities and the subject of this study: What was the nature of African involvement in the trade? Of European involvement? Was it always a trade? How can this agency be historicized? And what impact did such activities and relationships have on community members and institutions?

DESCRIPTION OF THE LAND

No story is complete without an understanding of the setting. The Anlo Ewes reside in an area that borders the Volta River in Ghana and extends through Aflao to the Ghana-Togo border. They comprise the groups Anlo, Some, Aflao Klikor, Dzodze, Wheta, Ave, and Whenyi.[1] They have a long tradition of important migrations in their history. According to their traditions, the Anlo Ewes left other Ewe-speaking groups originally in the Yoruba-speaking areas of present-day Nigeria. (The towns of Belebele and Oyo are mentioned.) The second important migration was from Ketu in present-day Benin to Notsie, which is located in Togo. The last important exodus, from Notsie, took place in the late seventeenth century and represents a significant event in Ewe history.[2] Oral traditions explain in great detail the impetus for their departure from the walled city of Notsie. The kingdom was ruled well until the mid-seventeenth century, when King Agokoli came to power. Agokoli was a tyrant who imposed his will on the people. Because of his tyranny, the Anlo with other Ewes are said to have shattered the walls of the town and left in the middle of the night, migrating to their present location to settle in small villages and towns along the Volta River and the Keta Lagoon.[3] These scenes of oppression and flight are played out each year at the annual Hogbetsotso festival, in which actors challenge the oppressive "king."

It was in several venues in the Anlo Ewes' present location that the story of the slave trade was to come alive. These venues included the old slave fort, Fort Prinzenstein which, as mentioned before, has recently been renovated. Its partial remains are still to be found near the marketplace in Keta. From Anloga to Keta and beyond, neat rows of shallot crops are to be found on one side of the main road. The farming of shallots, as well as maize, cassava, pepper, and other vegetables, is the principal occupation. Bananas and sugar cane are also harvested for the production of gin. These farming plots are interspersed with diverse dwellings, from small mud huts with thatched roofs to two-story concrete buildings. On the other side of the main road are white sandy beaches that stretch along the Atlantic Ocean. There, fishermen are often seen pulling in their large seine nets that require the manpower of many men.[4] This area is also known for its unique pottery; red clay pots, finely carved or painted, can often be seen for sale on either side of the main road.

When I first visited in 1992 and 1993, I was struck by the erosion of the land, particularly in the town of Keta along this coastline. Community members spoke with sadness about this gradual erosion of the coast, which began in the early twentieth century. Some, such as former residents who have since moved to Accra or other cities, were visibly upset when discussing the situation, which at the time they felt they could hardly control. Residents of the area were just as aware of their diminishing land, often going to great lengths to explain just how big Keta had been only a few decades ago. In the early 1990s it was clearly just a narrow strip of land with a main road for vehicles, with the sea year by year approaching coastal homes and property. By 2003, however, marked changes had taken place. After years of talk about erecting a seawall, one is now being built by means of the Keta Sea Defense Project. Furthermore, the sea itself has receded, allowing room for a wide beach and much more breathing room for structures built along the ocean. Both are welcome developments that have already transformed these historical sea towns, bringing back a vibrancy and a hope that had been somewhat lost in recent years.

The Keta Lagoon is a major throughway to other towns in Anlo territory. It is a very shallow body of water that stretches about twenty miles from north to south, with some of its water coming from the Volta River. Its shallowness obscures the fact that it was in the time of the slave trade a locus of great activity. At that time it allowed safe passage to traders into Anlo country and allowed smugglers opportunities to conceal their goods.[5] Today's residents use the lagoon to go about their daily business as much as they use the bustling *trottros*. A staple of the Ghanaian transport economy, these small minibuses are often overstuffed with people and packages—and sometimes have seats that are halfway out the door. Canoes and sailboats are operated on either side of the lagoon by able "captains" who take their passengers back and forth each day. This lagoon is an important means by which the trading of goods takes place. It is used by traders from as far away as Togo who come to trade in the Keta marketplace.

The marketplace itself is in operation several days a week. It is a sea of highly organized transactions. All types of goods are traded here, including vegetables, fish, salt, fresh water, and livestock. Women are the chief operators, as Ghanaian women are known for being master traders. Some market women in Ghana and elsewhere in West Africa have made small fortunes plying their trade at similar markets. Shrewd and consummate professionals, they are very open to bargaining, but also know the worth of their goods.

What is noteworthy about the marketplace, however, is not simply these savvy traders and their transactions but also the diversity of the people, who come from miles away to participate in market activities. Many of them speak the same language, but they do not all share the same customs, particularly in the area of religion. Christians and members of the Yewe, Brekete, Nyigbla, and other local religious groups all work side by side. The Yewe are easily identified by marks on their faces or bodies. They traditionally mark both their cheeks with three deep black strokes, while members of the Brekete cult wear white and a chalklike substance on their faces and bodies at certain times of the week. All these groups have their own particular customs, yet there is a remarkable sense of tolerance at this marketplace.

Keta was one of the main slave markets in the area till the mid-nineteenth century. Here traders exchanged African slaves, primarily obtained from the hinterland, for salt from the coast.[6] Such activity is in stark contrast to the present state of most of the towns of the Anlo coast. In comparison to such a busy time, my observations in 1992 and 1993 were that many seemed underpopulated and much less active. Atorkor, for example, once a bustling center of the trade used by European and American traders as an outpost and supply station, was a quiet village. Its narrow roads and lanes, instead of being overrun by the business of daily activity, were dusty and bare. Here and there children could be seen playing in a compound or a few petty traders selling fruit from their sparsely stocked stands. "Where are the people?" I found myself asking my guides and translators. As often as I asked, I received a wistful answer. "Atorkor was such a bustling town, so long ago."[7] Others would add that many of the town's inhabitants had moved to the capital of Accra to look for work. They were part of a phenomenon common to most postcolonial African villages and towns. Areas that were once nerve centers have become almost deserted. This desertion had economic and political implications as well as physical ones. By 2003 I observed some small but important changes. The building of the seawall and other efforts have done much to alleviate some of this attrition; still, these towns and villages remain a shadow of their former selves.

Finally, Eweland is a region that cannot be simply described by its physical features. It is also characterized by the sounds of the land. From the roosters that require one's attention each morning to the drumbeats at night, this is a place that is rich in sound. In fact, as we shall see later, there are certain drum styles and rhythms that break the silence on a subject too often buried —the story of the Atlantic slave trade. Finally, there is the sound of the ocean, which is significant not only on a physical level but on a spiritual level as well. Its waves, like heartbeats, are constant. As such, the community's relationship with the ocean, as shown in Emmanuel Akyeampong's *Between the Sea and the Lagoon,* is very much a part of Anlo Ewe identity.

In this chapter, I have related a few important versions of the Atorkor incident as they were told to me, with minimal analysis and comment. Perhaps the most important of these was the version of Togbui Awusa III, chief of Atorkor, with whom I spoke on two different occasions.[8] I have placed the incident in the context of other historical accounts, including contemporary sources and travelers' records. I analyze the story in terms of the central issues of this book—impact and agency. I also look at the metaphorical connotations of the story as well as the ways in which these different versions, as memories of the past, may have been affected by events of the recent past and present. Finally, I attempt to situate the story in broader historical discussions about the utility of oral history.

TOGBUI AWUSA'S VERSION
OF THE INCIDENT

It is said that the chief's great-grandfather of the same name, Togbui Awusa Ndorkutsu of Atorkor, was the first to allow the Danes to come ashore to ply their trade.[10] As the trade progressed, Atorkor became known as a major way station for slaves. Its very name comes from the Asante *meto meko,* meaning "I will buy and I will go." It was thus named because of the experience of a royal visitor of Kumasi with mosquitoes along the coast.[9] A system developed whereby Ndorkutsu, through his agents stationed near Anyako, Hatorgodo, and further inland, collected slaves in the hinterland and brought them to the coast. These agents brought the slaves to Ndorkutsu's "big house" on the shore of Atorkor. There, they awaited European and American ships. Most of the slaves, then, came from the interior; they were not from the coast. They were, however, mainly Ewe-speaking people.

One day a group of drummers, famous drummers from the area, were playing their drums on the shores of Atorkor. The type of drum they were playing was called the *adekpetsi* drum. On this day the group included two of Togbui's relatives—Ndorkutsu's grandson and his grandfather. As the drummers played, the Europeans came to collect the slaves. As he was preparing to go, the captain of the ship invited these drummers to come aboard and play. He offered them barrels of drink, giving the same to the crowd that had begun to assemble on the Atorkor shore. An atmosphere of merriment ensued, and many became drunk. Thus were the drummers lured onto the

European ship. Before they knew what was happening, the ship set sail, taking them away. According to Togbui, "They were tricked into going on the boats to play their drums." They, too, joined the newly captured Africans of the hinterland as slaves to be sold in the Americas.[11]

Togbui heard the story from his grandfather—the son of Ndorkutsu. He stressed the fact that this story was a secret; that the details were told to him not all at once but little by little. He emphasized how sensitive a subject this was since several of the descendants of these drummers had since changed their family names. "It will be insensitive to try to question their descendants about the incident and they will not be willing to talk about the unfortunate event in history. Furthermore, they have since changed the family name of the chief drummer. A new chief was installed in place of the one who was taken away and a new name, Tretu, was chosen."[12]

The story goes that emotions ran so high about this incident that the neighboring towns of Atorkor and Srogbe almost went to war. No one wanted to go to war, but it was a distinct possibility since it was widely thought that this incident was prearranged. The captain of the drummers was said to have offended one of the wives of Chief Tamaklo from the neighboring town of Wuti.[13] In response, Chief Tamaklo arranged with Ndorkutsu for the drummers to play on the Atorkor shore. In any event, Togbui stated, "This was the first time that people from this area were taken as slaves."[14] Slaves were always from the hinterland, not from the coast.

OTHER VERSIONS OF THE INCIDENT

As stated previously, this story was told to me by several different sources, particularly elders in formal and informal settings. Many agreed with most of what Togbui Awusa of Atorkor recalled in his interviews. Others, such as Mama Dzagba of An-loga, added a few other details to essentially a similar base. Some of these are worth mentioning here.

> They [the Anlo] were stolen by white people; there was a higher ratio of men to women. The Europeans brought a sailing ship and anchored off the coast of Anlo. They started drumming, dancing, drinking, and merrymaking in the ship. The people of Atorkor were amazed and gathered on the beach to watch them. The Europeans then invited the people on the beach to join them in the drumming and merrymaking on the ship. The people entered their fishing boats and rowed over to the ship. They used about four surf boats. They then joined the whites in the ship and danced and drummed with them. At the end of the dance, the Europeans offered the people of Atorkor some kind of large biscuits, believed to be German biscuits. At the time of the incident there was a slight famine in the region. When they were given the biscuits, they were also given beef and rice and other gifts, and then they left the ship and went back to their homes. They showed all the food and gifts they had received on the European ship to others at home (husbands to wives, wives to husbands). They ate this food for about a month. The European ship then sailed away and then they returned later with more gifts for the people of Atorkor. They came a third time with food and gifts for the people, and when the people entered the ship they gave them a lot of alcohol to drink and lots of food to eat and whilst they were drumming and having a good time, the ship set sail and took them away. They were unaware of the time that the ship set sail.[15]

Mama Dzagba emphasizes something that was not raised in other accounts: that this was a planned effort on the part of European traders to gradually entice and solicit the trust of the Anlo people, only to kidnap them at a later date. Food as well as drinks were offered, and as this was a time of famine, the people were vulnerable to this enticement.[16]

Scenes from the incident at Atorkor dramatized in sculpture
at the Atorkor Slave Memorial Site, Atorkor, Ghana.

Photos: James O'Neill.

The paramount chief, Togbui Adeladza, concurred in his interview with Togbui Awusa's account that there was some sort of collusion on the part of local inhabitants. He also claims that the cause of this incident was a dispute over a woman called Enunato—the wife of one of the senior drummers. The drummer, seeking revenge, quickly arranged to sell the other drummers, including his enemy, to the slave traders. They were told that the white men wanted them to play. When they obliged, they were taken away. Some resisted by jumping into the sea, but most remained on board. In the end the woman in question left for Ada and got married to an Ada man. They changed their name to Kanase.[17]

Still another perspective comes from Chief James Ocloo of Keta, whose family played a great role in the history of the Anlo coast. His version suggests that the cause of the conflict was not a woman; it was because the town of Atorkor was in debt to the Europeans. "Chief Nditsi [short for Chief Ndorkutsu] used to buy tobacco from the Europeans and send to others; he would come and leave goods for the chief to sell. Later on, he would come and collect the money. The town of Atorkor became indebted to the Europeans. They saw some people drumming, they asked them to make the same drumming on the ship." From this point James Ocloo's story is the same as the other versions.

HISTORICAL CONFIRMATION OF THE INCIDENT

In spite of the fact that this story is told all over Eweland, it is a footnote in the European and American historical record. The most significant source of information comes from a Rev. Chas Thomas, whose contemporary account, *Adventures and Observations on the West Coast of Africa and Its Islands* (1860), provides detailed information about trading on the coast of Africa. He records a journey that originated in America on a sloop called the *Jamestown*. The *Jamestown* was a flagship of the African Squadron, which was established by the American and British governments to suppress slave-trading activities on the high seas. The squadron was established in 1843 as a result of the Treaty of Washington, which gave the American and British navies the right to patrol the coast in pursuit of slave ships:

> Article 8—The parties mutually stipulate that each prepare, equip and maintain in service on the coast of Africa a sufficient and adequate squadron, or naval force of vessels, of suitable numbers and descriptions . . . to enforce separately and respectively the laws, rights and obligations of each of the two countries for the suppression of the slave trade; the said squadrons to be independent of each other; but the two governments stipulating nevertheless, to give such orders to the officers commanding their respective forces

as shall enable them most effectively to act in concert and cooperation, upon mutual consultation as exigencies may arise, for the attainment of the true object of this article etc.[18]

The *Jamestown* sloop was commanded on this particular voyage by a Captain James Ward.[19] The sloop sailed from 1855–57, stopping at various ports in Africa and its islands. Rev. Thomas was chaplain of the sloop during this period. His chapter on the old Slave Coast situates and gives the closest approximate date of the Atorkor incident. In a December 23, 1856 entry, Thomas says that the peoples of the old Slave Coast tell the story of

> a Yankee captain who visited this river lately. After paying the headmen, or traders, for five hundred lively darkeys, he invited them into his cabin to take a drink. He was profuse in his hospitality, made them all drunk, put them in irons, sank their canoes, pocketed their money and got under weigh. Two of the twenty five thus taken jumped overboard shortly after, and were drowned; the remainder he sold in Cuba for four hundred dollars each.[20]

This account, though secondhand, is the most direct written evidence we have of this story. We can deduce from Thomas's book that the incident must have taken place within the past year, 1856, because he says in his entry that they had crossed the Volta River twelve months before and there was no mention made of the incident. Thus, the Atorkor incident probably took place in 1856.

Other information that we gain here is that the ship was American, or at least it sailed under the American flag. This is highly possible given the immense amount of slave-trading activities carried out by Americans at this time. There is an enormous amount of archival material on the use of the American flag in the continuation of the slave trade. The American flag was used in part because the Treaty of Washington protected the rights of Americans doing legitimate business off the coast of Africa. The squadron—both the English and the American vessels—was not legally allowed to arbitrarily search American vessels, yet these vessels were principally involved in the slave trade.

It is possible, however, that the ship that took the drummers had a number of different European and American nationals on board. Ironically, the system that prevailed at the time was one in which the nations of Europe and America joined forces in much the same way that Anlo elders and chiefs refer to them in their oral history accounts. This system, called an "abuse of the American flag" by many U.S. Navy officials, was one in which a vessel would be fitted in New York under the American flag for legitimate trade.[21] On board would be a Spanish crewmember. On the coast of Africa, this Spaniard would oversee the embarkment of equipment, cargo, and crew (more Spanish and Portuguese). This crew would then take charge of the vessel for the rest of the voyage.[22] Most of the trade in this period of the 1850s was thus being carried on as a "multinational" effort. Still, the lion's share of this effort was carried out by Americans in American-built ships. A British officer of the African Squadron stated that "at least one-half of the successful part of the Slave Trade is carried on under the American flag, since the number of the American cruisers in the station is so small in proportion to the immense extent of the slave dealing coast."[23] Thus it is highly probable that Thomas's recorded account is accurate—that it was a Yankee captain involved in the Atorkor incident.

Rev. Thomas's account also helps to confirm two other parts of this story, including that those kidnapped included relatives of the chief. ("After paying the headmen, . . . he [the Captain] invited them into his cabin to take a drink.") This corresponds well to Togbui Awusa's account and that of others in which we learn that the chief and his relatives were the main traders or headmen. Finally, in terms of what we can establish as probable facts, we have the mention of Cuba as the destination of the drummers in Thomas's account. This also corresponds with some of the oral accounts, which point to Cuba as the destination of the ship.[24]

These are the facts of the incident according to Rev. Thomas. Kofi Awoonor, in his own research, uncovered the story as told to him by people along the Anlo coast: "In the little village of Vuti in Anlo-Ewe country, the story is told of how a group of drummers were persuaded to come aboard an English ship to drum for the Captain. Those on the shore saw the ship vanish over the horizon. The song, 'On which shores are they are going to land' is still sung today."[25]

This account places the village of Vuti (Wuti), which is a neighbor to Atorkor, at the center of the story. Though it does not say that the ship left from Wuti, it is possible that the reason the story is told in Wuti is that some of the drummers were residents of this town. This would be consistent with the oral accounts, which indicate that the drummers hailed from a number of neighboring towns. Still, the major difference here is that the ship is said to be an English ship, not an American one. This may, however, be attributed to the fact, as said before, that local people tended to use the terms *American* and *European* interchangeably. Finally, the existence of the song, "On which shores are we going to land" fits with the practice of local people recording important aspects of their history in song texts and drumming styles. This song in its entirety goes as follows:

Go ka nu dze ge woyina?
Go ka nu dze ge woyina?
Go ka nu?
Adose kple Afedima woe yina daa
Adose kple Afedima woe yina daa

Go ka nu dze ge woyina?
(On which shores are we going to land
On which shores we are going to land
On which shore?
There go Adose and Afedima far away
There go Adose and Afedima far away). [26]

There is a similar reference to this incident in Charles Mammattah's *The Eves of West Africa*:

> When the slaves of yore first saw the blue waters of the Atlantic and realised that their fate was sealed and that they were leaving home and kindred for good for a journey into the dark unknown, one of them was borne on the wings of song, and granted the gift of a visionary, he composed the words and tune instinctively to this most moving of Eve [*sic*] atrikpi" war songs. You can imagine the exuberance with which they all danced a final farewell to their homeland. Hands, feet and body vigorously danced the dance of destiny at either the entrance to the Baguida (Badzida) wharf (port) near Be—Beach in Togo or at "Madzikli Beach" at Atoko, a renowned slave port in Ghana, situated near Anloga, "Madzikli" being the corrupted name of a Glasgow slave trader "Major King." (The translation of the song sung is as follows:) "Beholding the wharf, we now know we have come face to face with the grim inevitable realities of fate." [27]

From this account we may deduce once again that it was most probably a multinational ship that came to the Atorkor shore. It may have had an American captain to shield its activities, but the ship almost certainly included an Englishman or a Scotsman. Mammattah's reference to "Madzikli Beach" at Atorkor, which was named after Major King—a Glasgow slave trader—is one of several similar references that suggest that there must have been some involvement of traders from those areas. Atorkor is also referred to as New Glasgow in the diary of

Christian Jacobson, a merchant in Keta in the mid- to late nineteenth century.[28] This suggests that there were substantial business dealings between the residents of Atorkor and England/Scotland.

These three accounts are the only sources of written literature on the incident at Atorkor. Though sketchy and incomplete, they confirm four basic facts about this incident: (1) it took place in or around 1856; (2) the kidnapping of local residents did take place and included the chief's relatives or headmen; (3) it was most likely a ship with a multinational crew with English and/or American crew members; and (4) Cuba was the likely destination of the ship. It is on these central facts that most of the following analysis hinges.

HISTORY AND MEMORY

As discussed earlier, there are few recorded memories of the Atlantic slave trade from the African perspective. This story is significant in that it has been remembered at all. Rosalind Shaw's recent book, *Memories of the Slave Trade: Ritual and the Historical Imagination in Sierra Leone,* is a welcome addition to this line of study. She concentrates on memory through ritual practices with an emphasis on the "spirit landscape" of Sierra Leone with respect to the slave trade. As such, she is not only interested in what is remembered in words or discursive practices but in images and nondiscursive practices such as the cosmologies of witchcraft, practices of witch finding, and the negotiations between diviners and their clients. This is a fascinating and important study in that it looks beyond the apparent silence on slavery to practices within a society that speak about the subject in coded ways.[29]

The Atorkor incident and other stories in this volume, by contrast, are oral narratives with a focus on that which has been remembered in words. In terms of categorization, this story is an actual account of a historical event that forms part of the personal traditions of the Ndorkutsu family. It is also, to some extent, historical gossip, in that the story has been told within the community for generations.[30]

Although we may be assured that the essential facts are correct, issues of memory must be addressed. We have two major markers of the story—a contemporary account by Thomas writing in 1857 and today's accounts by elders and chiefs in Ewe villages along the coast. An extensive review of archives in Africa, America, and Europe did not reveal any other record of this story in the interim years. What is noteworthy, however, is that from the time of that original record till now, there has been little change in the basic facts. The four pieces of the story that can be confirmed (the date, the ship, composition of those who were taken away, and the destination) have not been altered. Furthermore, the versions of the story that Kofi Awoonor and Charles Mammattah collected in the early 1970s show little difference from the accounts told to me (Awooner and Mammattah's works were both published in 1976). The other elements of the story, however—the cause of the conflict, the exact names of people involved, and so on may have been altered over the years.

The many important events that have occurred in the history of Ghana and of Africa in general between 1856 and 1976 to the present may indeed have had an effect on the telling of this story. These include the onset of the colonial era, Ghana's independence under Nkrumah in 1957 and the coming to power of Jerry Rawlings in 1981. Without concrete evidence of the changes in the story that may have occurred during these periods, we may only speculate how past events may have affected present-day versions. For example, one of the results of colonial rule was an intensified effort to unite on the part of the Anlo and other Ewe-speaking people. The Ewe Unification Movement was a response to historical events of the latter part of the nineteenth century and the early years of the twentieth. By 1890 the British, after encountering years of fierce resistance from the Ewes, were finally able to extend their rule over coastal Ewe territory in what was then the Gold Coast. Around the same time, the Germans also became players on the coast and competed with the British for control of the land. This resulted in an agreement to split Ewe territory—the Gold Coast (Ghana) territory going to Britain and the Togo territory going to Germany. The territory that went to Britain included the Volta region. At the end of World War I, Germany's territory in Togo was ceded to France, much to the consternation of local Ewe chiefs, and the Volta region was ceded to the British and incorporated into the Gold Coast. Advocates of the Ewe Unification Movement concentrated their efforts on the unification of Ewe territory in both countries from the 1920s till well after World War II.[31]

We know from early work done in this area by Sandra Greene that Ewe traditions of origin were altered during this period to emphasize the unity of the Anlo with other Ewe-speaking peoples.[32] With the exception of the Blu clan, all Anlo clans then claimed they had participated in the great exodus of the Ewe from Notsie in the late seventeenth century. Furthermore, the *Ewe Newsletter,* launched by Daniel Chapman in 1947, was used to assist in forging an Ewe consciousness. It enjoyed a wide distribution in Anlo territory. Notwithstanding these efforts, to this day, the goal of unification has not been achieved.

In light of this colonial record it is possible, then, that certain elements of this story were adapted to the spirit of the age. From the standpoint of colonialism, it would be important for Anlos to portray themselves not as slave dealers who sold other Ewes to the Europeans but as unified with other Ewes in Ghana and Togo in opposition to foreign forces; it would be important to emphasize the elements of the story that suggest that the Anlos were *tricked* by European traders. It would be important to point to the negative impact of dissension and division within the community. This could then be seen as a lesson regarding the value of unity.

In a similar way, the period before, during, and after independence—which is almost synonymous with Kwame Nkrumah—can be seen to have influenced this story as well. From his years in London prior to his return to the Gold Coast in 1947, Nkrumah was an agitator for the freedom of black people not only on the African continent but all over the world. His eventual victory for Ghana in 1957 he saw as a victory for all those under the colonial yoke in Africa, the West Indies, and beyond.[33] His Pan-African ideology had a profound effect on the population of Ghana, including residents on the Anlo coast. The desire for internal unity as well as the building of bridges with other Africans, African Americans, West Indians, and others may very well have led elders and others to emphasize certain parts of the story.

Finally, Rawlings's assumption of power in 1981 may have influenced adaptations of the story. First, on his maternal side Rawlings hails from this part of Ghana, although he himself was born in Accra in 1947. Second, in the years before 1993 he attempted to forge international ties with the West Indies and others in the African Diaspora.[34] Domestically, he encouraged the growth of heritage tourism and the preservation of historical sites such as Ghana's many slave forts and castles.[35]

The truth of the matter is, however, that the four basic facts of the story that can be confirmed have not changed since 1857. Furthermore, what is striking about present-day accounts is the presence of balance. Even Mama Dzagba's account, which directly accuses Europeans of trickery in the slave trade and is perhaps the least balanced of the interviews, includes information on the role of African traders. At one point she explains that the Anlos did regular business in Dzodze in the interior and other places, exchanging slaves for salt.

However, it is true that our ancestors went to Dzodze [northern parts of Ghana] to buy slaves. They used salt as a means of exchange, and this sort of trade was not common. There was no salt water to make salt, so salt was of major importance. They introduced salt to the northerners, who ate without salt before then. After they tasted the salt, they asked Anlos to bring them some more on the next trip. They were obliged to exchange the salt for something else so the Dzodze people offered slaves in exchange. One cup of salt was equivalent to one slave. So the more salt you carried the more people you bought. For example, if you could carry twenty cups of salt there, you could return with twenty slaves whom you sold expensively to others [the rich] along the coast.[36]

Chief Ndorkutsu, likewise, gives a detailed account of the fact that his ancestor had agents in the interior whose job it was to collect slaves. Both sides of the story are shown. There are thus no apologies given for African involvement in the supply side of slave trade in these accounts. Furthermore, the presence of such balance suggests that if informants happened to hold strong Pan-African views and were particularly sensitive to African American sensibilities, such views appeared not to have played an important role in our discussions.

On a broader level, this story brings us back to the discussion of silences in history. As shown in the growth of the social history movement, history is not only about "great men and presidents."[37] Events and everyday people that are not typically remembered in history texts nonetheless play an important role in history. At the same time, in the case of oral history, getting people to speak about certain aspects of their past is sometimes very difficult. Hence Togbui Awusa's preface to his recounting of the incident: "It is an awful story; it is an awful story. Why do you want to bring it up now?"[38]

Those who have taken the testimonies of Holocaust survivors as well as victims of the Gulag have found a similar phenomenon. As Elie Wiesel says, "The inside is inconceivable even for those who were there. The victim's accounts of discrete events are often marked by absences: of idiom, of moral context and most powerfully, the absence of those who did not survive. . . . It can only be evoked obliquely or through silence because it is impossible to testify from inside the Holocaust world: the inside has no voice."[39]

The silence of the past is a factor also because of the unique relationship of the interviewer and the one testifying. To remember such traumatic events necessarily brings back the pain and the suffering. At the same time, there is the nagging doubt in the minds of those giving testimony that they may not be believed, that the horror and the terror that they describe as routine in Nazi Germany can never be fully believed unless personally witnessed. This doubt can lead to survivors silencing themselves. As Primo Levi writes, "Consciously or not, [the survivor] feels accused and judged, compelled to justify and defend himself."[40]

Journalist Irina Sherbakova found similar trends in her interviews with Gulag survivors. Since the 1970s she has been interviewing mostly female survivors of the Gulag who were part of the urban intelligentsia. Most of them were "Victims of 1936" (the height of the terror) who were repeatedly arrested and sentenced either to hard labor or to concentration camps throughout Russia. Their memories of those dark days, she says, exist as underground memories, a term very much applicable to the discussion at hand. This was particularly true of her first interviews in the 1970s, when it was not common for people to discuss these matters. Sherbakova found in these interviews that several of these victims, having been "rehabilitated," had never told their wives, husbands, or children of the horror they suffered at the hands of Stalin's government. A blanket of silence covered this past—a silence that only in more recent years has been broken.[41] According to Pal Aluwahlia in "To-

wards (Re)Conciliation: The Postcolonial Economy of Giving": "Traumatic recall is not merely a simple memory, for it is
a process that cannot be subjected to conscious recall. The para-
dox of trauma is that it is an experience that is repeated after its
forgetting and it is only through forgetting that it is experienced. In a sense, memory appears to repeat what it cannot
understand." He points out that this phenomenon was well documented by Freud, who showed that patients who had suffered
trauma were more concerned with *not* thinking of it.[42]

The testimonies of the Holocaust and Gulag survivors differ
from my oral history collection in one crucial aspect: the former
are testimonies of those who actually experienced or witnessed
these historical events. My collection represents stories passed
on from one family member to another or one chief to another
from generation to generation about a period that they did not
themselves witness. Still, in spite of this distinction, there are
many similarities in terms of history and memory.

THE INCIDENT AS A METAPHOR

"The first thing that makes oral history different is that it tells us
less about events than about their meaning."[43] After issues of historical corroboration and memory have been assessed, the Atorkor incident is best read as a metaphor for issues of agency and
impact in the Atlantic slave trade. First, it is a general metaphor
for transformations that took place during the slave-trade era.
The story represents the different phases of the trade, in particular the change in European and African agency from a period
of organized trading to disorganized and random activity: it is
a cultural marker or watershed between periods of order and
disorder.

In terms of European agency, it is additional evidence of
piracy along the African coastline. It shows that as late as the
1850s European and American ships were still engaged in the

slave trade, or in this case kidnapping, along the coast fifty years after the official abolition of the trade in 1807. It calls into question the nature and extent of the abolition—if some fifty years after it was legally abolished the slave trade enjoyed perhaps the greatest revival since its inception.

Numerous sources concur that the African Squadron commissioned by the Treaty of Washington in 1842 was ineffective in suppressing the trade. This incident is additional evidence of this fact. The ineffectiveness of the squadron can be attributed to many factors. First, no significant number of ships was deployed for the effort, suggesting an uneven commitment on the part of the British and American governments. For example, it was said that between 1,500 and 2,000 slave ships disembarked at Havana annually in those years; yet in 1853 there were only 19 ships in the African Squadron; there were 15 in 1854 and 14 in 1856. These few ships were expected to police over 2,000 miles of coast.[44] This was a feat that various commodores later testified was impossible.[45]

The continued debate regarding the method of policing the shores was also an impediment to the squadron's success. There were two general schools of thought: inshore versus offshore cruising. Offshore cruising, for reasons that are unclear, became the modus operandi, much to the consternation of some of the squadron commodores. Furthermore, U.S. administrations stood in the way of the more aggressive searches of various ships along the coast and in the West Indies. The question of the right to search and the specific limitations of this right prevented squadron commodores from doing an adequate job.

As seen in a letter written by the secretary of the U.S. Navy to Commodore Crabbe of the African Squadron, the navy was more concerned with protecting the individual rights of American businessmen engaged in "legitimate" commerce than in the pursuit of human rights in Africa. "The rights of our citizens engaged in lawful commerce are under the protection of our flag and it is the chief purpose,...the chief duty of our Naval power, to see that these rights are not improperly abridged or invaded."[46] Thus Crabbe was advised to use his "judgment and discretion" regarding ship searches. This view, coming from the highest ranks of the navy and, one may imagine, the president, suggests that their commitment was first to American traders and only second to the abolition of the trade.

Finally, it is clear from these records that there were no real "teeth" to the law. No real attempt was made to fully enforce the laws of 1807 and 1820, which declared that any breach of the law would be punishable by death. In fact, there exists on record only a few cases in which the captains of slavers were captured and actually punished beyond the loss of their ship and cargo.[47] The lack of true enforcement certainly did little to prevent and discourage individual traders from engaging in what at this time was one of the most lucrative business ventures in the world.

It is possible that traders themselves understood the limitations of the commitment to abolition, for not only was there insufficient policing of the African coast but also insufficient enforcement. Officials stationed in Cuba asserted that the problem was that slave-trade treaties stopped short of declaring participation in the slave trade as piracy subject to martial law: "General Serrano has several times expressed to me his opinion that, an advisable means of putting down the Slave Trade is that of declaring it piracy and treating the masters, crews and all concerned as pirates, subject to Martial law. He has several times repeated to me his determination to propose and recommend the adoption of that measure to his government [i.e., Spain]."[48]

Furthermore, if as it is estimated, approximately 300,000 slaves were imported into America between 1806 and 1860, how were these slavers allowed to disembark their cargo in American ports if the trade was indeed illegal? How were the ports of New Orleans, Florida, and the Mississippi Delta policed?[49] What messages were being sent about the reality of the trade? Was it really illegal if few were prevented from pursuing it and those captured were not punished to the full extent of the law?

The Atorkor incident is also significant because it suggests that during this period in the nineteenth century the trade was not always a trade—an exchange of goods and resources. It sometimes involved theft, trickery, and kidnapping. Brodie Cruickshank, a member of the Legislative Council at Cape Coast Castle during this period, recorded similar impressions of the Gold Coast in *Eighteen Years on the Gold Coast of Africa*: "We see the white man, at one time, having recourse to the grossest dissimulation, enticing the unsuspecting African within his power and breaking his pledged faith without compunction; at another, we behold him leagued with a friendly tribe, carrying fire and sword into defenceless hamlets and bearing off to his boats the shrieking natives."[50]

Later in his narrative he talks about the sense of arbitrariness and constant state of fear and chaos that developed as the trade continued:

> During the continuance of the slave trade, which added ten-fold to the general lawlessness of men, opportunities of disposing of such stray waifs as the solitary traveller, the hunter who had wandered too far from his home, the labourer in his plantation, and the water carrier returning form the distant pond, were so frequent and attended with so little chance of detection (where fear, for the most part, detained every one within the limits of a small circle of friendly intercourse), that it was certain slavery to venture beyond the short precincts without sufficient numbers to maintain their freedom."[51]

This incident and other sources strongly suggest that the trade did not always involve mutual exchange between more or less equal parties. Africans in this context did not have the upper hand in a sophisticated system of slave supply. The significance of the Atorkor incident is that it stands as one piece of compelling evidence that shows clearly that the trade involved a certain amount of arbitrariness and a certain number of unsystematic actions on the part of Europeans *and* African traders.

QUESTIONS OF IMPACT AND THE INCIDENT AS A CAUTIONARY TALE

The Atorkor story not only sheds light on the question of agency but also addresses the issue of the impact of the slave trade on the Ewe community. Anlo indigenous institutions were profoundly affected by the Atlantic slave trade. This is particularly evident in the discussion of the causes of the incident. Though the exact cause of the conflict is difficult to discern, two explanations stated by informants shed some light on the issue. One version suggests that the trade became a corrupting force in the society. Paramount chief Togbui Adeladza says in his account that eventually the chiefs and other inhabitants began to use the slave trade as a means of disposing of people with whom they had a quarrel.[52] In this case there was a dispute between two residents of the area that was resolved in the "kidnapping" of the drummers. Instead of resorting to traditional legal means of redress, they turned to the slave trade. The custom of *Nyiko,* which included a trial and whose verdict had to be approved by the chief and elders, was summarily bypassed. This issue will be discussed in further detail in chapter 6, on the effects of the trade on political and legal institutions, but suffice it to say here that one effect of the slave trade was to corrupt indigenous legal institutions.

One source says that the town of Atorkor was in debt to white traders and thus arranged to pay this debt by the "kidnapping" of the drummers.[53] If this indeed were the case and if such cases were widespread, then it augurs the future role of debt vis-à-vis the African continent and first world nations. It

prefigures what has now become a standard relationship between developing nations and Europe and America: whereby
these nations are heavily burdened with debt, which is paid for
by the raw material and resources of their land. This notion of a
town being indebted to traders, then, could possibly have started
this disturbing spiral trend. Furthermore, if indeed the move
toward becoming a debt-carrying nation began in the era of
the slave trade, then it is possible to say that this is one extremely
devastating effect of the Atlantic slave trade. Though not within
the purview of this study, these issues are suggestive of areas in
which more research could be done in an attempt to answer
the following: Did entire African towns become indebted to
traders? Were towns encouraged to become indebted? Did they
ever repay these debts or did such debts have the effect of prolonging slave-trade activities? Did the current process of globalization, which includes the carrying of enormous debt for many
developing nations, begin with the operations of the Atlantic
slave trade?

At the same time, this is also a colorful story told by many
people in a dramatic way. Though it is not an invented tradition,
given that the basic facts of the story can be confirmed, certain
elements of the story have been invented. These elements are
reminiscent of the great tradition of West African folklore as
cautionary tales. Among its most colorful aspects, which are
perhaps also fictionalized, is the mention of crowds of people
drinking and making merry on the shore as the drummers were
taken away. Though this was described in almost every account,
it is possible that the mention of the merrymaking was added
by storytellers in part to add a sense of drama and suspense to
the story. It often occasioned a laugh from informants at the
thought of the local people drinking and making merry without any idea that respected members of the community were
being kidnapped. The drinking and the merrymaking seem to
be the community's poetic way of saying that they were oblivi-

ous to what was happening in their midst. *It is a way to dramatize the fact that they did not expect such a thing to happen, given the relationships that had been previously established with white traders.* After all, Ndorkutsu's "big house," where the slaves were housed as they waited for the arrival of European ships, stood in the community as a constant reminder of the strength of this relationship.

The Atorkor story shows that by the mid-nineteenth century almost anyone was vulnerable. This may be one reason that the story is remembered to this day: the fact that before the incident the coastal people felt a certain immunity from the vagaries of the trade. Perhaps members of the community felt confident that there was an established system of slave supply. "Other" Africans from the interior were taken and shipped abroad, not those along the coast and certainly not the drummers and the chief's relatives. Certainly they would never be sold or kidnapped. Or so they thought.

The story thus appears to be the community's way of grappling with their involvement in the trade. The reference to drummers in particular, which at present is not independently confirmed by other sources, is probably a way to suggest that important people in the community were equally oblivious. Most communities rely on their leadership for guidance and direction; there seems to be a subtle suggestion here that as their leaders were misled ("taken away"), so were the people. They did not understand that their active involvement in the trade would eventually have a profound and negative impact on the land and its people. At the same time, the story itself may be a statement about the leadership or loss of leadership in the community.

As quoted in the introduction, the Okyenhene (chief of Oken) testified to Basel missionaries in 1870 that if his drummers, pipers, and sword bearers became Christians and thus effectively left the fold, "then I can no longer carry out my ceremonies nor can I receive foreign embassies worthily."[54] If this statement is applied to the Atorkor incident, the loss of the drummers meant the loss of the mouthpiece of the chiefs and the community—and by extension, then, the loss of leadership. If the chief is a chief because of those who attend him, when an important faction of this group is taken, what happens to the authority of the chief? Does he not lose his authority as well?

The story thus represents a watershed of revelation that no one was immune from this cruel trade in human beings. Even the highest social classes were not exempt. Given the increasingly arbitrary nature of the trade, if some were not free, all were not free. If they could take the drummers, including the chief's relatives, they could take anyone. This was the stark reality of the transatlantic slave trade.

CHAPTER 3

African Agency in the Atlantic Slave Trade

Realities and Perceptions

A lot of people think the chiefs were selling their subjects. In the beginning, decisions [were made] regarding bad characters. When selling came in, society got to know that it was anybody being sold.
Togbui (Paramount Chief) Adeladza, Anlo Ga

In my almost fifteen years of working in this field, after every talk or reading of my work in various venues in the United States and abroad, one question invariably dominates any ensuing discussion: Why did Africans sell other Africans into slavery? The incident at Atorkor and the fact of Chief Ndorkutsu's trading relationships with European slavers clearly raise this question. It is a vexing question asked by many—not only descendants of Africa in the African Diaspora, not only historians of slavery and the slave trade—but by all who seek answers to some of the great tragedies of human history. For some, there is a sense that if we could answer this question, we could somehow understand motives and assign responsibility, if not blame, for this awful era. For others, in particular Diasporan communities whose heritage has been shaped by these events, there is a sense that the answer to this question would facilitate reconciliation with their African past. It is as if this question is a bridge—a bridge that one must cross in order to make sense of realities past and present. Still, beyond the actual and concrete details of the answer lie a wordless longing and a determined search for a scattered identity.

The answer is by no means a simple one. The reality is that in an era of shifting allegiances, fierce competition on land and on the high seas, sporadic and sustained conflicts, a diversity of players moving in and out of the trade, much of the slave-trade era reads like a spy novel or a suspense thriller whose ending is unclear. It is also often unclear through much of this period who are the "good guys" and who are the "bad guys." Such was the complexity of this era. What we can say, however, in partial answer to the question, is that the fact of the dual involvement of Europeans and Africans in the slave trade did not imply *equal* partnership but rather parallel lines of activity originating from different cultural and political spaces. The simple fact also that no European was ever enslaved on a plantation in the Americas refutes this notion of equal partnership. We can also say that the answer to this question depends on the particular period of the slave-trade era. The operations of the slave trade varied greatly depending on the period. As evidenced by the Atorkor kidnapping incident and other random kidnapping incidents of the nineteenth century, many of these African traders, even the most influential and powerful among them, often found themselves, like their captives, in insecure and precarious positions.

Still, before a thorough review can be undertaken, the question itself is worthy of interrogation. Embedded within it are several faulty assumptions. First, there is the assumption that during the era of the slave trade Africans conceived of themselves as one people and one continent as opposed to numerous communities large and small. The fact is that Africa became a continental force only in the modern era. Ironically, before the onset of the transatlantic slave trade in the fifteenth century and through much of the ensuing centuries, the many regions of Africa—North, South, East, and West—though interconnected by trade, the spread of religion, and constant intercontinental migration, these regions and communities were largely distinct and separate from one another.[1] The Sudanic kingdoms of Ghana, Mali, and Songhay in West Africa, for example, had little or nothing to do with the great stone kingdoms of Zimbabwe in southern Africa, which thrived from the thirteenth to the fifteenth centuries. Diversity was, as it still is today, great, and the sheer expanse of the continent allowed for many communities to live in relative isolation from each other and sometimes even without knowledge of the other's existence.

At the same time, African notions of community even within the same ethnic group were often complex. As we see in the Anlo Ewe example in the incident at Atorkor and also later in this chapter, Ewes on the coast were not averse to selling Ewes from the interior. Notions of community often did not extend beyond a group of villages or towns in a particular area. The ties that bound these communities were clan and kinship networks more than language and customs. In other words, kinship networks were a major determinant of social behavior, even including the way people engaged the institution of slavery.[2]

Many slaves, though not all, had the opportunity to become a part of the master's kinship network and so could enjoy some of the privileges of the family.[3] Whereas this was doubtless true for many domestic slaves, the fact is that many oral accounts, as shown above, still testify to a stigma associated with this status even in cases where slaves were fully integrated into their master's family through marriage or childbirth. In this regard, one of my informants in the Volta region spoke of his ancestor's marriage to one of these domestic slaves in the nineteenth century. Even today, this line of the family is still quietly associated with slavery, although its members have long been integrated into the family. As a result, it is almost a crime to say to someone in Ewe, "Togbuiwo nye amefefleor Mamawo nye amefefle" (They bought your grandfather or they bought your grand- mother). From the Cape Coast side there are similar stories: "Slavery is always talked about in secrecy. The person [accused] would take you to traditional court and you will be asked to prove beyond reasonable doubt the origin of the person." It was not uncommon, according to one informant, for chiefs when they meet to sometimes quietly say, "Oh, don't mind this guy, his grandfather was bought by my grandfather."[4]

I contend that though the concept of clan and kinship networks has the appearance of being inclusive, it paradoxically is also a way of excluding others. It is a way of saying, "These are our kin, and then there are others." These are two diametri- cally different communities, and methods of behavior in and between them are often completely different. This was certainly the reality of the slave-trade era, and some would argue that remnants of this tradition are still strong today.

The modern concept of Pan-Africanism—or the unity of the African continent and its Diaspora—germinated from the political philosophy of Trinidadian George Padmore (1901–59, *The International African Opinion*), Jamaica-born Marcus Garvey, and African American scholar and activist W. E. B. DuBois. Pan- Africanism was concretized by Kwame Nkrumah, president of Ghana, which was the first colony to gain its independence from Europe, in 1957.[5] Pan-Africanism today, however, is still very much an ideal that has yet to come to full fruition. The new Af- rican Union, founded in 1999 as a successor to the Organization of African States and set up to promote greater social, political, and particularly economic cooperation among African states, has made some progress in its drive to promote an African Renaissance.[6] Still, the Pan-Africanism that was promoted by DuBois, Nkrumah, and others—which envisioned an Africa that did not divide itself along ethnic lines—is not evident in many places today (the Democratic Republic of the Congo, Liberia, the Côte d'Ivoire, to name a few recent examples at the time of this writing). If such unity beyond ethnic and language barriers does not exist today, we can only imagine the climate of yesterday, which is the reason that such a question—why did Africans sell each other into slavery—needs to be greatly problematized.

This question is also faulty as stated because it assumes that Africans had exclusive control over the supply of slaves on the coast and over slave-trade operations in general. It assumes wrongly that no slave was ever kidnapped by European nationals, when in fact kidnapping played a major role in the early stages of the slave trade in the fifteenth century and then again in the last phase of its operation in the nineteenth century—arguably one of its peaks. As such, the question itself is one-sided. It speaks of the agency of Africans without reference to the agency of Europeans and Americans, which will be explored in part in this chapter and in greater depth in others. The fact is that European and American nationals played a critical role in the operations of the Atlantic slave trade on four continents in six legs of the trade, including the persistent demand for labor in the New World and the willingness to meet this demand by any means. And so the shared responsibility for this catastrophe is not evident in the very question itself.

Finally, there is another assumption that is often made when this question is asked: Why did chiefs sell their subjects to these white traders? As shall be seen in this chapter, not all chiefs were slave traders, and not all slave traders were chiefs. Depending on the period, the size of the community, and the depth and level of trade, there was a diverse group of people involved in transatlantic slave-trade operations. In the Anlo Ewe example, which we will examine in detail, some local chiefs had to jostle with individual rogue traders who in many ways threatened their power bases. In the case of the larger Asante kingdom, on the other hand, power was much more concentrated in the hands of the king and his appointees.

Such are the popular misconceptions regarding the slave

trade. These are due to many factors. First, it should be said that historians from W. E. B. DuBois to more recent authors Edward Reynolds, Boubacar Barry, Paul Lovejoy, Patrick Manning, and others—have provided a broader context to the answer to this question in the ongoing body of research on the slave trade. But much of this work, though celebrated and appreciated in academic circles, has not penetrated the perceptions of the general public. Some of this work, like the important research of John Thornton in *Africa and Africans in the Making of the Atlantic World,* suggests that Africans were equal partners with Europeans in the transatlantic system. But to see Africans as partners implies equal terms and equal influence on the global and intercontinental processes of the trade. This was simply not the case. Africans had great influence on the processes of enslavement on the continent itself, but they had no direct influence on the engines behind the trade in the capital firms, the shipping and insurance companies of Europe and America, or on the plantation system in the Americas. Likewise, they did not wield any influence on the budding manufacturing centers of the West. Furthermore, this influence on the continent was by no means an exclusive one, as evidenced by the presence of over fifty European-built and -manned slave forts and castles in Ghana alone. Finally, even Thornton's own research and analysis of the range of small- and large-scale kingdoms in Africa at the time suggests that equal partnership between Europeans and Africans was not possible. As he shows in the following excerpt: "In all, only perhaps 30 per cent of Atlantic Africa's area was occupied by states with a surface area larger than 50,000 square kilometers and at least half of that area was occupied by states in the medium sized range (50,000–150,000). The rest of Atlantic Africa was occupied by small even *tiny* states."[7]

Given the different makeup of communities and kingdoms on the continent, African agency could not have meant the same thing for all these societies. Furthermore, the effects of the trade were different on these groups in part because of their difference in size and organization. Large-scale kingdoms (few as they were at the time) like the Asante kingdom, the Akwamus, or the kingdom of Benin were in a position to exercise some control over slave supply, but the majority of the communities in Africa at that time—small-scale societies, like the Ewes —were not in exclusive control of their fates. For example, early in the slave-trade era in the fifteenth century, the *oba* (king) of Benin was able to maintain a certain control over his end of the trade. He dictated his terms to the Europeans on which he wanted to trade. These terms initially involved trading in pepper and other products. Even later, with the trade in slaves, the oba opened and closed the market at will. This he did because in his quest for more territory, he needed to retain a large male population. At one point the oba put a total embargo on male slaves, which continued well into the seventeenth century. He was able to dictate trading policy in part because of his control over specialized trading associations in the kingdom. Finally, this control allowed him to maintain balance among these associations. All this was clearly possible because of the centralizing nature of power resident in the oba's position in the Benin kingdom.[8]

Another reason for misconceptions about this issue has to do with the sparse treatment of slavery and the slave trade in American and African textbooks. A cursory look at popular history texts in the United States shows that Africa in general is not a high priority even in world history courses. The same is true in American history texts.[9] In spite of some changes and additions in recent years, the subject is still relegated to a few paragraphs, without the richness, complexity, and sensitivity needed to explore this period.

Finally, these limited perceptions are also the result of documentaries and films on the subject of slavery. Though it can be said that there has been marked interest in the subject since the enthusiastic public reception of television series *Roots* in 1976 and intermittently since then, there is still much room for improvement in the way the subject is treated. Even well-researched films like Spielberg's *Amistad* (1997) used simple flashbacks to make references to the initial capture in Africa of Cinque, the rebel slave leader and main protagonist, without giving the audience a sense of the full context of this capture. The travel documentary *Wonders of the African World,* by Henry Louis Gates Jr. has also made an important contribution to this field by placing Africa at the center stage of world history with captivating shots of places and events and enlightening interviews with diverse parties.

The problem here as elsewhere is that this series asks the question regarding African involvement in the slave trade but does not fully answer it in terms of pointing out the intense pressures of European demand for free labor as well as the continental forces behind such pressures. Europe, unlike Africa, was united in its desire for this labor to settle and develop the Americas and to bring European nations into the mercantile powers they are today. In fact, economists of the day revealed that up to 36 percent of Britain's commercial profits in the seventeenth century—that is, more than one-third—was due to the triangular trade and the indispensable contribution of slaves and their labor.[10] To acknowledge the role of the kingdoms of the Asante and the Dahomeans in the trade as was done in Gates's series is a worthy and important effort, but without addressing issues of European agency in like detail as well as discussing African resistance to the trade in the same conversation, viewers are left with more questions than answers.

So what is the answer to this question of African involvement, and how does the Ewe example provide a window into this issue? How do the few stories that are still told along the Atlantic coast of Ghana provide pieces to a puzzle previously hidden or misunderstood? If the above represents a brief outline of the misconceptions and the reasons behind them, what were the realities of African involvement in the slave trade?

DANGEROUS LIAISONS: DEVASTATING IMPACT

The fact of the dual involvement of Europeans and Africans in the slave trade, at least in the Ewe example, did not imply *equal* partnership but rather parallel lines of activity originating from different cultural and political spaces. The best evidence to support this claim comes from the fact that one of the region's most important slave traders—Geraldo de Lima—was imprisoned by European officials for part of this period. Other traders were obliged to continually move their bases from one town to another to avoid suppression, so much so that one author has called their pursuits one of "pluck and risk."[11] Such events in the nineteenth century exposed the essential vulnerability of African trading efforts, as any systems that may have previously been in place broke down in the face of external interests.

Another major point is the fact that involvement in the slave trade differed greatly depending on the period. There were several transformations of the slave trade from its beginning in the late fifteenth century to its slow end in the nineteenth. The Anlo Ewe example demonstrates this well. Finally, the larger context of slave trading in Ghana is important as a means of seeing how the activities of the Anlo Ewe on the southeastern coast fit into the broader picture.

At first glance, oral traditions do not say much about slave supply on the Anlo Ewe coast. Much of the information available is about slave traders, and there is very little on the slaves themselves. Important traditions, however, have been collected by Reindorf, Aduamah, and more recently Ghanaian sociologist

G. K. Nukunya that do reveal some general information about slave-supply activities on the Anlo coast. Such traditions suggest that slave traders were rich men who in some cases possessed important stools. (*Stools* are the actual and symbolic representation of political power, usually chieftaincy positions. *Stoolhouse* refers to the seat of power, so to speak, and the actual place where the chief presides over his court.) Still, the community seemed to have an ambivalent reaction to these men. On the one hand they were regarded with a certain respect. As an Ewe proverb confirms: "Wealth commands respect."[12] On the other hand they were feared and thought to be hard, if not evil, men. One of the prayers and libations recorded at Tagba Xevi, an Ewe traditional area, goes as follows:

> *And I salute you ablotsu, the uneasy to handle one*
> *I do not know which is male*
> *I do not know which is female.*[13]

Ablotsu refers to a stool possessed by slave dealers. This passage is said to mean that these were men who drove a hard bargain. Other references to the wealth and status of slave dealers are to be found in the oral account of the stoolhouse at Denu. The ancestor of this town is known as Baku. According to the description of the stoolhouse: "The other stool according to the elders was made by Baku's grandson, Ayivor Akposoe as a mark of his wealth which he had acquired by the slave trade. He was installed on the stool as the first chief of Denu soon after 'the Aguedzigo war.' Akposoe's stool bears a string of thirty six cowries all blackened and decaying due to exposure of weather."[14] No doubt these cowries were representative of his wealth and status, as is also evidenced by one of the oral traditions of this study that describes the stoolhouse of the slave trader, Antonio of Woe. His cowries represented not only his wealth but the number of slaves in his household.[15]

Slaves in the Family

Still, most of what has been collected on the subject is about those who profited from slavery and not about the slaves themselves. This is understandable since the majority of the slaves would have been taken from the interior and the Anlo territory is along the coast. Nukunya's "A Note on Anlo Ewe Slavery and the History of a Slave" is one exception. Here he tells the story of a slave girl, originally from Krobo territory, who was kidnapped by Anlo raiders and taken to the slave town of Woe on the coast. Her capture took place well after the abolition of the slave trade in 1807. She was captured in the 1890s, which is again suggestive of the idiosyncratic and arbitrary nature of the slave trade in this period. Her story also suggests that slaves were largely incorporated into the general society. When after puberty her owner wanted her to become one of his wives, she said, "How can I marry one who said that he would be like a father to me?" In fact, she had become part of her owner's descent group and had subsequently declined to discuss her origins even with her own children. Also remarkably, she did not return to her original home even though it was not a great distance away.[16]

In my recent collection of oral histories in the Volta region, I heard similarly amazing stories from informants about slaves in the family. Given the sensitivity of this issue it would be inappropriate to name specific names, but in two significant cases two interviewees told me that their relatives had bought slaves and then subsequently married them, thereby integrating them into the family. This information, it should be noted, was not offered early in the interviewing process but only after repeated visits—in one case after several years. One interviewee confessed that her ancestor of the same name had bought and married her aunt's mother. This was a subject, she admitted, that no one freely discussed. As she said, "They can harm you if you are calling them slave descendants."

Another prominent informant in the area also confessed, after several conversations and interactions, that indeed his ancestor, a chief, had bought and married a slave from Agortime Kpetoe Afegame, a town near Ho, the center of the inland Ewe-speaking region. This woman became one of the sixteen wives of the chief and was given a new name by her husband. According to those who knew her, she was a tall woman indistinguishable from other women in the area except for a certain mark on her face that displayed her origin. Interestingly, the informant said that he had learned from his mother that it was her sister who had consulted a local shrine called Fofui to find out why the family was at that time having certain problems. The priest of the shrine then revealed to them that their ancestor was originally brought as a slave from the Ho area. Family representatives subsequently visited the town of Agortime Kpetoe Afegame and poured libations as a way of making reconciliation with the past. The informant then said that as a consequence of this event, things improved for the family. Also of interest about this story was the fact that other family members, including a younger relative who was present at the time of my interview, were not aware of having slaves in the family—yet another testimony as to the secrecy surrounding such origins.[17]

These admissions regarding slave heritage were remarkable in that it is rarely the case in Ghana that anyone confesses to having slave ancestry. Ironically, it is much more permissable to confess to some connection to slave traders—but an absolute taboo to mention slave ancestry. This made these admissions all the more phenomenal given the past and current discomfort with raising this issue publicly.

TRANSFORMATIONS OF THE
SLAVE TRADE: THE EWE EXAMPLE

Slavery and the slave trade were not the same in every period of the Anlo's past. In fact, by the nineteenth century, according to oral traditions and other sources, the slave trade on the Anlo coast had undergone a number of transformations.[18] It can be said that there were four distinct stages of the Atlantic slave trade along the Anlo coast. The first stage, in the seventeenth century, was characterized by very little activity. The Dutch trader Bosman recorded in his visit in 1698 regarding "the land of Coto" (Keta): "Their trade is that of slaves, of which they are able to deliver a good number but yet not so many to lade a ship. . . . By reason their Trade is small they are very poor; very few of them being rich."[19] He goes on to contrast the trading pursuits of Keta with those of Popo (farther along the coast) praising the inhabitants of the latter for their ability to "rob more successfully and consequently by that means encrease their trade."[20] Still, in spite of this activity, Bosman, found that filling a ship required months of waiting. For that reason, he appears to have found more ample trading activity at Whydah (Dahomey) in the seventeenth century.[21] Further evidence of the relatively few numbers of slaves that were garnered from this area in the seventeenth century comes from Bosman's statements about the other resources in the area: "This land is tolerably provided with cattle, at least as many as are sufficient to supply its inhabitants. . . . River fish is not wanting here, but they can get none out of the sea by reason of the violent burnings which extends from this place to Accra and farther along the whole coast."[22]

It is clear, then, that cattle breeding and fishing in the Volta and Mona rivers as well as the Keta Lagoon were sufficient occupations for the Anlo people. We know also from other sources that the farming of sorghum, millet, sweet potatoes, and bambara groundnuts also formed an important part of the community's staple diet.[23] They were self-sufficient but not wealthy.

The second distinct period of the slave trade in this area is associated with the domination of the Akwamu state over Anlo territory from 1702 to 1730. Akwamu rose to become an imperial power in the second half of the seventeenth century. European records (Barbot and Romer) comment on the Akwamus's famous attack on Greater Accra, Ghana's current capital, in 1687.[24] Long before its domination of Anlo territory, the Akwamu state had an expansionist policy and ruled over the modern-day Akwapim and as far east as Larteh. Constantly seeking more territory and power, the Akwamus engaged in many wars and conflicts with their neighbors and even expanded their powers as far east as Dahomey under the leadership of Ado.[25] In Akwamu even today there is a song on the drums that records these exploits: "Woadi Dahome ade ammeewo?" In the Twi language, this means: "You have eaten Dahomey and it hasn't satisfied you."[26]

The Anlos, because of their tributary relationship with the Akwamus, were also on hand in these pursuits. These quarrels, however, were not exclusively about control over the slave trade. For example, they fought over possession of lands at the mouth of the Volta River in their quest for exclusive access to the salt lakes. Still, the Akwamus's expansionist policies led them to raid for slaves, and to that extent, they drew on the assistance of the Anlos. Raiding of the Krepi states (small Ewe states to the north) took place during this period, when slaves would regularly be deposited at the Keta slave market for sale.[27] It is also worth noting that the Akwamu state during this period formed a strong alliance with the Asante that was to last many years. This was significant in that the Asante state, as will be discussed in greater detail later, was to become a major player in the slave trade in the years that followed.[28]

The next period, 1730–1830, represents perhaps the beginning of an organized process of slave supply along the Anlo coast. Not coincidentally, this period was also a time of increased European presence. It was during this phase that European forts were established in the area, including Fort Prinzenstein at Keta in 1784.[29] According to the tour guide of the now renovated fort, James Ocloo, "victims were marched to Atorkor and Adina

Fort Prinzenstein, Keta, Ghana, built by the Danes in 1784.

Photo: James O'Neill.

markets, and then marched on foot to the fort to await transport." Though Fort Prinzenstein does not have the same commanding presence of Cape Coast Castle or Elmina Castle, the basic setup of the fort is similar. It has the same narrow, windowless stone dungeons for males and females respectively as well as a place for the residence of the European agents of the fort. These residences conveniently overlooked bathing sites where slave women were forced to bathe in the open. There are also rooms for incoming cargo and trade items such as guns, ammunition, and liquor. Though relatively small in size, the structure of the fort is the same as its larger counterparts.[30]

There was, then, a correlation between European intervention and level of trade. During periods of little European intervention, as in the seventeenth century, there was not much transatlantic trading in this area, but with increased European intervention in the eighteenth century, there was organized and systematic trading on both ends. It would appear that one of the principal motivations to sell slaves came directly from the European presence on the coast. In other words, Europeans did not make Africans sell slaves, but their persistent efforts on the coast intensified slave traffic. As seen in the accounts of Bosman and others, traders were prepared to wait *months* for the successful loading of their ships. Even John Newton, author of the famous hymn "Amazing Grace," when he retired from his life as a slave trader confessed, "I verily believe that the far greater part of wars in Africa would cease if the Europeans would cease to tempt them by offering goods for slaves."[31] Other authors have likened the European presence to a disease that was brought to the continent, wreaking havoc on its institutions.[32] My preferred analogy, given that a trade in human beings, though marginal, did exist prior to European arrival, is to view the European and American presence as a match that was lit to bits of paper on the African coast. Once lit, it became a fire. If there had been no match, perhaps there would have been no fire.

The other factor to consider here is whether or not the overwhelming demand for slaves sufficiently obscured other occupations that had previously been important in the area.[33] According to evidence given by Chief Akolatse to the Crowther Commission in the early twentieth century: "There was no work, we had to sell slaves."[34] This statement by itself is not conclusive about the state of other occupations at the time, but it does suggest that slave trading, coinciding as it did with an increased European presence on the coast, took on a more dominant role. And so it was that in the one hundred years between the time that Bosman visited the coast and this period, the dominant activity had shifted from cattle, farming, and fishing to include a heavy emphasis on slave trading.

Still, this is where the level of organization and systemization began and ended—in the one hundred years after the end of Akwamu domination over the Anlo. This century, when the Anlo as a people were more free to determine their own political and economic agendas, represents the most organized period of slave supply. Finally, we see a very different picture in the nineteenth century. The Danes in 1792 abolished the slave trade, and the British did the same in 1807.

The last phase of the Atlantic trade in the nineteenth century, beginning in 1830, represented an unprecedented growth in slave-trading activities.[35] This phase on the Anlo coast was dominated by a small group of individual traders, some of whom enjoyed limited partnerships. In many ways, their organization mirrored the organization of Ewe society in general —small groups of semiautonomous entities without a major centralizing force. These traders often had strong connections to Europeans and largely operated independently of one another. Even at the height of their activities, they did not engage in large-scale partnerships as was the case with their European counterparts. At the same time, they increasingly found themselves subject to the intense suppression efforts of the English and the Danes during this period. Finally, as evidenced by the Atorkor kidnapping incident and other random kidnapping incidents that will be discussed, many of these traders, like their captives, found themselves in uncertain and vulnerable positions.

Chief Ndorkutsu of Atorkor perhaps best represents the end of the most organized period of trade along the Ewe coast. According to the testimony of Ndorkutsu's descendant, there was an established trade route, with stations at Atito, Alakple, and Hatorgodo, among others. The chief had agents at these stations who would stay three or four days till they received enough slaves and brought them to the coast. On the coast itself they were kept in the "big house" while awaiting the arrival of European and American trading vessels. Ndorkutsu worked largely alone or in limited partnerships with his brother, Chief Gbele, and later his nephew Kumodji of nearby Srogbe.[36] The slaves were obtained from the interior—from Krepi and beyond—where slaves were exchanged for salt from the coast. The slave trade was fed by a network of trade routes that linked various parts of the Ewe territory with one another. The main route from Keta northward up to Salaga and Kebou went from Sadame on the Keta Lagoon into Adaklu at Toda, and thence through Waya to Peki, Ho, Kpando, Nkonya, and Buem to Salaga. KetaKratchi, Salaga, and Atakpame were important salt-slave centers.[37]

Another limited partnership that characterized this period existed between the traders Doe and Afedima of the town of Woe. Both were of the Anatsi family. According to oral sources, Afedima was known for her fishing ventures along the coast and was in need of many laborers to help her in her efforts. "She had both domestic slaves and others whom she sold." So her business efforts also brought her into contact with the Atlantic system. In fact, it is clear from the record that she was to some extent on an equal footing with her European counterparts in this end of the system. "She dealt a lot with the Danes and Portuguese and other European traders and even got married to one of them, who took her to Europe and she came back alone. . . . When she came back she was the first person to own a European fishing net."[38] According to other sources, it was Afedima, along with a man called John Tay, that introduced the seine net, also known as *yevudor,* in the mid-nineteenth century (*yevu* refers to white in Ewe). This net did much to increase Anlo fishing ventures.[39] Doe was said to have brought the Yewe god from Dahomey; this he used to acquire slaves for sale on the open market.[40]

The European that Afedima married was reportedly Don Jose Mora—an important trader in his own right. He is referred to most often as a Spaniard.[41] His Ewe name is Adohose. Oral histories and European records (particularly the Danish records) attest to his activities in the middle of the nineteenth century. In the Anlo area he was based at Woe, where he had close associations with the Chief Gbodzo.[42] Mora was known for being extremely persistent in his pursuit of the trade, thereby frustrating Danish attempts at suppression. Governor Carstensen in his diary tracked his activities in several places: "Mora had been at Vay [Woe] to where a North American vessel laded with goods had brought him from Havana." In another entry in October 1842, he pinpoints Woe as a hotbed of slave dealing activity: "During the last decade, especially the towns of Atorkor and Vay have called for strict measures especially because of the stay there of the Spaniard Mora—a man who like at present de Sawa at Whydah, persistently resisted the measures which again and again were taken against his unlawful trade."[43]

Mora is an excellent example of the complicated nature of African agency as it relates to activities on the coast. What we see here is a European who established his residence on the coast and was so active in the acquisition of slaves that he is often discussed in the context of African traders. Though we know few details about his association by marriage to the African trader Afedima, it is likely that this association gave him a certain access to the community he might not otherwise have had. At the same time, this close association with African traders by marriage, residence, and common activities also had its costs. He ended up being subject to some of the same constraints placed on African traders at this time. Like the other African traders of this period, he was obliged to keep moving his base of operations to avoid suppression efforts by Europeans on the coast. He moved alternatively from Woe, Blekusu, and Atorkor.[44] Such was his kinship with the community that it was said of him and others like him: "The natives obstructed the Danes from capturing these daring individuals. Danish threats and suspending of payments to local chiefs were of no avail."[45] Time and again, the record shows that he was helped by the Anlos in concealing his slave bounty as he was pursued by European officials.[46]

Chief Gbodzo of Woe, closely associated with Mora, also played an important role in this period. He had apportioned areas where he assembled the slaves on the seashore and another further in the interior. "Whenever a slave ship arrived, a cannon was fired, and the other station will answer with firing of a cannon, too."[47] Then the shackled slaves were brought to the shore to be sold. During one of my research trips to the coast I was shown some of these shackles. Regarding the origin of these slaves, it is further said that: "In the Anlo area, whenever there were disobedient people or people who behaved criminally, they were got rid of by selling them to the Danes along the coast together with palm kernel. . . . Well, they knew that slaves were being sold along the coast, so any criminals or disobedient people were brought down from the interior [all over the Volta region]."[48]

These key figures notwithstanding, perhaps the slave trader who best represents the trade at this time was Geraldo de Lima. Geraldo was originally from Agoue in Dahomey. His given name was Adzoviehlo Attiogbe. According to the oral accounts he was educated by his father at Grand Popo.[49] In his early days as a trader he operated in the Whydah and Agoue areas. By the 1850s he joined the employ of an established slave trader in Anlo called Cosar Cequira Geraldo de Lima.[50] They worked from a base at Vodza, where Attiogbe help trade local and European products for slaves.[51] Geraldo was like many of the Brazilian-born traders who had for years done business not only along the Ewe coast but also along the coast in Dahomey. Some of these traders were former slaves who took advantage of opportunities to return to their homeland. They then set up along the coast and actively pursued the most booming business of the day: the trade in slaves. In Dahomey Geraldo's counterparts were Dom Francisco, Domingos Jose Martin, and Joaquim D'Almeida.[52]

As a result of his increasingly close association with the Brazilian de Lima and the growth of their business ventures,

Attiogbe became the natural successor to his employer when de Lima died in 1862. Not only did he take over his employer's personal and business affairs, he also assumed his name: henceforth, he was known as Geraldo de Lima.[53] His reasons for doing this were unclear, but it is ironic that an African trader on the continent assumed the name of a slave trader by choice when Africans in the New World were forced to give up their African names in exchange for European ones. In any event, as his trading efforts continued to thrive he diversified into trading palm oil products, cotton materials, tobacco, guns, gunpowder, and liquor.[54] He added greatly to his wealth and reputation to such an extent that the Anlos both revered and feared him. It is for this reason that when asked about the slave traders in the area, his name was often the first answer given by informants.[55]

Some of the oral histories reveal that the chiefs and traditional priests did indeed have a certain respect for Geraldo. "They only sit down quietly and show him respect since he was a war captain."[56] However, some authors have suggested that any support he received from the Anlo establishment was based on self-interest. When it was useful to be associated with one of the wealthiest men of the day, Anlos embraced such an association. When it was more useful to consider him an outsider, they did so.[57] In general, it can be said that while he inspired simultaneous fear and respect from the populace, his relationship with the local chiefs depended on their allegiances.[58] Those that were allied with the British were naturally Geraldo's enemies. Those who had strong trading interests that coincided with those of Geraldo supported or at least tolerated him.

Another bit of evidence regarding his close relationship with the Anlos is his association with supernatural powers and phenomena. In this respect he is treated like other important figures in the community.[59] Again, the oral histories strongly corroborate his supernatural gifts. His eighty-odd-year-old granddaughter, Lucy Geraldo revealed in a 1993 interview that once

Geraldo had been asked by the people to provide rain. So much rain ensued that "the townspeople begged him that they were having floods and that the rain was enough. He then stopped the rain; at this point Geraldo [who had been imprisoned] was released from prison."[60] Finally, Geraldo solidified his connection with the Anlos through marriage. One of his wives was said to be woman from Atorkor called Nyamewu. Given Atorkor's involvement in slave traffic, this marriage may also have helped him in his business dealings.[61]

But his granddaughter and other informants also speak of his European connections. "He traveled to Vodza and built a story building; downstairs was divided in two. One half had the women and the second half had the men. They did not mix and they did not dress up." Here her description of the European-style building (the remnants of which are still there today) shows de Lima's adoption of European ways. Furthermore, she says, "He dressed up like a European" and he was a Catholic.[62]

Geraldo may have adopted a Europeanized personal style, but his relationship with the British authorities was combative at best. First, Geraldo attempted to thwart British attempts to enforce the abolition laws. Second, even when he diversified his trading interests, he still refused to comply with the law that required traders to pay custom dues to the government.[63] This law came into effect when in 1874 the British formally extended their colonial rule to the Anlo territory. Furthermore, Geraldo, in seeking to further thwart British influence, made overtures to the Germans, who by 1884 had declared a protectorate in neighboring Togo. The British were highly suspicious of Geraldo's dealings and, in fact, accused him of plotting to kill Captain Campbell, the British district consul. As a result of such tensions, they demolished his two-story house at Vodza and set out to arrest him. His arrest in Vodza in January 1885 effectively ended his career as a major trader in the area since he was detained (without much of a trial) till 1893. He was imprisoned in part because of his ability to wield a certain power over political and economic activities on the coast. The British, fearing such power, decided to imprison him, thus allowing themselves more room to solidify their base in the area.[64]

I contend here that even though British rule at this time might have been somewhat tenuous—enough so that they perceived Geraldo as a threat—they had sufficient control of the area to arrest Geraldo and to keep him detained for a period of eight years. This is to say that even given de Lima's acknowledged power in the area, he was still subject to the constraints of British rule, first in terms of the direction of his trade (from slaves to oil, etc.) and second in terms of the final curtailment of his activities through imprisonment. If one of the most powerful traders of the time was placed in such a position, what does that say of others who were less powerful? It is true that he maintained a power base from the 1850s to 1885, but as we have seen, this required a careful juggling between local Anlo chiefs and the British authorities. Given this fact he was not able to control slave supply, but he did expertly negotiate a complicated set of variables to his own benefit. In the end, the British asserted their ultimate control over the area by not only extending their rule but imprisoning Geraldo, who perhaps more than anyone could have seriously challenged their goals. This example shows the complex reality of trading ventures along the Upper Slave Coast in the nineteenth century. Even their most powerful trader was subject to internal and external constraints that eventually ended his tenure as a major player.

If the constraints placed on individual traders were symptomatic of this period of transformation from a more organized trade to a disorganized one, then so were incidents of kidnapping. Unfortunately, there is not much literature on the subject. The ship surgeon Falconbridge asserted that kidnapping seemed to play a major role in the slave trade. "All the information I could procure confirmed me in the belief that to kidnapping and other crimes the slave trade owes its chief support."[65] Furthermore, there exists very little statistical information regarding how slaves were acquired. Among the little that exists is the information collected by the linguist Koelle in the 1850s—the time period of this study. Koelle looked at records of slaves that were captured then released and brought to Sierra Leone in the 1850s. Subsequent analysis of this data shows that 30 percent of the slaves had been kidnapped, 34 percent had been taken in war, 11 percent had become slaves as a result of the judicial process, 7 percent were debtors, and 7 percent were sold by "relatives and superiors."[66] We do not know, of course, the extent to which his tally of one-third of the slave supply acquired by kidnapping was typical. We also do not have conclusive evidence as to who would have been responsible for the kidnapping—Europeans or Africans.

Still, there is no question that kidnapping was one method used by Europeans in procuring slaves, particularly in the beginning of the era; but in the main, these random acts soon gave way to more organized trade. That the Atorkor incident happened as late as 1856 suggests that Europeans did engage in some random acts of kidnapping in the postabolition period. Though the claim of one oral source, Mama Dzagba, that "they [Africans] were stolen by the white people . . . the Europeans did not buy the slaves," can easily be challenged by the data, it is clear that such incidents did not take place only in the early years of the trade.[67]

In terms of African agency, two names surfaced the most frequently in the oral accounts with respect to kidnapping incidents. These were Kpego (Pogo) and Kajani. Both were professional slave catchers. There are several important references to these men that shed some light on their activities and their effects on Anlo society. Kpego was said to be "the leader" in slave dealings. He was from Asamara, an Anlo town near Tsiame. "He caught anybody, any stranger, any citizen, and sold Anlos to the Danes."[68] In another account it is said that "he went by the roadside to collect whomever, give them drink, keep them for some time, sold them at the coast...his station at Atorkor, Adina, or Keta."[69] Kajani was supposedly not an Anlo but from the northern region. "He would arrest people and chain them together. Anlos went and bought slaves and sold them to the Danes."[70] There are few sources of information on these individuals. From the scant knowledge we have about them, we may assume that they acted as individual traders who did not engage in any large-scale partnerships. What is particularly significant here is the fact that the activities of these men and others created a certain insecurity among the Anlos given the knowledge that people could be randomly captured and sold away from their communities against their will.

These two names are as well known as two others associated with slave catching elsewhere in Ghana in the nineteenth century—Babatu and Samori. Both did much of their slave raiding in the northern region of Ghana.[71] They had large armed groups at their disposal and essentially terrorized the people and waged numerous battles in order to obtain slaves. Babatu, in particular, was much feared by villages in the region, who were required to pay heavy tributes in order to avoid capture. The groups whose villages he and others raided included the Sisselas, the Dagartis, the Konkombas, the Frafras, the Kassenas, the Grunshi, and the Namdams, among others.[72] He was eventually cornered and forced to flee to the northern town of Yendi, where his grave may still be found. In fact, there is a folk festival that commemorates even today the capture of Babatu and thus the end of his evil exploits.[73] What is interesting here is that Babatu, like his counterpart Geraldo de Lima in southeastern Ghana, acted as an individual trader, notwithstanding the fact that both worked with others to accomplish their aims. Babatu, in fact, was from Niger and Geraldo de Lima from Agoue (present-day Benin)—both places outside of Ghana. They did not represent any particular ethnic group, and their allegiances varied according to their purpose. The role of these rogue traders as well as the fluidity of regional boundaries demonstrate the complexity of the issue of slave supply, which could not always be attributed to particular ethnic groups or even chiefs.

THE ROLE OF THE ASANTE

If slave supply *was* to be controlled by any one group in south-eastern Ghana, it would have to have been a large state like the Asante. In fact, if one looks at any map of the slave markets and routes, Kumasi—the center of Asante control—is central to all these routes. All roads seem to lead to Kumasi. A small group like the Ewes of loosely organized local chiefdoms could not exert total control over slave supply in the nineteenth century. As seen above, they had much more sway over the direction of the trade in the period when there were more organized systems in place. It is possible that only a large centralized state with a standing military operation could have dominated the trade during the turbulent period that followed the abolition of the trade.

Certainly there is evidence that the Asante and their allies, the Akwamus, played an important role in slave trading throughout the era of the slave trade. As one oral source confirmed: "The Asante were the main traders and the name Atorkor is derived from the Akan, meaning 'let me buy and go.' "[74] Before this time, the town was called by the Ewe name *Akplorkplorti,* which refers to a particular tree that grows in the area.[75] The Asante in the eighteenth century, in effect, renamed the town in their own language in much the same way as was done by Christopher Columbus and the conquistadors of old with America, Jamaica, Puerto Rico, and so on. Still, even at the height of their activities in the eighteenth century, for them to have been in control of slave supply suggests that slave trading was their primary activity. There is to date much debate regarding this issue. Several authors, after careful analysis, confirm the importance of the Asante and the Akwamus as slave traders but see this activity as part of a larger economic and political agenda.

In other words, the Asante and the Akwamus, continuing into the nineteenth century, were also known traders of cotton, salt, oil, pottery, and particularly gold.[76] In terms of their political aspirations, there is evidence that they pursued an expansionist policy, with slaves and other end products simply the result of their consistent warfare as opposed to the reason for it.[77] Throughout the years from the slave-trade era till now, they have been sometimes accused of going to war to acquire and then to sell slaves. However, Asante leaders like Osei Bonsu, Asantehene in 1820 contended: "I cannot make war to catch slaves in the bush like a thief. My ancestors never did so. But if I fight like a king and kill him when he is insolent, then certainly I must have his gold, and his slaves and the people are mine too. Do not the white kings act like this?"[78]

This assertion was backed by other observers such as the English official Cruikshank, who in 1853 said, "The Ashantee wars are never undertaken expressly to supply this demand [for slaves]"[79] Kwame Arhin in his work shows that slaves who were captured in war would be sold as slaves. He further claims that Asante chiefs tried in many ways to limit the influence of traders. This they did out of their belief that trading would destroy an appetite for war. There was even a concern that professional traders would sell arms to the enemies of the Asante, thus threatening the welfare of the state.[80] The Kumasi chiefs confirmed as much in Bowdich's nineteenth-century account: "Were [the chiefs] to encourage commerce, pomp (to which they are much inclined) would soon cease to be their preroga-

tive because it would be attainable by others; the traders growing wealthy, would vie with them: and for their own security,
stimulated by reflections they now have too little at risk to originate, they would unite to repress the arbitrary power of the
Aristocracy; and even if they did not, inevitably (as the chiefs
conceive) divert the people's genius for war."[81]

That said, there was still a connection between periods of
high incidence of warfare and voluminous slave traffic. The king
of Salaga in northern Ghana asserted in 1876: "The Ashanti
often sold into slavery a whole village full of his people and...
no one's life or property was safe when the Ashantees were in
the country."[82] The Salaga slave market was indeed the most
famous of all the slave markets. Salaga, founded by the Mande
leader Dyakpa Nde wura in the Gonja kingdom in the sixteenth
century, was overrun by Asante forces in 1744 who subsequently
conquered much of the surrounding areas and made them tributary states of the Asante kingdom.

As a result, the Asante maintained control over the Salaga
market, Dagbon, and other regions in the north and in this way
were able to administer their trading operations. Salaga and
the northern slave routes in general (which includes three of
Ghana's ten administrative regions—the northern, upper east-
ern, and the upper western regions) were important outposts
not only for the movement of slaves to the south (who would
then be transported across the Atlantic) but also for the movement of slaves along the Trans-Saharan routes—the western
route, a central route, and two easterly routes spanning across
West Africa, the Sahara, and North Africa. Even today in these
areas there are many physical reminders of this past, including
a pond in Salaga called *wonkan bawa* (Hausa for "the bathing
place of slaves") and the old slave camp of Paga in the upper east
region where holes dug in rocks (which served as drinking
troughs), graves, and auction blocks can still be seen today.[83]

Bono Manso slave market, commemorative plaque.

Photo: Anne C. Bailey.

The Bono Manso slave market was also one of the major markets for the Asante, and remnants of this history can be found there today. In fact, the inhabitants still tell and reenact a story from this period that records a bit of this history. Briefly, Bono Manso, which according to local tradition was once a major town called Techiman with 277 streets, during the slave trade became a way station for slaves from the north who were being transported to Kumasi and further south. There they would be sold either internally or across the Atlantic. According to oral sources, "Here the sick and tired were left with the chief [of Bono Manso] to take care of them. They also captured people from Bono Manso to replace the sick and tired." [84]

In general, when there were periods of relative peace and retrenchment in this area, such as early in the nineteenth century, there was a decline in the trade. [85] There is no denying, then, the great and pervasive Asante influence in slave trading. This influence was felt indirectly as well. Europeans on the coast recorded the growth of organizations of slave catchers that they called "Siccadingers"—from *Fika din* in the Ga language, which means "black gold." In this climate of state warfare and raiding as well as the overwhelming European demand for slaves, these individuals got in the business for themselves and illegally enslaved many free men on the coast and sold them to European traders. Ironically, some of these slaves were laborers on Akwamu farms.[86] This paints a somewhat bleak picture of how destabilizing and insecure life must have been for many communities within and without these centralized and expansionist states. In plain terms, if those who belonged to these large states were not safe, then who was?

In terms of the specific relationship between the Asante, the Akwamus, and the Anlo Ewe, they were often allies. In 1730, when Anlo was no longer tributary to the Akan state Akwamu, they continued a relationship based on trade. Later, with the rise of the Asante empire, this relationship greatly involved the trading of prisoners of war. By the turn of the nineteenth century, evidence of their relations could be detected in the existence of Ewe envoys that were sent via Akwamu to the Asante stronghold of Kumasi.[87] After the abolition of the slave trade, the Asante and the Akwamus depended on the Anlos in their prime location on the coast for the continuity of trade in the face of British restrictions. They also depended on the Anlos for military support.[88] This role caused the Anlos to be caught between Asante conflicts with the British—conflicts that were heating up in the 1850s and 1860s. Colonial records of this period show that the British were constantly concerned that there would be an Asante invasion. In fact, the offering of gifts to the king was one way of neutralizing tensions. A decision to send representatives of the Asante king to Cape Coast to sit in on court appearances of Asante citizens was another measure used to ensure peace and to increase trade.[89]

By 1866 the British took steps to curb this relationship, having acknowledged: "There are but two modes through which the Ashantees... can receive supplies from the coast during war, the Assinee and the Volta [Anlos]." In that year, the British troops entered into a conflict between the Anlos and the Adas, This conflict was spearheaded by the trader Geraldo de Lima. As a result of a trading dispute with an Ada man, Geraldo rallied the Anlos to support him in battle. According to reports, "they had provided him with an army of 3000 and 4000 men which he led against the Addas."[90] The British, in turn, rallied their own troops, including support from Accra, Christianborg, and surrounding villages. The end result was that British troops successfully routed the Anlos.[91]

Still, even after peace agreements were drawn up, the Asante continued to have influence in Anlo Ewe territory.[92] This influence did not mean, however, that the Asante controlled trade routes in the area. In the end, it was not until the British asserted more control over the Gold Coast area by the burning of Kumasi in 1874 that this influence substantially decreased.[93]

Finally, as we will see in chapter 5 on European agency, all these conflicts and wars waged by the Asante and the Akwamu states, among others, cannot be seen in isolation. European agents on the coast, often from their bases in coastal forts and castles, introduced guns and gunpowder at an alarming rate, which greatly increased the incidence of warfare in the area that is now modern-day Ghana and the rest of the West African region.[94]

TWO LINGERING CONTROVERSIAL ISSUES

Such is the general outline of Anlo Ewe slave-trading activity in the larger context of slave-trading processes in Ghana during the era of the slave trade. In the midst of this discussion of African agency, two important issues regarding such involvement are

worth further interrogation. These two issues point to the difficulty that many have in understanding this involvement under
any circumstances. First, there is the issue of one ethnic group
selling other members of the same ethnic group into slavery.
Some say they may have understood how communities with
different languages and cultural heritages that were isolated from
one another could sell others into slavery, but how do we explain the phenomenon as in this case of Ewes selling other Ewes
into slavery?

Second, another important yet irksome question, connected
to the first, is: Why did some of those slaves who were transported to the Americas who later had an opportunity to come
back to Africa turn around and become slave traders themselves?
How do we explain this phenomenon?

Cultural Motivations versus Universal Motivations

As already mentioned elsewhere and evidenced in the quote
from Togbui Adeladza at the beginning of this chapter, in terms
of cultural motivations unique to the African experience, domestic slavery functioned much as prisons do in contemporary
society. It was a means to rid a community of someone undesir-
able. It was a way to exercise the right to punish that individual
while keeping him in the community. It was also a means of social ostracism that was thought to protect the community from
criminals who would commit adultery, stealing, and so forth.
Furthermore, domestic slavery was a means to incorporate and
strengthen a labor system for great and large empires like the
Asante, whose tributary states to the north and elsewhere were
often forced to work on their plantations. As Bowdich notably
remarked in his *Mission from Cape Coast Castle to Ashantee* in
1819: "The extent and order of the Ashantee plantations sur-
prised us yet I do not think they were adequate to the popula-

tion; in a military government they were not likely to be so. Their neatness and method have been already noticed in our route up. They use no implements but the hoe...and a hut at each wicker gate where a slave and his family resided to protect the plantation."[95]

But domestic slavery also served the needs of small traders and farmers such as those on the Anlo Ewe coast of southeastern Ghana. Slaves, as we see in oral testimony on the trader Afedima, were used for farming and fishing ventures. In this way, African societies thus did not differ from societies from time immemorial that have used slaves in a similar way. They were also used to build and extend family structures, as when a master would marry his female slave. Finally, slaves were sold for the same reasons that Europeans bought and sold them—money and goods. Human greed and desire for wealth were clearly motivations—universal motivations, if you will—in Ghana and elsewhere in West and Central Africa that encouraged cooperation with European traders of like mind.

Notwithstanding all these factors, I contend here that class issues were at the heart of the level and depth of slave trading that became systematized in the eighteenth century in the Ewe example and at other periods in other regions. What is clear from the record is that everyone in these societies did not enjoy equal status. There a was a dichotomy not only between chiefs and others but also, as mentioned earlier, between kin and others. The African concept of community was extremely small. A complex system of kin networks determined in large part the way in which individuals interacted with others. Among the Anlo Ewe, kinship networks on the Atlantic coast were preeminent in their understanding of community. Even other Ewes to the north were largely excluded from these networks except in cases of intermarriage.

This situation was not unlike prerevolutionary Europe and

America, where the ideals of "all men are created equal" and "liberté, fraternité, and egalité" were unequivocally groundbreaking at the time of their introduction. These ideals were explicitly set forth in the American Revolution in 1776 and the French Revolution in 1789—notwithstanding the irony that slavery and colonialism played a dominant role in both European and American societies at the time. The supreme irony is that it was the very question of slavery that engendered the debate around these issues of freedom and equality. Before this period, in much of Europe serfdom was predominant till the fourteenth century. Serfs, though not slaves, had limited rights. They were largely tied to the land of their masters, who could arbitrarily discipline and dispose of them. And so, though chattel slavery in Europe, as such was rare, serfs with few privileges were doomed to a fixed class system. It was not till the fifteenth and sixteenth centuries that this system gave way to rents, free contracts, and monetary payments and serfdom thus became a thing of the past.[96]

The inequalities that existed in prerevolutionary Europe that sustained a feudal economy were not unlike the inequalities present in some African societies. Historian Walter Rodney in his seminal book, *How Europe Underdeveloped Africa,* argues that before the advent of the European on the continent, communalism—understood as equal and cooperative relationships within African communities—was the rule and not the exception. Though in general I agree with many of Rodney's arguments, particularly his conclusions regarding the devastating effects of the trade on the continent, I do not fully concur that communalism was as dominant as he claims. There may have been a *veneer* of communalism in some African societies, but this did not take away from the underlying presence of different social relationships. These social relationships during the slave-trade era became socioeconomic relationships. The reason the

Atorkor incident is still remembered and told in a sea of relative forgetfulness on this subject in the Anlo Ewe region is because the chiefs and the headmen had now become victims. Given their social status, the unthinkable had taken place. This is what makes this incident in the mid-nineteenth century an important turning point—the realization that no one was immune from the trade and that in the eyes of the slave trader everyone was a potential slave, everyone was judged equally in spite of social status. Issues of class, then, are one explanation and an answer to the question of why Africans sold other Africans into slavery.

Ex-slaves in the Slave Trade

We know, as mentioned before, that certain ex-slaves, particularly some Brazilian slaves in the nineteenth century, returned to Africa and engaged in slave traffic. At the same time, in terms of balance, it should be said that not all the ex-Brazilian slaves who returned to Africa got involved in the slave trade. For example, a very interesting group in Ghana, called the Tabon, had a great desire to return to Africa and thus made the journey to Ghana in 1829. Tabon comes from the Portuguese *Ta bom?* (Is it okay?). They were originally seven families under the leadership of one Azumah Nelson, and they were all former slaves who had bought their freedom. Skilled craftsmen and farmers in Brazil, they brought these skills with them when they arrived in Jamestown, Accra. They were well received by the local chiefs and eventually were absorbed into the Otublohum Section of the Ga State. Today, they are considered a part of the Ga ethnic group, native to Accra, but maintain their own distinct identity and have their own chief, called the Tabon Mantse. The structure and people of Brazil House on Brazil Lane, their original residence in Jamestown, still stands as a testimony to the contributions that these ex-slaves made to their new home communities. Other Brazilian ex-slaves also migrated to other areas in Africa, including Lagos, and formed similar communities, in which they built schools, churches, and other public buildings.[97]

Why did others take a different turn? On one level, it adds to the comment made by Chief Akolatse to the Crowther Commission in the early twentieth century: "There was no work, we had to sell slaves."[98] It may say something about the predominance of slave tracking, hunting, and selling activities on the African continent in the nineteenth century that even some of those who returned were drawn into the trade. What had been a marginal activity in the sixteenth century became a predominant one in the nineteenth in no small part due to the overwhelming influence of European and American traders and their African counterparts. This type of climate could encourage such activity even on a small scale. Still, this is an area that, though troubling, is worthy of further research to truly understand the motivations and the circumstances of those traders who were themselves ex-slaves.

This last point demonstrates, as was said in the beginning, the true complexity of this era and the absolute necessity of not painting a picture in starkly black-and-white, "good guy"/ "bad guy" terms. The attacks, the counterattacks, the raids, the subterfuge, the kidnapping, and the rest add up to one very disturbing and confused time in history. Relationships and identities were constantly shifting in response to changing circumstances. On the one hand, there were universal motivations for involvement in the slave trade—simple human greed and desire for wealth. Other motivations were more culturally nuanced and particular to groups and individuals who participated in the trade. Still other reasons may never fully be known or understood. One thing that is clear, however, is that there were always those Africans who chose not to participate and who resisted the trade. As such, no discussion of African agency is complete without a look at the other side of that agency: resistance to slave traffic on the continent. This we will look at in the following chapter in the context of resistance to slavery in the African Diaspora.

CHAPTER 4

African Resistance

The Slave Who Whipt her mistress and Ganed Her Fredom *and Other Oral and Written Tales*

It happened in the barroom. There was some grand folks stopping there, and she wanted things to look pretty stylish, and so she set me to scrubbing up the barroom. I felt a little glum and didn't do it to suit her. She scolded me about it and I sauced her. She struck me with her hand. Thinks, I, it's a good time now to dress you out, and damned if I won't do it. I set down my tools and squared for a fight. The first whack, I struck her a hell of a blow with my fist. I didn't knock her entirely through the panels of the door but her landing against the door made a terrible smash and I hurt her so badly that all were frightened out of their wits, and I didn't know myself but that I'd killed the old devil.

Sylvia Dubois, The Slave Who Whipt her mistress

So says the self-proclaimed "saucy" and slightly irreverent Sylvia Dubois in what has to be one of the most colorful slave narratives in existence, with a title that jumps off the page: *A Biography of Sylvia Dubois, the Slave Who Whipt her mistress and Ganed Her Fredom.* What follows this dramatic scene, according to Sylvia's recollections, is the return of her frustrated master, Munical Dubois, the tavern owner, from an out-of-town trip and his resignation that his wife and slave could no longer get along. He then determined that the best remedy would be to offer Sylvia her freedom and send her to New Jersey. This offer she happily accepted and with her small child headed on foot to New Jersey, where she proudly declared to an onlooker: "I'm no man's nigger—I belong to God—I belong to no man."[1]

This narrative, which some say lies somewhere between folklore and history, is not unlike many of the African oral narratives in my collection.[2] Though this slave narrative is not necessarily typical, it demonstrates unequivocally that resistance was a constant theme throughout the history of slavery and the slave trade. Africans and their counterparts in the African Diaspora did not sit idly by while families were being torn apart, social and political institutions were being undermined, and, in the New World, untold cruelties were being meted out to slaves and their children on a daily basis. The answer to the question of whether they resisted is, then, a resounding yes. They resisted in every way they could—with mind, body, and spirit. They resisted on both sides of the Atlantic consistently and persistently until the slave trade was abolished and until the institution of slavery itself came to an end.

It is important to note that not only was this resistance widespread and intercontinental, it was multifaceted. Resistance was not relegated to armed efforts and other physical types of resistance. African resistance also and especially included what we may call a "nonviolent disengagement." Such disengagement took many forms on the continent and elsewhere where Africans were transported. Finally, Africans used words as weapons. Their words—whether in text or in speech—gave voice to their oppression and, in the midst of such a process, restored to them their dignity and personhood.

But how do you defy a system that has several legs and is operational on several continents? Africans chose to do so in many ways, starting from their own particular bases in the Caribbean, America, or in Africa itself. The history of black resistance is well documented in the United States and the Caribbean in part because of the emphasis in the historiography on armed resistance efforts. C. L. R. James and more recently Eugene Genovese documented the efforts of Toussaint-Louverture and others in the Haitian Revolution as perhaps the best example of black triumph in this regard. Haitian slaves rose up in 1791 and fought a bitter revolution with their French masters to take control of the island by the formation of the Haitian Republic in 1804.[3] This date is remembered in history as perhaps the most important milestone in the struggle against slavery. The United Nations and UNESCO have in fact declared 2004, the bicentennial, as the International Year to Commemorate the Struggle against Slavery and Its Abolition.[4]

James and others did concede that several of the revolts in the United States were "ill organized uprisings which were always crushed with comparative ease."[5] In addition to the fact the slave owners had all the government and military power on their side, the failure of several of these insurrections was because of the presence of a few of what might be called black Benedict Arnolds who changed sides at critical junctures in the struggle. Slaves who informed their masters of plots against them or who even fought alongside their masters against other slaves undermined black efforts to gain their freedom; at the same time, they managed to bolster white efforts to sustain the institution indefinitely. Still, the consistency and frequency of such incidents such as the Stono Rebellion in 1739 attest to the determination of blacks to struggle for their freedom.

Likewise, the many instances of black protest throughout U.S. history in the face of white suppression, as recorded by Dr. Mary Frances Berry in *Black Resistance, White Law,* also give testimony to the same. Berry shows through case after case and incident after incident how blacks continued to resist injustice in America as sanctioned by government policies and the Constitution itself. The many large and small rebellions in the West

Indies and the Americas in general also bolstered the abolitionists' cause and greatly influenced the British Parliament to abolish slavery in 1834. Records show that Parliament originally
preferred a gradual abolition of slavery. The timing of pivotal
rebellions, such as the renowned "Emancipation Rebellion" led
by Sam Sharpe in Jamaica in 1831–32, prompted the British
government to take action sooner than planned. As Hart says,
"the rebellious slaves re-set the time table for emancipation."[6]
Other significant rebellions that took place in the early nineteenth century that also contributed to a climate for abolition
included: the Ibo conspiracy in St. Elizabeth, Jamaica in 1815;
the Barbados rebellion of 1816; the rebellion of Demerara in
1823; and widespread conspiracies in Jamaica in 1823 and 1824,
culminating with the Sam Sharpe rebellion that galvanized a
large section of the slave population in 1831–32.[7] These rebellions, coupled with virulent public reaction, suggest that these
and other events did play a key role in the ending of slavery.

   Still, there were at the same time many examples of nonviolent resistance. Though many of these incidents would not
typically be recorded in history books, they were nonetheless
pivotal in the long exercise of chipping away at the operations of
the slave trade and the institution of slavery. During slavery,
blacks engaged in everything from work slowdowns to crop
sabotages. The termination of unwanted pregnancies by slave
women was also viewed by some an act of defiance, as they
thereby deprived the master of yet another child born into slavery.[8] The determination of many slaves, such as Frederick Douglass, to read and write in spite of the fact that slave literacy was
illegal was also an example of black defiance.

   In Africa, we likewise have examples of both armed and
nonviolent resistance. Dutch trader Bosman describes the violent resistance of slaves from the interior who thought they
would be eaten by white traders: "When we are so unhappy as
to be pestered with many of this sort, they resolve and agree to-

gether (and bring over the rest of their party) to run away from the ship, kill the Europeans and set the vessel ashore by which means they design to free themselves from being our food." Bosman says that twice they met with such misfortune, but the Portuguese were more unfortunate, losing four ships in four consecutive years in this manner.[9] And so it is clear that some armed resistance did take place on the continent. In the main, however, as the records of Bosman and others show, slave rebellions of this sort could easily be put down with the assistance of other armed European ships on the coast.

But there were many examples of nonviolent disengagement on the continent. As mentioned earlier, large states such as the Benin or the Congo kingdom may have been in a better position to attempt to curtail the slave trade, but smaller polities could not mount major resistance efforts. Even Benin and the Congo eventually succumbed to slave-trading activities, at least in part because of their inability to control what was fast developing into a worldwide system. It is perhaps not coincidental that their attempts to curtail the trade (whether by the king of Congo's letters to the king of Portugal or by the oba of Benin's temporary embargo on male slaves) took place in the early sixteenth century—the beginning years of the slave trade. Even then this system (as will be described in detail in later chapters), which spanned several continents and included multifaceted interests worldwide, would hardly have given them room to maneuver out of the trade even if they were obstinately against it.

Various Muslim polities, including the Bondu and the Futa Jallon, are noteworthy for their resistance efforts. The Balanta, the Djola, and other groups are also known for their anti-slave-trade efforts.[10] On the Ewe coast resistance came in the form of the voluntary disengagement of the people from various community institutions that became involved in the slave trade. As will be discussed in chapter 7 on religion, young girls were typically sent to one of several religious cult houses for instruction in the ways of the group. Their time there was intended to last anywhere from six months to a year. This period, much as in the case of a novice in a nunnery, was a period of learning the ways to worship the god in question from priests and other elders. When in the early nineteenth century parents discovered that religious leaders had used the cult as a means of acquiring and selling slaves, they stopped sending their children to the religious cult houses. In fact, the Yewe cult rose to prominence in Eweland in part because of the scandal of a previous cult that had been involved with the trade. In this way residents showed their quiet defiance and distaste for the cruel traffic. They could do little to influence the worldwide systems of trade already in place; similarly, as women in a society where men held most of the leadership positions, they were hardly in a position to openly defy their leadership, but they could use their own personal circumstances as a means of protest. They could disengage themselves from culpable institutions. Such were their brave attempts at resistance. The oral narrators in my collection specify that it was the mothers who pointedly refused to send their children to these religious cult houses after some had lost their children because of this egregious breach of trust. It was the mothers who protested with their feet. It was the mothers who simply kept their daughters home.[11]

These acts of defiance from African women on the continent foreshadow and in some cases mirror similar acts by their New World counterparts. Although many slave women may not have had the opportunity to whip their mistresses and win their freedom, they did find ways to defy a cruel system. They may not have been able to strike at the system with full frontal blows, but their writings and later their oral histories took up the fight. They spoke their piece—and in so doing, spoke for peace. Writers like Carol Boyce Davies and Henry Louis Gates Jr. show us that out of the silence of women's voices comes agency through transgressive writing or speech. "Transgressive speech, bell hooks would assert, challenges situations of oppression, challenges power and talks back to authority when necessary regardless of the consequences.... One may argue then that black women's writing occupies the position of transgressive speech because it transgresses the boundaries and locations for black women within the context of societal authorities and norms."[12]

They break the silence on the oppression they experienced as both blacks and women, and are thus to be counted along with the Nat Turners and Toussaint-Louvertures as agents of their own fate. In this regard, the narratives recorded by ex-slave Octavia V. Rogers Albert are particularly interesting, as is the narrative of West Indian slave Mary Prince, one of the first of its kind.

IN THEIR OWN VOICES: EX-SLAVES SPEAK OUT AGAINST SLAVERY

The full title of Octavia Albert's narrative tells a story in itself: *The House of Bondage, or, Charlotte Brooks and Other Slaves, Original and Life like, As they Appeared in Their Old Plantation and City Slave Life: Together with Pen-Pictures of the Peculiar Institution, with Sights and Insights into Their New Relations as Freedmen, Freemen and Citizens* (1890). Albert's title, like many other titles of narratives (almost as long as the narratives themselves), suggest the real human drama that was slavery—the arbitrariness of life, the chaos, the fear—all of which mirrored to some extent what was taking place in the continent they left behind. Another good example of this drama is the narrative of William J. Anderson (b. 1811): *Life and Narrative of William J. Anderson, Twenty-Four Years a Slave, Sold Eight Times! In Jail Sixty Times! Whipped Three Hundred Times!!! Or the Dark Deeds of American Slavery Revealed. Containing Scriptural Views of the Origin of the Black and the White*

Man. Also a Simple and Easy Plan to Abolish Slavery in the United States. Together with an Account of the Services of Colored Men in the Revolutionary War—Day and date and Interesting Facts.

Mrs. Albert, who was born a slave but was a child at the time of Emancipation, grew up to be a teacher in rural Georgia who eventually married a preacher. It was in their home that she began to take in older ex-slaves and eventually recorded their stories. So we have that rarest of circumstances—an ex-slave who becomes an interpreter of her own experience and the experience of others. Unlike the WPA narratives, which were collections of interviews of ex-slaves in the 1930s taken by largely white interviewers, this book stands out in terms of the agency of the ex-slave in having the foresight some forty years earlier in 1890 (the start of the Black Woman's Literary Era) to record the insights of fellow ex-slaves. Given the time period, it is all the more remarkable an achievement because such recordings were done by a woman.

She begins her book with a strong voice that establishes her authority on the subject: "NONE but those who resided in the South during the time of slavery can realize the terrible punishments that were visited upon the slaves. Virtue and self-respect were denied them.... Much has been written concerning the negro, and we must confess that the moral standing of the race is far from what it should be; but who is responsible for the sadly immoral condition of this illiterate race in the South? I answer unhesitatingly, Their masters."[13]

With such an introduction, she goes on to detail some of those cruelties suffered by the likes of Charlotte Brooks (Aunt Charlotte) and other slaves. Lest there be any who would whitewash the evils of slavery, as was already being done so few years after Emancipation, she quotes Brooks as saying:[14]

> Why, old marster used to make me go out before day, in high grass and heavy dews, and I caught cold. I lost all of my health. I tell

you, nobody knows the trouble I have seen. I have been sold three times. I had a little baby when my second marster sold me, and my last old marster would make me leave my child before day to go to the cane-field; and he would not allow me to come back till ten o'clock in the morning to nurse my child. When I did go I could hear my poor child crying long before I got to it. And la, me! my poor child would be so hungry when I'd get to it! Sometimes I would have to walk more than a mile to get to my child, and when I did get there I would be so tired I'd fall asleep while my baby was sucking.[15]

She further talks about the separation of families that was routine during slavery—the cruelest of acts for a people with such a strong tradition of kinship: "I have never seen or heard from them [my relatives] since I left old Virginia. That's been more than thirty-five years ago. When I left old Virginia my mother cried for me, and when I saw my poor mother with tears in her eyes I thought I would die. O, it was a sad day for me when I was to leave my mother in old Virginia."[16]

We see in these fragments of stories a picture of the cruel hand of slavery—especially as it affected women. Mothers of young children were forced to deal not only with the hardships of forced labor but also the separation from babies long before they were weaned. Such separation would only be a precursor to the permanent separation that children would experience when they or their parents were sold. Aunt Jane, who was sold to a master in Louisiana, also told how she had to leave her kin, in her case because her master needed to pay his debts. Even if the children were not sold, parents and children were subject to the whims of the master when it came to discipline. As says ex-slave Caroline Hunter of Virginia, "Many a day, my ole mama has stood by an' watched massa beat her chillun till dey bled an' she couldn' open her mouf."[17] Life for a slave meant arbitrary subjection to variables well beyond their physical control.

It is no wonder that many slaves turned to the world of the

spirit to understand and to exercise some authority, if only moral authority, in their powerless worlds. Hence the plethora of religious references in this book and many other slave narratives. Religion was not just an esoteric spiritual experience, it was an opportunity to transcend and overcome present-day circumstances. Some had a genuine encounter with what we call today liberation theology. Thus worshipping their God in their way was a major act of defiance. After one of the several hymns referenced in the narrative, Aunt Charlotte says: "Yes, my dear child, that hymn filled me with joy many a time when I'd be in prison on Sunday. I'd sit all day singing and praying. I tell you, Jesus did come and bless me in there. I was sorry for marster. I wanted to tell him sometimes about how sweet Jesus was to my soul; but he did not care for nothing in this world but getting rich."[18] Furthermore, regarding her mistress, she said the following: Old mistress used to have balls on Sunday. She had me and her cook fixing all day Sunday for the ball on Sunday night sometimes. Mistress's religion did not make her happy like my religion did. I was a poor slave, and every body knowed I had religion, for it was Jesus with me every-where I went. I could never hear her talk about that heavenly journey."[19]

In these two quotes, we see two phenomenal things at work. First, Aunt Charlotte is boldly declaring through the spoken word how her faith literally got her through the worst of times. You can almost see her smiling at the thought that her Master, as she says, did not know "how sweet Jesus was to my soul." For Charlotte, as for so many of slave narrators, it was as if they had some hidden treasure, not just in the nether world but right there under the noses of those who oppressed them. A secret world to retreat to that no one could disrupt. A world within a world of hate and normalized cruelty. Second, we see Charlotte making another bold statement against organized religion of the day. In a quietly subversive way, she clearly makes it known that though she was a simple slave woman, she knew that the religion of her mistress was hollow. This juxtaposes with her own confidence in her" heavenly journey." Again, to her mind, she had something that those with all the power and the money could never have—not as long as they participated in her oppression. This was resistance of a very high order.

But this line of thinking did not end here. As convinced as Charlotte and many other slaves were of their faith in Jesus, so were they convinced that there would be justice or divine retribution for those who kept them under the iron heel of slavery. A conversation between the author, Mrs. Albert, and Aunt Charlotte regarding the death of her mistress reveals as much:

> "Mistress did not live right, and she did not die right. The old saying, 'Just as the tree falls, just so it lies.' So many times I used to want to talk to her about her religion; but she seemed to know every thing, and I was a poor creature that knowed nothing but how to work for marster in the cane-field. Marster had mass for mistress, I don't know how many times; but what good did it do her soul?"
>
> "None whatever, Aunt Charlotte; we must make our peace with God before we leave the world. This world is our dressing-room, and if we are not dressed up and prepared to meet God when we die we can never enter the promised land; for there is no preparation beyond the grave. The Bible tells us, 'Whatsoever a man soweth, that shall he also reap.' "[20]

At the same time, we see that some blacks did not view themselves as exempt from review on Judgment Day because of their victimization at the hands of whites. They were not wholly perfect beings subject to cruel and imperfect masters. Interestingly, as evidenced from some of the slave narratives, they too struggled with the notion of a "sinful heart" as a peculiar human condition and would require moments of repentance before their God.[21]

Such sentiments are very apparent in the narrative of Mary Prince, a West Indian slave—a narrative that shares several of the key elements of Mrs. Albert's book. Noteworthy is the statement by the publisher in the preface: "The idea of writing Mary Prince's history was first suggested by herself. She wished it to be done, she said, that good people in England might hear from a slave what a slave had felt and suffered."[22] That in 1831, a few years before the official abolition of slavery in the West Indies and a full generation before its abolition in the United States, Prince should have the boldness to believe that she had a story worth telling and that it should be told is remarkable. In so doing, she becomes one of the first ex-slaves to tell the truth about the British West Indian version of slavery. She also ends up being an important voice for female slaves.[23]

Prince's narrative is, the publisher asserts, from her own lips. She dictated it to someone in his family, who then wrote down her words. So, like many of the other slave narratives, it is literally a spoken text or a talking book.[24] After detailing the many cruelties that she suffered at the hands of her master and mistress on various islands and in England, where they eventually brought her, she makes a passionate and effective argument against the evils of slavery:

> How can slaves be happy when they have the halter round their neck and the whip upon their back? and are disgraced and thought no more of than beasts?—and are separated from their mothers, and husbands, and children, and sisters, just as cattle are sold and separated? Is it happiness for a driver in the field to take down his wife or sister or child, and strip them, and whip them in such a disgraceful manner?—women that have had children exposed in the open field to shame! There is no modesty or decency shown by the owner to his slaves; men, women, and children are exposed alike. Since I have been here I have often wondered how English people can go out into the West Indies and act in such a beastly

manner. But when they go to the West Indies, they forget God and all feeling of shame, I think, since they can see and do such things.... All slaves want to be free—to be free is very sweet. I will say the truth to English people who may read this history that my good friend, Miss S——, is now writing down for me. I have been a slave myself—I know what slaves feel—I can tell by myself what other slaves feel, and by what they have told me.[25]

Here we see Prince accomplishing many things in giving voice to her struggle. First, her declaration that "to be free is very sweet" is almost like a manifesto. This is the second time that she has used the same phrase in the narrative, as if to underscore the fact that she understood only too well the nature and desirability of freedom.[26] Second, Prince turns to her audience and defiantly questions their hypocritical civility. When she wonders out loud how the English can go and behave in such a "beastly" manner in the West Indies, she is taking aim at what was commonly known as English civility. The good English gentleman and his fine Christian wife and mistress of the house in England—who were they *really,* she seems to be asking. And who did they become in parts far away?

This is a subtle argument but a strong weapon of resistance because Prince is here asking English readers and listeners alike to search and question their own morals and values. What were these values if they could not be upheld in every land and in every territory and in and among every people? Were they, like the religion of Aunt Charlotte's mistress in Louisiana, hollow and empty, or were they principles to live by? And so, there is a double-edged sword to Prince's words. While declaring her own desire for freedom and her understanding of what that means, she asks readers at the same time to examine their own values—and in so doing makes an effective antislavery argument on *their* terms. With that, she brilliantly closes her case.

THE RED CLOTH TALES AND
OTHER TALES OF CAPTURE

In the same subtle way, ex-slaves who told their stories to interviewers for the WPA collection in the 1930s made strong accusations against their former masters, particularly with regard to how their ancestors were captured. Many of these narratives are not quite as forthright as the preceding ones, perhaps because of the way in which the interviews were done. An ex-slave in the South would naturally be very cautious with a white interviewer in a period that was only two generations after Emancipation. However, as Michael Gomez found in his extensive review of some of these tales of capture, ex-slaves used metaphor and imagery to convey substantial critiques of their masters and of the institution of slavery in general.

"Dey stole her frum Africa wid a red pocket handkerchief." So says eighty-four-year-old Hannah Crasson about her great-grandmother, Granny Flora, in one of the many tales told by ex-slaves about the initial capture of their ancestors. This and other tales about the use of red cloths or flags by whites to entice blacks onto the slave ships was a means to say unequivocally that whites were primarily responsible for the slave trade and slavery. Black slaves were not unaware of African complicity but chose, in view of what evils they lived and endured every day, to emphasize the agency of whites. As Gomez says: "Versions were compared and edited by 'the committee of the whole.' Accounts passed from mouth to ear all the way from Virginia to Texas. White southerners, so engaged in managing the machinery of plantation agriculture and slavery as the principal means of social control (at least from 1830 on), were quite unaware that right beneath their noses their *supposed chattel* were engaged in a complicated process of analyzing, debating and collating their experiences."[27]

But their resistance through the use of language did not end with slavery; it continued even in these interviews with largely white interviewers. Whether or not they were conscious of the way in which slavery, only a few decades after its abolition, was being recast by the general public we do not know, but it was as if they were not taking any chances. They would, in telling their version of events as it was told to them and as they understood it, make a clear statement about the culpability of whites even if it was cloaked in metaphors. In short, in the shadow of their emancipation, they boldly used a time-honored African tradition—the art of storytelling—to resist their oppressors. From African oral histories to today's spoken word movement, literally from time immemorial, language and voice have been used as effective tools of communication.

Finally, we look closely at one other very intriguing tale of capture: *The Story of the Blind African Slave, or, Memoirs of Boyrereau Brinch*. There is no specific mention of a red cloth here, but Brinch does detail the manner in which he was kidnapped by the English and "a brief account of the custom of civilized nations, in luring the innocent natives of Africa into the net of slavery."[28] This account is included here in part because there are sections of it that are eerily similar to the tale of the Incident of Atorkor told by the Ewe community in Ghana as detailed in Chapter 2. Here, too, deception and guile play a major role.

Brinch first gives an extensive account of his original home in Africa—the Bow Woo kingdom in the county of Hughlough, which in his words was positioned somewhere along the Niger River "in that part of Africa called Ethiopia, and of that race of people denominated negroes, whom we as a civilized christian, and enlightened people, presume to call heathen savages, and hold them in chains of bondage, who are our fellow mortals, and children of the same grand-parent of the universe."[29] Though it is difficult to determine the exact location and ethnic group to which Brinch belonged, we can generally place him in Central Africa in a region closest to the place where the Niger River empties into the Gulf of Guinea. According to Brinch, the Bow Woo kingdom was one of the tributary states of the empire of Morocco in the mid-eighteenth century. Furthermore, he claims he was from a very important family in the region since his father was the governor of the county.

In fact, it is after his father's return from the seat of the empire in Morocco that Brinch's capture takes place. The year is 1758, and an English vessel engaged in the slave trade is stationed on the Niger River. The setting is a major feast in celebration of the sun, after which Brinch, then about sixteen years old, and several companions go down with great excitement to bathe in the Niger River.

> But Lo! when we had passed the borders and entered the body thereof [of the woods], to our utter astonishment and dismay, instead of pursuers we found ourselves waylayed by thirty or forty more of the same pale race of white *Vultures,* whom to pass was impossible, we attempted without deliberation to force their ranks. But alas! we were unsuccessful, eleven out of fourteen were made captives, bound instantly, and notwithstanding our unintelligible intreaties, cries & lamentations, were hurried to their boat, and within five minutes were on board, gagged, and carried down the stream like a sluice; fastened down in the boat with cramped jaws, added to a horrid stench occasioned by filth and stinking fish; while all were groaning, crying and praying, but poor creatures to no effect.[30]

Brinch goes on to describe the process by which the English traders came to capture him and his comrades. First, the English captain remained in the area for many months, ingratiating himself with the inhabitants, and then, he says:

> We had not remained many days, in this situation before we learned by the Interperter [*sic*], that the officers were courting

some of the women, and were almost idolized by the natives, who were *making public feasts for their amusement, and entertainment.* At length it was announced that a grand feast was to be held on board of the ship; apparent preparations, were made accordingly, and all the principal inhabitants of the Town were to attend. This was considered as a civility due from that deluded people, to the officers of the vessel, while the blackest perfidy rankled in the hearts of those traitrous villains, who conceived and executed the plot. A general invitation was accordingly given to all classes, without distinction. The day arrived, the boats of the ship were busily employed in bringing on board the visitors. The principal inhabitants of the Town came on board; in short, but few staid behind only the sick, lame, aged and children; they brought with them many valuable articles of plate, &c. when all were on board, the festivity commenced, but mark, the slaves were cautiously concealed in the cockpit, that vigilance might be kept asleep and suspicion lulled into security. When they had regailed themselves with Food, Brandy, Spirits and Wine, were introduced and prepared in many ways to make it the more delicious. When they had drank freely, laudinum was secretly conveyed into their liquor, a general intoxication, and sound sleep soon prevailed, and insensibility was the consequence. These dexterous dealers in iniquity seized upon the moment, fastened with implements already prepared, each individual down upon their backs, with poles across their breasts and leggs, with hands and feet drawn up by cords to certain loop holes therein.[31]

And so we see the same pattern here as in the Atorkor incident in southeastern Ghana, though this incident reportedly took place at least one hundred years earlier: a kidnapping, not mutual trade; ingratiation with the inhabitants of the area; luring Africans onto the slave ship under the pretense of a feast; much drinking and amusement follows; the Africans are proverbially asleep; and the slave traders take full advantage. Again, as in the incident of Atorkor, this event may be understood on different levels. On the one hand, the capture of the Africans may indeed have taken place in much the way Brinch describes it. This may even have been a well-known modus operandi of slave traders on the coast—not unlike how their counterparts in the Americas developed time-proven techniques for seasoning slaves and other methods of guaranteeing subordination. For traders who felt they had exhausted that particular "supply post," this may have been a last stand. At the same time, this event most surely can be seen in a metaphorical light as well. "When they had drank freely...a general intoxication, and sound sleep soon prevailed, and insensibility was the consequence." Is this not a way of saying that the Africans, caught up in the excitement and the merriment of the occasion, played right into the hands of their enemies? That they were asleep instead of being awake to the drastic circumstances that were about to befall them? That they were unaware of the devastating effects of their neglect for generations and generations to come?

This may well be some of what Brinch (as other narrators) intended to convey by means of this tale, which reads almost like a trope of the slave trade. Consistently, he uses words like "luring," "demon of seduction," "pretension," and "traitor" to refer to whites in the classic trickster tradition, with which Brinch was no doubt familiar. Even in his lurid descriptions of his life as a slave in Barbados and in several parts of the United States, his masters and mistresses are often described in this light.

At the heart of this tale, however, is Brinch's cry for freedom—a freedom that he eventually receives after fighting in the American Revolution against the British. The irony of the situation was not lost on him: "Thus was I a slave for five years fighting for liberty."[32]

Brinch's narrative demonstrates his commitment to resisting on every level the institution of slavery. But as we have seen, he was not alone. More slaves than history has recorded went to great lengths to secure their own freedom. Not only did the likes of Boyrereau Brinch and Sylvia Dubois so dramatically fight their way to freedom, but then there was the inimitable Henry "Box" Brown, who escaped slavery in 1848 by mailing himself to Philadelphia in a packing case and lived to tell the tale on the transatlantic abolitionist lecture circuit. Such was their overwhelming determination to be free, for, as Mary Prince said, "To be free is very sweet."[33]

CHAPTER 5

European and American Agency in the Atlantic Slave Trade

From Raid and Trade to Operational Breakdown

It turned out that the Europeans used the same trick in other places along the coast [in Cape Coast, Elmina, etc.]. In the early days, the people who were taken to America were not bought.... They [Europeans] used trickery to obtain slaves initially.
Mama Dzagba

There is a word in Ewe used to refer to whites—*yevu*. Formed from the contraction of *aye* and *avu*, it literally means "tricky dog." This term is not very flattering and very much reflects if not agreement with the above quote then some sympathy with the sentiments behind it. In traditional Eweland some believe that Europeans have been able to achieve their technological advantage by means of trickery. This is interesting in and of itself but is particularly significant coming as it does from a people with a strong trickster trope in their storytelling traditions.[1] Ironically, as we discussed in the previous chapter, African American ex-slaves who told their stories for the WPA collection also draw attention to this issue of European trickery and deceit. In recalling the tales their forefathers told of their initial capture in Africa, they consistently speak of being lured onto European ships by red cloths, handkerchiefs, or flags only to be then taken on the dreaded Middle Passage trip to the Americas.[2]

The Ewe terms are also revealing because throughout their oral records there are few explicit references to Europeans or whites in general. This is all the more surprising given the major role played by European and white American traders in the pursuit of the slave trade. As some authors have said, there was a "ruthless efficiency" about slave-trade operations that spanned four continents and adversely affected every people they encountered from the Native Americans in the Americas to the Africans on the continent. Yet though we know much about European operations from their *own* records and some published slave narratives, we learn very little about the subject from African oral historical accounts.

Other references to whites suggest that the Anlo Ewe, in recalling the history of this period, simply conflate all the different European nations as well as America into one nation and one people.[3] Though in the primary account of the kidnapping incident of Atorkor, Chief Ndorkutsu specifies that it was a Danish ship that had kidnapped the drummers, in many of the other recollections of the incident there was no distinction made when referring to white traders. Furthermore, there was no recall of whether the ship that took the drummers away was a French, Danish, or even a North American one.

In some accounts, an interviewee might specify the Danes and mention that they were the first to ply their trade in the area; others might mention the later involvement of the English, especially in their belated attempts to control and stop the slave trade after abolition in 1807. The complex interplay of various European nations, including the French and the Americans, all in fierce competition with one another, however, is not evident in the oral record. The Ewes are not alone in this phenomenon. It appears that the same can be said for several other groups in

Mural at Fort Prinzenstein after renovation.

West and Central Africa that had contact with white slave traders. There is little memory of the actual ships and their names or of the nations that sponsored them. Slave ships from abroad are all treated as if they originated from the same place, and this in itself is very telling. This is to be understood against a backdrop of the many slave forts and castles that continue to dominate Africa's shores and the over 100,000 slave ships that bombarded the continent during the era of the Atlantic slave trade.[4]

What information we have from oral histories in other regions centers on the pervasive belief in West Africa that whites bought slaves in order to eat them. This belief was enough to cause many captives to commit suicide if they had the opportunity to do so. Olaudah Equiano's very famous slave narrative, published in 1789, is revealing in this respect as are the written sources of European traders such as Bosman, Snelgrave, and even John Newton, who reported that Africans in Sierra Leone shared the same sentiment. Of boarding the slave ship, Equiano writes:

> When I looked round the ship…, and saw a large furnace of copper boiling, and a multitude of black people of every description chained together, every one of their countenances expressing dejection and sorrow, I no longer doubted of my fate, and, quite overpowered with horror and anguish, I fell motionless on the deck and fainted. When I recovered a little, I found some black people about me, who I believed were some of those who brought me on board, and had been receiving their pay; they talked to me in order to cheer me, but all in vain. I asked them if we were not to be eaten by those white men with horrible looks, red faces, and long hair? They told me I was not; and one of the crew brought me a small portion of spirituous liquor in a wine glass; but, being afraid of him, I would not take it out his hand.[5]

Likewise, in the sixteenth century, Portuguese traders were told by the Africans they encountered on the Guinea coast that "they knew well how the trade had been carried on on the Canaga and the Christians ate human flesh and that all the slaves they bought they carried away to eat."[6] This notion of white cannibalism represented not only the real fears that Africans had of their captors but also metaphorically was a statement about how the trade had literally enveloped and destroyed their land.[7] Apart from these cryptic references, however, we have only a few clues in the oral record as to how Africans perceived European slave traders.

This represents a huge gap and points once again to my proposition that the historical memory of Africa on this subject is deeply fragmented. This is significant because it means that what we know of European and white American involvement in the trade comes largely from their own records—replete with their own biases. For me as a researcher, this necessitated several trips to England to look at records there. I went to the Public Records Office, among other places in London, and found at least part of the story from the British perspective. This is largely what I have detailed below—the operations of the slave trade on the European and American side, with a final discussion of some specific interactions with the Anlo on the old "Slave Coast" gleaned from the fragments of oral narratives that were available to me.

The role of external interests was indeed comprehensive and wide ranging. Such interests spanned several continents and constituted five of a total of six major legs of the Atlantic slave trade: (1) demand; (2) organization or setup of the trade in Europe/America; (3) trading activities on the African coast; (4) the Middle Passage voyage; (5) landing in the Caribbean; and (6) industrialization in Europe.[8] This all-encompassing role underwent several transformations during the era of the slave trade.

Above all, this role was dynamic. As the trade grew, it penetrated many different levels of society. This is evidenced not by statistics but rather by the fact that the business of the slave trade came to involve almost all areas of European/American society. Finally, over a period of time, this role became entrenched. We know, for example, that when Europeans first arrived in Africa, they came seeking a diversified trade with Africans. Those early ventures, from about 1445 onward, were characterized by a trade in gold, pepper, and other spices. It was not until Christopher Columbus's encounter with the New World that there was impetus on the part of Europe to pursue a trade in slaves.

There was little systemization in the first years of the encounter. For example, Sir John Hawkins, a captain during the reign of Queen Elizabeth, in 1554 was the first Englishman to engage in the slave trade. On his second voyage, prompted by "the sight of so much black ivory," he randomly seized a number of Africans and sold them to the Spanish to work in mines and plantations.[9] And so the trade began with almost random events of kidnapping. As it progressed, however, from a diversified trade in gold, pepper, and other products to almost exclusively a trade in slaves, systematized trading practices became the rule of the day. This was particularly necessary because of the stiff opposition to kidnapping by Africans and competition among all the European countries as well as America. This entrenchment is similar to the antebellum period in American history (1830–60). At this time, when slavery was most profitable, it became more systematized and entrenched. Likewise, the trade in slaves on the African continent, particularly during the rise of the sugar colonies, also became systematized and entrenched. This entrenchment of operational practices further facilitated and ensured the success of trading ventures.

The Atorkor incident discussed in chapter 2 and various inferences that can be drawn from it can be used as a starting point. Sources from the eighteenth and the nineteenth centuries also provide a context for evaluating the European/American role in slave trading.[10] It is fair to say that they are voluminous and stand in stark contrast to the fragmented history of the trade from the African perspective. There is no silence here, at least not in the historical record.

LEG I, DEMAND: THE ENGINE DRIVING THE TRAIN

Without the demand for slaves, there would have been no transatlantic slave trade, no competition between rival nations, no laws of interdiction, no illegal piracy along the coast— but, most of all, none of the terror and degradation suffered by slaves on their journey from the coast of Africa to the Americas. The firsthand account of Alexander Falconbridge, a ship doctor on slavers in the eighteenth century, corroborates this view. In his *Account of the Slave Trade on the Coast of Africa* (1788), he describes two incidents in which temporary suspension of the trade did much to "restore peace and confidence among the natives, which upon the arrival of the ships, is immediately destroyed by the inducement then held forth in the purchase of slaves."[11] This was his description of the peoples along the River Ambris in Angola, an area that at the time had experienced a five-year suspension of the trade. Likewise, when the same situation occurred at Bonny, he says, "The reduction of the price of negroes and the poverty of the black traders appear to have been the only bad effects of the discontinuance of trade; the good ones were, most probably, the restoration of peace and confidence among the natives and a suspension of kidnapping."[12]

The demand was like the engine that powers a train of railway cars. It was the motor that determined the nature and extent of the trade and ultimately the price of slaves. Before 1850 there had been many trading highs and lows. Abolition in 1807 did little to deter slave traders, and, in fact, in the 1820s and 1830s, there was an unprecedented increase in the traffic. It is estimated that more slaves crossed the Atlantic at that time than at any other period in history.[13] This was due to the fact that Cuba and Brazil, with their large planter economies, had a high demand for slaves. At the same time, the high mortality rates of blacks in both places created an increased demand. Such a demand in conjunction with the atmosphere of abolition drove up prices and profits because it was now more difficult for slavers to get their cargoes safely disembarked at ports in the Americas. The import figures for Cuba for example, rose dramatically at this time: 13,911 in 1853 (the highest for twelve years); 16,092 in 1858; 30,473 in 1859.[14]

If we use the Atorkor incident as an example, the American or European ship that came to the Slave Coast in 1856 was probably sailing with the intent to sell its cargo in Cuba. At the point at which other colonies ceased to have a high demand for slaves,

Cuba's demand increased greatly.[15] Fresh labor was constantly needed to cultivate the huge sugar and coffee plantations on the island. Cuban colonials believed that England's abolition policies were set up expressly to suppress competition on islands other than their West India properties. This suspicion, combined with the fact that by this period partnerships were forged between planters and Havana businessmen, tended to support the increase in slave-trade traffic and importation of fresh labor into Cuban estates. Havana businessmen began to make investments in the planters' estates by way of loans, giving them a vested interest in making the estates as profitable as possible. Spain, depending as it did on these commercial sources in Havana, also did little to openly suppress the traffic in slaves.[16] And so we see, for good or for bad, Cuba has long nurtured an independent spirit.

Given such demand, it was inevitable that prices would be driven up. "Rich traders would no doubt willingly pay much larger sums than was hitherto the custom to secure the landing of such profitable cargoes as those of Negroes have hitherto have been."[17] This quote is from a record dated 1852, contemporaneous with the time period of the Atorkor incident; the price of those slaves was estimated to $400 each. But records from as early as 1819 show that 15,147 "negroes" were sold in Havana at $400 dollars each, for a grand total of over $16 million! These prices were astronomical given the fact that prices on the coast, according to the British annual report in 1849, ranged from $5 to $25.[18] It is clear, then, that the demand made the trade much more profitable for Europe and American traders and investors. In effect, the abolition of the trade in the forty plus years since the turn of the century had elicited the opposite effect. It increased the level of demand, thus increasing the numbers of slaves imported as well as slave prices and profit margins. The greater the risk, the greater the potential profit. This was one very important transformation.

LEG 2, ORGANIZATION AND SETUP OF
THE TRADE IN ENGLAND AND AMERICA

In order to understand how the trade underwent such an important transformation in the nineteenth century, it is necessary to briefly look at what took place in the seventeenth and eighteenth centuries. At that time, the trade was dominated by European state-chartered companies, among whom competition was stiff. In the seventeenth century alone, eight nations—Portugal, France, England, Sweden, Denmark, the United Provinces, Brandenburgh, and Scotland—all had committed substantial interests to the trade. Each tried with limited success to achieve a monopoly over the other nations.

In 1672, England's Royal African Company came into existence. The company's main forts and castles were on the Gold Coast, though it also had holdings in northwest Africa and Whydah. On the Gold Coast, Cape Coast Castle was the Royal African Company's primary base, the "capital" of all its other Gold Coast settlements. There, it maintained a sizeable workforce including civilian and military employees. In 1721 the Royal African Company also established a lodge at Keta along the Anlo coast in order to facilitate communications with the castle.[19] At the same time, by 1700, the field had already expanded to include private interests and the level of competition had substantially increased. The result was that the Royal African Company found itself in conflict with interlopers of its own nation and of others, notably the Dutch and French.[20] Still, according to Davies, "Both contractors and licensees traded within a framework of royal regulations and royal officials were appointed to reside on the African coast."[21] Private traders were also required by Parliament to pay the *assiento* company 10 percent to defray expenses of the forts and factories on the African coast.[22] In this way, the state continued to be involved in the business of the trade. Finally, each enterprise, even though private, sailed under its national flag, be it French, Portuguese, English, or otherwise.

In England, London was initially the center for all this activity in the eighteenth century, but by the 1720s Bristol had become the leading slave port, encompassing half of all English clearances on an annual basis. As London was replaced by Bristol, so was Bristol later replaced by Liverpool.[23] Liverpool remained the leading port from the mid-eighteenth century till abolition in 1807. During this period Britain, and thus in the main Liverpool, had a very large interest in slave traffic, with 40 to 110 ships doing business on the African coast each year.[24]

Even though these companies were pursuing profits for their investors, technically independent of their governments, there was a distinct nationalistic element to their efforts. In the nineteenth century there occurred a drastic transformation in that an unprecedented number of ships leaving New York, Baltimore, and other areas in the States as well as Europe were operating on a *multinational* basis. It became the norm to have several different European nationals sailing with one or two Americans under the American flag. It was precisely because the American flag meant protection from the intrusions of the African Squadron (in effect abolition police) that this practice became widespread. The context of the illegality of the trade also must have encouraged traders, now pirates of all nations, to form alliances in order to ensure the continued success of their efforts. This was in stark contrast to the intense nationalistic competition that characterized the first two centuries of the slave trade. These collaborations also make it impossible for North America, for example, to distance itself from the awful business of slave trading, even though that is exactly what was done in the years prior to the Civil War.

What follows is a delineation of this process, taken largely from trading records and accounts of the city of Liverpool. Liv-

erpool is used in part because one version of the Atorkor incident identified the slave ship in question as an English ship. It is
also a good example because it provides insight into the height
of trading operations in that city and shows just how ruthlessly
efficient this trade was. Little was left to chance. Everything,
from the investor's potential profit to the insurance premiums
on African slaves, was calculated to the last degree.

Before a slave ship left the port of Liverpool, there were
seven aspects of the trade that had to be in place: These were the
securing of: (1) investors; (2) agents; (3) captains; (4) ships; (5)
outlay; (6) surgeons; and (7) crew. The first piece of business was
securing investors. Without investors and their capital, there
would have been no trade. Without individuals or firms backing
these pursuits, it would have been impossible for such expensive
yet ultimately profitable ventures to take place. Given the importance of investors, there has been surprisingly little research
done in this area. It is known, however, that these voyages were
usually financed by partnerships.[25] We also know that there
were many sleeping partners. They funded the slave trade, but
otherwise may have had little contact with the actual voyages.
This allowed many to keep their heads above the fray with an
air of "respectability" when in reality, their deeds suggested
otherwise.[26]

What is interesting about these sleeping partners is the fact
that they came from all walks of life. In fact, in an examination
of the records of Liverpool slave trader William Davenport, historian David Richardson asserts that "given the quite substantial
outlay of capital involved in each slaving venture, rapid expan-
sion of the trade depended to some extent upon the attraction
into it of 'outside' sources of capital."[27] Furthermore, according
to another source, "it is well known that many of the small vessels that import about one hundred slaves are fitted out by at-
tornies [sic], drapers, ropers, grocers, tallow chandlers, barbers,

tailors etc. Some have one eighth, some a fifteenth and some a thirty second."[28] Many politicians were also heavily involved. Several members of Parliament, the town council, and mayors were involved at some point. This group included all of Liverpool's mayors between 1787 and 1807.[29]

And so we see that an important transformation took place. The trade slowly became one that affected many areas of society, so much so that Gomer Williams says "that every man in Liverpool is a merchant, and he who cannot send a bale will send a bandbox. . . . that almost every order of people is interested in a Guinea cargo."[30] The business of the slave trade was not just the business of slave merchants, it involved others in more traditional areas of life. There was a distinct commingling between legitimate interests and "illegitimate" interests before the ships left port. In many ways, these partnerships enjoyed the anonymity of investors in today's stock market. Just as millions of people invest every day on the world market in companies that they have no direct involvement in running and operating, so did investors—large and small—traders, and others participate in the Liverpool trade. The business behind the business of the trade thus affected many important areas of the general society, and so though not everyone in British society was involved in the slave trade, *all* benefited from it in one way or another.

This view is consistent with Eric Williams's in his famous book, *Capitalism and Slavery*. Britain's growth as a great maritime and economic power was intrinsically linked to the slave trade. Furthermore, the islands in the West Indies were the basis of Britain's economic strength, which was thus derived from the labor of the slaves. The seaport towns of Bristol and Liverpool grew as a result of the capital accumulated from the trade as well as the growth of subsidiary industries such as shipbuilding.[31] Liverpool was just a small town with 138 households before slave trading turned it into one of the major ports of the world.[32]

For years, many scholars have debated the Williams thesis, with some suggesting that the slave trade was not solely responsible for Britain's power. Whether his thesis is accepted in its entirety or not, it is possible to say that traders and investors were not the only ones to profit from the Atlantic system. British society as a whole also derived many benefits.

Still, much of the investment came from companies with access to large-scale capital. Capital from European bankers and merchant houses was the crucial ingredient that enabled plantations to be developed and Africans to be bought and transported.[33] The Bank of England, for example, played a critical role as banker to merchants and planters alike. Some of the bank's officers were even more directly involved; Humphrey Morice, for example, who was director in the early 1700s, owned six slave ships.[34] In terms of large partnerships, about ten houses, each with a few partners, accounted for almost two-thirds of the traffic. They were among the Fortune 500 of their day. Since their outlay was greater, they could engage in the sale of at least one thousand slaves a year.[35] The firms Peter Baker and John Dawson and William Boast and Co. were the largest and second-largest in the slave trade from 1783 to 1792. A review of the voyages they underwrote in the appendixes of Williams's book shows that they had substantial returns on their initial investments. Many used their profits to gain large extensions of credit for outfitting new ventures.[36] In the main, it was these firms, according to some authors, who facilitated the development of a systematized merchant class and the growth of British industry.

Agents

Liverpool records show that partnerships usually depended on the ship's agent or "purser" to do the actual organization of everything needed for the voyage. Often the agent was also a partner closely identified with the firm. These agents were a small group of trusted men who (1) supervised the outfitting of the ship; (2) arranged for outward-bound cargoes; (3) worked with the captains as well as the commission houses in the New World; and (4) kept accounts.[37] They thus played an extremely important role, which could be likened to that of a chief ombudsman or liaison.

Captains

Captains, on the whole, did not leave many records of their voyages, but we gain insight into their experience and the operations of the trade from selected autobiographies such as that of Hugh Crow, a slave-trade captain in the eighteenth and nineteenth centuries, and that of the Frenchman Captain Theodore Canot. Furthermore, from Stephen Behrendt's "The Captains in the British Slave Trade from 1785–1807" we gain some valuable information. Behrendt compiled a database of some 2,876 slave voyages during this time period, pulling information from Liverpool and Bristol muster rolls, among other sources. He then identified the number of captains involved in these voyages (946) and sought to piece together important biographical information (age, years at sea, etc.).

From this study we learn the process by which men became slave-trade captains. Generally, there was an informal procedure of boys being apprenticed to experienced slave captains. Often, in fact, young men followed their fathers into the business. Many initially gained their experience as mates in the West India trade, eventually taking command of their first voyage at around the age of thirty. These seafarers made their money largely from "privilege slaves"—slaves that they could in turn exchange for cash and "coast commissions," which reflected a percentage of the gross proceeds.[38]

Shipping

The shipping industry also received a significant boost from involvement in the slave trade. Liverpool slave ships came to be known as "guineamen," named after the famed Guinea Coast, the Atlantic coast of Africa. These were designed to hold large cargoes above all else. Ships such as the Liverpool ship called *Brookes* (1789) are well known in the literature. The image of rows and rows of Africans in the hold of the ship, without room at their heads and with their feet piled on one another, was to become one of the most powerful antislavery images.[39] The inhumanity of the trade in human cargo comes across fully in this image, which leaves few details to the imagination. It is clear that slave traders at that time did not consider the issue of mortality rates and in fact were narrowly concerned with packing in as many Africans as possible. In so doing, they disregarded the fact that such conditions would inevitably bring about the loss of a great number of slaves before they reached their destinations.

Ironically, after the abolition of the trade, the industry saw a number of innovations in trading vessels. These later models were designed for maximum speed so that slavers could avoid capture. At the same time, there were attempts made to design ships that could carry the necessary armaments while still accommodating substantial cargo.[40] The clipper was reputed to be the fastest and the most modern ship at that time. In fact, these ships for a while were able to elude the African Squadron because of their efficiency and speed.[41] The evolution of the trade also saw improvements that may have resulted in better conditions for slaves on board. These were linked to various statutes enacted by Parliament in part as a reaction to the abolitionist crusade and in part due to the increased connection between high profitability and low mortality rates. Before the late 1780s, by statute, slavers were not to exceed two slaves per ton. By 1788 the law declared, even more favorably, that for every vessel of up to 207 tons, there were to be five slaves per three tons.[42] How much of these "improvements" were for the purpose of safeguarding profits, we will never know.

Outlay

A good example of the outlay of traders comes from Captain Theodore Canot's nineteenth-century account, *Adventures of an African Slaver*. Expenses in general included the cost of cargo to be exchanged, insurance costs, wages for captain and crew and, as Canot's records show, hush money for every leg of the journey. Cargo on these ships included a massive number of guns. In the eighteenth century alone, between 283,000 and 394,000 guns were imported into Africa each year by European traders. These guns played an important role in the enhancement of slave-trade activities. Furthermore, the cotton goods that were manufactured in places like Manchester in England were widely traded along the coast.[43] Other goods included many products from countries with which Europe traded. These included iron, copper, brass bars, silk—and most especially liquor. The many references to the latter in the oral histories attest heavily to the role of liquor in slave-trade pursuits. Finally, over time Africa became a large market for Europe's trading goods—those manufactured on the continent and those acquired from its trading partners around the world. Some go so far as to say that Africa was simply a dumping ground for cheaply made materials and bric-a-brac. In this way, the seeds of the Industrial Revolution were sown.[44]

In a response to a question regarding the kind of currency that was used in Eweland by the Danes, the oral record revealed the following: "First they were using cowries (not the ones on the ground now). Later they give them pieces of cloth, drinks, whiskey in barrels, pieces of tobacco. Though the Danes brought the cowries, they usually don't pay in money, they exchanged goods."[45]

In addition to the costs for cargo there were insurance costs. Slave ships were generally insured against loss of their cargo—human and material. Investors who lost a part of their cargo for various reasons could expect to recoup up to 95 percent of their losses. Liverpool merchant Richard Davenport's records show that for seventy-four of his voyages, he paid £34,000 in insurance costs and recovered £26,000 for losses incurred.[46]

The famous case *Gregson v. Gilbert,* more commonly known as the *Zong* case, changed the nature of insuring slave ships against loss of cargo. The *Zong,* owned by a Liverpool trading company, had already made several slave voyages by the 1780s. On one particular voyage from West Africa to Jamaica, the *Zong* lost more than 60 Africans to illness from an original group of 470. The ship also lost almost half its crew. The captain, Luke Collingwood, in assessing the tremendous loss, instructed his crew to throw overboard all the sick slaves to save on water rations and to put them in a position to claim insurance losses. Over three successive days, 131 slaves were systematically thrown overboard and drowned. Such were the circumstances of the unfortunate men and women aboard the *Zong* that the case engendered in the public nothing short of sheer horror. Public opinion, as a result, was swayed in favor of the abolitionists. Furthermore, the case forced jurists to confront the ever-present dilemma of regarding men as chattel who could be disposed of at will. In the end, the owners of the *Zong* ship won the battle for compensation, but this decision was later overturned on appeal.[47]

The *Zong* case was not the only case of this nature. *A Complete Digest of the Laws, Theory, and Practice of Insurance* was published in Great Britain in 1781, the same year as the *Zong* case, partially as a result of such controversies. This digest was deemed necessary because there were apparently no definitive ordinances regarding the matter; "everything being left up to the insurer's "uniformed opinion." As a consequence, traders and insurers alike felt dissatisfied with the disorder of the system. "We appear to be adrift without pilot or compass, driving before the wind of Accident, amidst Quicksands and Rocks so that if we long escape shipwreck, we shall have wonderful good luck."[48] By 1790 Parliament intervened, decreeing that "no loss or damage shall be recoverable on account of the mortality of slaves by natural death or ill treatment or against loss by throwing overboard of slaves on any account whatsoever."[49]

By the mid-eighteenth century, some slave traders took to the practice of insuring among themselves.[50] We do not know if this was due in part to the growing lack of support from the court system or if traders eventually had problems securing insurance policies for their cargo. Aimes cites contemporary sources suggesting that by the 1840s the reason was the latter. Suppression efforts increased the risk of loss of cargo and thus made insurance companies wary of insuring slave ships.[51] In any event, the issue of insurance, though it underwent several transformations, remained important to the maintenance of the trade.

Finally, another important development in terms of outlay was "hush money." Canot's record of his voyage in 1827 is a good example of what we may expect was quite common given the volume of trade during the years of the official abolition. In his record of expenses he budgets for hush money to be given to officials at his port of departure in Europe and at the port in Havana. Under "Expenses out," he has $200 for "clearance and hush money"; under "Expense in Havana," he has a category "Government officers at $8 a head."[52] Though we have few examples as explicit as this one, we may extrapolate that the slave trade could not have continued to the degree that it did without a certain amount of corruption. Officials at both ends of the transatlantic voyage had to be paid off quietly.

Surgeons

Surgeons, or ship doctors, played a very important part in the slave trade. In general they were responsible for first, ensuring that traders chose only able-bodied slaves on the coast of Africa and second, that these slaves remained in reasonable health during the Middle Passage voyage. They checked teeth and limbs and oversaw the process of branding the slaves before they set out to sea.[53] From Alexander Falconbridge's famous account, we learn not only about the role of the ship doctor but also much about conditions of the slaves on slave ships as well as how they were captured. Many of these doctors ended by contributing greatly to the more traditional branches of their profession.[54] Another important development was the practice of promoting surgeons to the command of ships. This developed in part as a consequence of the Dolben Act, which privileged experienced seafarers and acknowledged the connection between high profitability and low mortality rates.[55] Thus as the trade became more entrenched, the surgeon's role became increasingly important both on the slave ships, in terms of enhanced responsibilities, and on land, in terms of contributions to the field of tropical diseases. Again we see how ruthlessly efficient this system came to be. It was no longer a question of haphazard kidnapping as in the early years of the trade. Those involved in the slave trade became students of the trade, if you will, who carefully studied what was the best way to bring about their desired profits. In such a system there was no room for remembering that the cargo, after all, was human—flesh and blood like themselves.

Crew

Crew members on slave ships came from a variety of sources. It was unpleasant work, so often they had to be enticed or coerced into service. The first crew members on slave ships were undoubtedly poor boys who started out as apprentices and were subsequently promoted to second and first mates.[56] Others were "impressed" into service on a slave ship. Some were even drugged and kidnapped.[57] Still others were criminal offenders who were attempting to escape the law by service on a slave ship.[58] In fact, many captains had agreements with rooming-house landlords and tavern keepers that provided them with a steady supply of men at all times.[59]

Eventually, as the trade became more entrenched, a system developed in which Africans were given opportunities to join the crew. Brodie Cruikshank describes the black "kroo" of Sierra Leone, for example, as being particularly adept at rowing the small boats of newly acquired slaves to the ship, docked at a distance from the shore. Many of them became efficient seamen but others found themselves, as men with black skin, victim to the same cruel trade in which they participated; they could easily be captured and sold by those who saw their worth as cargo and not as seamen. Other writers of the time suggested that Negroes could be useful in the loading and unloading of cargo, thereby protecting white sailors from exposure to coastal fevers and diseases.[60] In any event, this development clearly came toward the end of trade, after substantial contact with the African coast had taught traders how best to pursue their efforts.

LEG 3, ACTIVITIES ON THE AFRICAN COAST

In the beginning of the European encounter, there were no explicit rules of operation. As discussed previously, the first traders, like Sir John Hawkins, pillaged villages and engaged in kidnapping. Still, we know that European and American traders through their sustained contact figured out a systematic mode of operation that had several components. This system still included kidnapping to some degree, whether by Africans or by their white counterparts, as seen in the Atorkor example. Furthermore, as the African oral histories and the narratives of ex-slaves reveal, deception and guile were sometimes used to lure Africans onto slave ships.

Records also show that "buying obedience" was very important. Sums were routinely paid to villages for commercial purposes. These are usually listed as "coustomes." This would in turn give traders the right to pursue their efforts without interference. This practice eventually gave way to others. According to Governor Carstensen, Danish governor of the Gold Coast in the mid-nineteenth century, the system underwent a number of changes, moving away from giving cash stipends to chiefs in favor of giving goods.[61] Carstensen goes on to complain that the Danish were the only Europeans still paying these stipends when the English, for example, who benefited from the very peace and order that the stipends ensured, had long since stopped paying them.[62]

Another mode of operation was to distribute to chiefs and others what Carstensen calls "ridiculous titles." The title of "Duke," for example, was given to the chief of Aquapim. Carstensen, in mockery of this system, says that he personally chose to address these newly titled natives simply as chiefs. Ridiculous as it may have seemed to the governor, however, these titles served an important purpose. They facilitated a process of acculturation of Africans into the European way of life. Europeans exported not only guns and liquor but also these outward signs of status, with all their pomp and finery. This was clearly evident in another mode of operation, the gift of flags.[63] From other accounts we learn that "much ceremony and many presents" were used to secure loyalty and support. These included things like "a Spanish hat or a piece of silk."[64] In fact, ironically, this is one area in which the oral record is not silent. In several of the accounts in my collection there was mention of "gifts" that had been given to chiefs and others from Europeans. They were usually mentioned with great pride. For example, in my interview with the elder Mr. Benedictus Tamakloe in 1993, he enthusiastically showed me the top hat that was reportedly given to his ancestor by Queen Victoria in recognition for his bravery and valor.[65]

Another way of gaining the locals' acceptance was the employment of several of the residents along the coast. Clearly, this was one of the main reasons that a small town like Atorkor became a major trading depot. It was not simply the case that African traders were involved in the actual sale of Africans but that others in the town, as in many of the coastal towns, also participated in the economy generated by slavery. Traders needed a long list of items and people to assist them on the coast: canoes, canoe men, servants, messengers, gong beaters, washerwomen, porters, and translators. Fees were also paid for "renting" the beach and for entertainment expenses. The employment of all these people as well as the infusion of currency and goods played an important role in trading efforts.

Perhaps most important, however, was the establishment of a permanent physical presence in the form of the forts or slave castles along the coast. The first forts were built by the Portuguese at Mina (1482) and Axim (1503). The British Royal African Company followed suit with Cape Coast Castle at Fetu and other sites at Sekondi, Accra, Dixcove, Kommenda, Winneba, and Anomabu.[66] The closest fort to Atorkor was Fort Prinzenstein, established at Keta in 1714. The fort changed hands several times between the Danish and the Dutch, with the former rebuilding the present site in 1784. Carstensen confirms of Danish occupation in its heyday: "The Danish governor and civil servants were privileged slave traders."[67] They continued to occupy it till 1850, when they sold all their Gold Coast possessions to the British.[68]

The official purposes of the forts were to set up a defense against other European nations (evidenced by the big guns and cannons facing the sea), to establish a permanent staff that would develop good relations with local peoples, and to accumulate slaves and cargo in readiness for trade. The forts were, then, generally trading posts that included storage and meeting rooms.[69] But the forts had many unofficial purposes as well. They were also bases of operation for systematized intervention in local affairs of governance, particularly in the period following abolition. In many ways, these forts were early precursors of colonial institutions, whose administrators undoubtedly learned much from the hundreds of years of sustained contact during the slave trade. This fact alone shows the importance of breaking the silence on the trade in Africa, where there is much academic and popular interest in the impact of colonialism but a fragmented memory on the slave trade. Yet as we see here, the two were intimately connected.

Another unofficial purpose of the forts is closely tied to the above. As discussed earlier, it is clear that European nations along the coast took more than a passing interest in the outcome of local wars. From early on, there is evidence that the nations would invest their money and guns in support of one group over the other. Sometimes this was done for political purposes only —in order to secure loyalty or to sustain support of a particular group. More often than not, however, it was done to assist in the process of obtaining captives who would later be sold as slaves. This appears to have been an important mode of operation throughout the slave-trade era. In 1689, the English sided with the Fetu in their war against the Abrembo (Abrem) by giving them "six field pieces and sixty white soldiers." This was done with the understanding that they would receive all slaves captured by the Fetu. Furthermore, in 1706 the English were said to have hoped for the victory of the Akani in a local war because this would mean "there will be a glorious trade in slaves."[70]

The role of missions and schools was also crucial. As we know from the Atorkor sources, some of Ndorkutsu's relatives were sent to European schools. It is clear also from documents such as Carstensen's diary that an unofficial liaison was set up between trading institutions and missionaries. In his diary, he stressed the fact that all other European nations had long since realized that "civilizing the inhabitants" worked to their benefit in trading relations and urged the Danes to likewise establish a greater connection to missionaries on the Gold Coast.[71] Finally, there developed on the Gold Coast in the mid-nineteenth century what the Dutch called a system of "recruitment" of soldiers for their East Indian army. This system, some came to believe, was merely a veiled cover for slave dealings. It started in 1831 and continued intermittently till 1853. At its height in 1837, one thousand slaves at one hundred guilders a head were "recruited" from Elmina and sent to Java. In reality, these slaves were sold to the Dutch by the Asante.[72] It was incidents such as this that caused the Anlo Ewes to use the term *yevu* in reference to Europeans; a substantial amount of distrust, it is fair to say, was evident on both sides.

LEG 4, THE VOYAGE OF TERROR

In the last years of the twentieth century and now in the beginning of the twenty-first, there is much use of the word *terror.* Terror is designed to harm its object physically and psychologically. Without question, it would not be anachronistic to use this word to characterize the famed Middle Passage. Conditions on slave ships for Africans were truly something out of a horror movie. They were gruesome whether during the period of legal trading or after the abolition, but the period of suppression brought about unprecedented horrors for captured Africans.[73] Violence and death were a part of the journey from the beginning, but in the nineteenth century, as smugglers attempted to conceal their cargo from the watchful eye of the policing ships of the African Squadron, they held absolutely no regard for the sanctity of human life. This last stage of the trade thus had a devastating effect on the physical and mental well-being of Africans who were captured. Finally, given what we know from the oral sources, it is possible to surmise the extent of the blows that were dealt to African notions of kinship, death, dying, and burial.

In keeping with the tenor of this ruthlessly efficient system, conditions on slave voyages were closely linked to existing knowledge about slave mortality, technological advances in the shipping industry, and improved legislation. In the early years of the Atlantic system, the emphasis was on volume. Traders attempted to pack in as many slaves into a slave ship as possible without regard for proper ventilation or physical space. In the mid-eighteenth century, as traders and legislators witnessed the high mortality of such voyages, there were gradual changes in the kinds of ships that were built. New ships began to be built with lines of portholes below the gun deck or with large wind sails that facilitated the passage of air to the Africans below.[74] The English Parliament also contributed to this effort by requiring that slavers reduce the volume of slaves on board according to the tonnage of the ship.

It was in part the moral outcry generated by abolitionists regarding conditions on slave ships that helped to bring about these changes. Black and white abolitionists alike publicized the physical horrors of the Middle Passage in such graphic detail that legislators, shipbuilders, and others were forced to respond in some definitive way. As such, during this period, some forty years before the official abolition in 1807, there was a relatively greater sense of morality regarding conditions on the slave ships. Killings on board were less rampant and random, except in cases where revolts had to be put down.[75] The official end of the slave trade in the nineteenth century, however, witnessed a return to some of the more horrific aspects of the earlier trade.

We know much of the physical horrors on slave ships, although in recent years there has been a move away from narra-

tive tales of these horrors toward more statistical analysis.[76] No
statistic, however, could ever give us an accurate understanding
of not only the physical toll but the mental toll exacted on
African peoples. We gain much evidence of the physical toll
from accounts of the surgeon Alexander Falconbridge and the
slave narrative of Olaudah Equiano. In addition to the often-
noted lack of physical room for each slave, one key feature on
slave ships was the smell. Equiano speaks of "lavatory buckets
overflowing and slaves defecating where they lay."[77] Falconbridge likewise speaks of dreading his daily visit to the decks
below because of the stench.[78]

This noxious smell was exacerbated by the fact that there
was little ventilation in most slave ships. Even in the accounts
described by Falconbridge in the latter part of the eighteenth
century, which suggest that there had been improvements in
portholes and wind sails by this time, it can be seen that this was
not always sufficient to guarantee the health of the Africans on
board. "But whenever the sea is rough and the rain heavy it becomes necessary to shut these [portholes] and every other con-
veyance by which the air is admitted."[79] The lack of fresh air
mixed with the already noxious smells as well as the confine-
ment of space did much to cause rampant sickness on these
ships, leading to certain death. Various fevers and fluxes were
particularly pervasive on these ships. As the following account
by Falconbridge indicates, the physical toll on Africans during
these voyages was horrific:

> One instance will serve to convey some idea, though a very faint
> one, of their terrible sufferings. Some wet and blowing weather
> having occasioned the port-holes to be shut and the grating to be
> covered, fluxes and fevers among the negroes ensued. While they
> were in this situation, I frequently went down among them till at
> length their rooms became so extremely hot as to be only bearable
> for a very short time. But the excessive heat was not the only thing

that rendered their situation intolerable. The deck, that is, the floor of their rooms was so covered with the blood and mucus which had proceeded from them in consequence of the flux, that it resembled a slaughterhouse. It is not in the power of the human imagination to picture a situation more dreadful or disgusting. Numbers of the slaves having fainted they were carried upon deck where several of them died and the rest with great difficulty were restored.[80]

Dysentery proved to be a problem throughout the era not just for the slaves but for the slave traders, who knew that there would be no buyers for a slave thus stricken. This was the case because such slaves, even though they had survived the horrors of the Middle Passage and disembarked on shore, would almost certainly die within a few days after purchase. As a result, there were several cases of traders using various devious and degrading means to disguise the sickness of their cargo.[81]

Food was given to slaves on the slave ships twice a day. Traders learned early that to ensure survival of their cargo they could not serve Africans beans and other foods with which they were not familiar. In time, they learned to feed them African food, which did much to reduce the mortality rate. Still, the practice of feeding slaves (sick and healthy alike) from the same bucket contributed to the spread of infectious diseases.[82]

Another of the physical hardships slaves had to endure was the infamous "lash." Punishments for slaves did not originate on the plantations of the Americas. These punishments started on the slave ship. In the exhibit on the Atlantic Slave Trade at the Merseyside Museum in Liverpool, various implements, such as the lash and neck collars, are on view as testimony to the various methods of ensuring the obedience of slaves during the long voyage to shore.[83] The lash was used most pervasively, but neck collars were utilized as well. The numerous advertisements by goldsmiths in papers such as the *London Advertiser* bear testimony to the value placed on this equipment. "Silver, padlocks for Blacks or dogs," read one such advertisement in 1756.[84]

Violence on slave ships, then, was a way of life. One important observation noted by Equiano was that the crew was often not exempt from such violence: "For I had never seen among my people such instances of brutal cruelty and this not only shewn towards the blacks but also to some of the whites themselves. One white man, in particular I saw, when we were permitted to be on deck, flogged so unmercifully with a large rope near the foremast that he died in consequence of it; and they tossed him over the side as they would have done a brute."[85]

Perhaps the most inhumane aspect of the voyage, however, were the points at which the physical and the mental horrors of these trips collided. Given what we now know from oral sources of African views of death, burial, the body, and kinship ties, we may extrapolate to gain some sense of the actual suffering on these voyages and the effects they must have had on African—and in this case Ewe—culture and customs.

The proximity to death and dying must have been one such horror. Falconbridge describes, for example, that in his routine of checking the decks each morning, he would often find several dead slaves attached to the living by chains. What must that have been like for the living? What psychological terror must they have suffered throughout the night? Moreover, the dead were frequently thrown overboard by way of disposal. But the throwing of human beings into the treacherous seas of the Atlantic was not reserved for the dead; it happened also to the living, as the sensational *Zong* case had proved in the late eighteenth century. One may only wonder what it was like for those who were spared on the *Zong* and other ships where such incidents occurred. What did the willful killing of innocent men, women, and children do to the psyche of those left behind? For those who survived and made it to the Americas, must they not have brought with them the horror of seeing so much death?

Finally, the voyage of terror must have dealt a particularly strong blow to the African concept of kinship. Kinship plays a central role in Ewe traditional life. The community acknowledges patrilineal descent. and every Anlo belongs to one of fifteen clans *(hlo)*. One gains membership by birth, but strangers and slaves are often incorporated into existing clans. The Blu clan, for example, became a specific clan for strangers (people from outside the Ewe community). The word *hlo* itself means vengeance, as it refers to the fact that the clan could exact vengeance on those who had offended its members. In fact, *do hlo* means "to commit murder or an offence punishable by death or sale into slavery." Membership in a clan brought with its certain rights and responsibilities. Each clan member, for example, was expected to respect certain food taboos and funeral rites. At the same time, each was also entitled to specific land and fishing rights.[86] Given the meaning of the word *hlo*, some Ewes may even have attributed their awful plight to some wrongdoing done by them or their ancestors. Furthermore, on the slave ship there would be no respect for food taboos. This must have contributed to an overall sense of trauma. In addition to their extreme physical discomfort, they could only have experienced a deep sense of disruption and dislocation as they compared their new horrific reality to their previous lives.

Given this knowledge and the fact that many of these voyages, like that of the ship the *Wanderer* in 1857, contained a substantial number of children, we may also speculate that the children experienced the most trauma as a result of the voyage.[87] Additionally, from what we now know from the field of psychology about the importance of the formative years in shaping the future adult, again, we may only imagine the trauma of witnessing the constancy of death, dying, and violence without the palliative of traditional customs passed on by family and loved ones. Again, where the physical and the psychological horrors coincided, this must have dealt additional blows to African customs, values, and psyche.

LEG 5, LANDING IN CUBA: DESPERATE MEASURES AND DEVASTATING IMPACT

The terror of the Middle Passage continued upon landing in the Caribbean. Here, too, the system changed with the passage of time. The nineteenth-century period of abolition saw a reversion to some of the earlier horrors of the trade. This was due in large part to the smugglers' attempts to avoid capture. The laws of suppression were such that the African Squadron could not arrest the captain and crew of a suspected slaver if there were no slaves on board. Smugglers, knowing this fact, sought to get around the letter of the law by dumping all evidence of slave activity, including their innocent human cargo. This kind of activity, though it has been largely documented through isolated incidents, points to the horrific developments that took place at the end of the slave trade. Such developments could only have had a devastating impact on the African peoples aboard these vessels. What system did remain generally deteriorated into one in which there was little respect on the part of traders and plantation owners for the human beings in their charge. As such, in this leg of the trade Africans suffered some of the most devastating blows of all.[88]

Until the abolition, slavers would land at the major ports of Cuba, the reported destination of the ship in the Atorkor incident. By the mid-nineteenth century, however, to avoid capture slavers endeavored to find other ways to unload their cargo. According to Aimes, "Cargoes were run at a preconcerted time and place. The *bozales* [recently enslaved Africans] were put into rowboats, small sailing vessels, even steamers and distributed along the coast at places far from the original landing where

they were least expected."[89] The safe landing of slaves often required the collusion of selected government officials on the island who accepted bribes. Once landed, the ship would then be
burned to destroy all evidence of its existence.[90] One such case
was reported in the *Anti-Slavery Reporter* (September 1, 1858):
"The *W. D. Miller,* a vessel previously seen under American
colours in Cuba, escaped from her Majesty's ship *Teazer,* dis-
charged slaves in Cuba and was burned there to avoid subsequent condemnation."[91] Wealthy estate owners such as the
infamous Julian De Zuletta and other "Sugar Nobles," as they
were called, would eagerly await the ships' arrival.[93]

Another issue was the question of sale and prices. In the
years before the abolition, the "scramble" or the slave auction
were the methods of choice for selling slaves. A ship would dock
at the port of Havana and its slaves would disembark after having been washed and primed for sale. At an appointed time,
plantation owners would "scramble" around in an effort to
choose the best, most able-bodied slaves they could lay their
hands on. This apparent mayhem often engendered an overwhelming sense of panic and fear on the part of the slaves about
their fate and future.[94] Otherwise, there was the standard slave
auction, where landowners bid their best prices for the slave of
their choosing. By the mid-nineteenth century, however, such
public sales were too conspicuous for those illegally involved in
the trade.

For those slavers who were not successful and were captured
by the British cruisers, little was done in terms of enforcement.
According to Aimes, "Occasionally a slaver was unfortunate
enough to be caught. But the injustice of such cases was palpable. One Spanish captain who was sent to the Phillipine [*sic*] Islands for ten years in 1832 applied for pardon. The government
referred the case to Lord Palmerston, and on his acquiescence,
he was released in 1834."[95]

The status of freed slaves from such vessels was much better than that of the slave population on the island. At this crucial period a new system called *emancipados* was established by law, in which freed slaves were intended to work as paid apprentices. They would be commissioned to landowners for a specified period of time, during which they would be paid for their labor. But as archival sources repeatedly show, many of the landowners withheld wages from these apprentices. "It appears by a notice published officially in *The Gazette* of the 28th of June that many persons to whom emancipado apprentices had been assigned early in the year had some time after the expiration of the first few months neglected to pay in advance, as is ordered, the wages due for the second four months."[95]

And so it was that while superficially there appeared to have been progress achieved by the British cruisers and some conscientious Cuban officials in the freeing of slaves, this freedom was in effect quite hollow. Africans were effectively rendered "slaves" to the land and their new emancipado masters.

LEG 6, INDUSTRIALIZATION IN EUROPE

We may briefly refer to the last leg of the trade here insofar as it relates to the primary point of the control that Europe and America had over most slave-trading activities. In this case, as in others, Africans could exert little control. They neither owned the means of production nor did they have any direct influence on such means except for the crucial fact that it was by-products of their labor that contributed to the growth of industrialization in Europe. These products, taken to Manchester, Lancashire, and other centers of industry helped to transform European nations into the powers that they are today. As Eric Williams points out, "What the building of ships for the transport of slaves did for 18th century Liverpool, the manufacture of cotton goods for the purchase of slaves did for 18th century Manchester."[96] As noted before, though some may debate the *extent* to

which Britain and other nations owed their wealth to these activities, there can be no question that these goods, originating
from the by-products of slave labor, provided at the very least
a great benefit to British industry and the British nation as a
whole. It facilitated, in part if not in entirety, one of the most
important historical transformations of European society.[97]

EUROPEAN AND AMERICAN
RESISTANCE TO THE TRADE
IN THE ABOLITION MOVEMENT

Finally, no discussion of European and American agency is
complete without a review of abolition efforts. This movement, whose greatest advocates came from Britain and the
northern states of America, constituted a major form of resistance to the Atlantic slave trade. Pamphlets generated on both
sides of the Atlantic influenced public opinion and served to
illuminate the cruelties of the Atlantic system. In Britain and
in the United States, resistance came particularly from religious
groups, such as the Evangelicals, the Quakers, and the Mora-
vians, that had a moral objection to the trade and also from former slaves such as Frederick Douglass and Olaudah Equiano.
Rebellious slaves on plantations throughout the Americas also
put up formidable resistance efforts. The end result of these
efforts was that the British abolished the trade in 1807, the
Danes in 1803, and the United States declared the importation
of slaves illegal in 1808.[98]

The African oral record is relatively silent on the issue of
abolition efforts. The market for the abolitionist slave narratives
of Equiano, Mary Prince, and others was in Europe and North
America—the center of the slave trade and the institution of
slavery itself.[99] Africans were, of course, aware of what they
might have called a curious shift in policy of the Europeans, but
the abolitionist circles existed in locales outside of the conti-

nent. Still, in the midst of this silence there is one fascinating
oral narrative that illuminates once again the difficulty in sometimes differentiating European and African roles in the slave
trade on the continent. The story is told by Mr. Kofi Agyeman
Jantuah and confirmed by his mother, Mrs. Stella Jiagge, of the
Keta region. They are the direct descendants of the Danish
officer, Lt. Johannes Svedstrup, who was assigned to Fort Prinzenstein in Eweland to help enforce the abolition laws in the
mid-nineteenth century. Lt. Svedstrup also happened to be
married to an African woman named Miss Badger! Mr. Jantuah
and his mother now proudly tell the following story, which
reflects a mixture of oral history and archival research on the
part of Mr. Jantuah. It goes as follows:

> Lieutenant Johannes Wilhelm Svedstrup arrived in the then Dan-
> ish Guinea in 1844 as sergeant. He was responsible for arresting the
> Aquapim king Addum and the Osu grand interpreter Sebah Akim
> after they had sacrificed two of the rival chief Ussu Akim's chil-
> dren by cutting their throats in a fetish ceremony and smearing
> their blood over their big war drum. As punishment, the Danish
> governor Edward Carstensen exiled the culprits to the Fort Kastel-
> let in Copenhagen.
>
> Fort Prinzenstein became the scene of a dramatic event when
> at the request of the governor Carstensen it was reactivated in order
> to aid the suppression of the slave trade that had continued in the
> area under the influence of Portuguese slave trader Don Jose Mora.
>
> Guard-Chief Svedstrup was ordered to Prinzenstein to super-
> vise the restoration of the fort. When the Anlos realized that the
> intention of having the fort repaired was to prevent the slave trade,
> they got very angry because they profited out of having the slave
> transport passing through their land and camping there, partly they
> traded in slaves themselves. Svedstrup now realized that he was
> surrounded by enemies, and dared not go unarmed far away from
> the fort.
>
> One day he went into Keta town, which was only divided by
> a small square from the fort. Suddenly some Africans came rushing

towards him with spears, knives, and sticks. Svedstrup drew his saber and cut his way through them and ran to the fort, where some soldiers came to his aid. He then turned around and the Africans ran away, leaving two of them who were fatally wounded. Some hours later there were sounds of horn and drums in Keta. The fort was besieged by thousands of Anlo for several weeks who demanded that the culprit be turned over to them.

However, the commandant of Fort Prinzenstein, Svedstrup, and his garrison of mulatto soldiers and fort personnel took a courageous stand until the naval brig *Ornen* (the *Eagle*), under the command of Captain Irminger, came to rescue the garrison and bombarded Keta from the seaside.

In the autumn of 1848 came news that a war had begun in Denmark in the spring with Germany. Svedstrup sought permission for a year's leave.[100]

Another version of this incident, which could be called "The Siege," can be found in records from the archives of Denmark studied by the historian Georg Norregard in *Danish Settlements in West Africa*.[101] Though the details of the incident slightly differ, the Danish Lt. Svedstrup is also depicted here as an abolitionist crusader. When the Anlos besieged the fort, "Svedstrup was only able to keep them at a distance by means of hand grenades and rockets." Yet these records also show clearly that the Danes had little control of the area. Even when they were able to temporarily prevail over the Anlos and secure peace agreements and oaths sworn to the Danish king, Anlo traders remained defiant in their determination to continue the slave trade as they had before.[102]

In some ways, it is not hard to understand why the Anlos and Africans elsewhere on the continent would have been perplexed at what must have seemed like a curious change of heart on the part of the Europeans vis-à-vis the Atlantic slave trade. Why now, after they had profited from the trade for almost three hundred years, were they suddenly so interested in terminating it? If, as some of the oral histories suggest, they could hardly differentiate one group of Europeans from another, this must have been very confusing indeed. There were the slave-trading whites, the missionary whites, and now the abolitionist whites. The diversity of opinions coming from Europe and America must have been quite confusing. Elizabeth Isichei, in her book *Voices of the Poor in Africa,* quotes a white abolitionist as saying: "When I told one, this morning that the slave trade was a bad thing and that white people worked to put an end to it altogether, he gave me an excellent answer. 'Well, if white people give up buying, Black people will give up selling slaves.' "[103]

The trade was eventually stamped out, however, giving way to European efforts to sustain plantations on the Gold Coast itself. Some of these efforts had begun even before the trade was officially abolished by the English, such as the successful plantation scheme started by the Danish doctor Paul Isert.[104] These and other schemes in fact seemed to have had an influence on the decision to stop slave trafficking. As Isert asked: "Why did not our ancestors have the common sense to start plantations for the production of these commodities in Africa, where one can obtain plenty of labor at lower wages?"[105] If they had done so, there would have been no need to send the Africans off on the risky voyage across the Atlantic."

This issue raises a question that has been debated by scholars for years: whether abolition was a result of moral or economic objections to the trade. Eric Williams's claim in *Capitalism and Slavery* of the primacy of economic considerations has been reassessed by those who assert that industrial capitalists (those who some may say stood to gain much from abolition) did not play a large role in the abolition of the slave trade.[106]

It may well be that that the dividing line between these two sets of motives is artificial, but neither explanation takes away from the achievement of the abolition movement.[107] Given the fact that the trade was an entrenched part of European and American society and played a key role in African society, any arguments against its continuation faced vehement resistance.

Ironically, it was in this period of abolition that the kidnapping incident at Atorkor took place. In spite of the efforts of those who had advocated abolition of the trade, slave traffic continued vigorously. Still, there was a distinct shift from a period of largely systematized operations to a period of disorder and chaos where such random incidents could occur. As we have seen here, there may not be much in the African oral history record regarding European and American agency in the slave trade, but the fragments of information that do remain are enough to corroborate and add to the more extensive archival record in Europe and America. European and American actors in the slave trade manned a ruthlessly efficient system that spanned several continents and allowed them full control of five of six legs of the Atlantic slave trade. It was an all-encompassing role, which largely drove the actions of other players in the trade, including African traders on the coast. At the same time, there was much change and transformation from one period to the other in each leg of the trade. Such transformations, in the end, culminated in a devastating social and political impact on the Anlo Ewe community—on both its members on the continent and those transported to the New World. This will be the subject of the next two chapters.

The Social and Political Impact of the Atlantic Slave Trade on the Old Slave Coast

There was no rest in the land.
Mama Dzagba

THE SOCIAL EFFECTS OF THE ATLANTIC SLAVE TRADE: NO REST IN THE LAND

I can still remember the somber look on Mama Dzagba's face when she made this statement in her stoolhouse in the capital town of Anlo Ga near the sea. It was midday, but yet we sat in the dark in a dimly lit room discussing a subject that too often lies in the shadows. Mama Dzagba, an important Queen Mother in Eweland, seemed to want to convey more than anything the instability that was a direct result of the slave trade. I would take away from our meeting a sense of the chaos, the uncertainty, and the fragility of those days. It was in her words—and even more so in the lines on her face. As she said the words, "There was no rest in the land," she shook her head in dismay. Suddenly, I was not just a researcher taking notes in an interview. I was brought back for one long moment to a disquieting time. No rest, as in the absence of peace. No rest, as in the absence of stability. It was the kind of time, like moments of regret in a life, that people would want to put behind them and forget—and maybe then, just maybe, find some rest.

It was a time, Mama Dzagba goes on to say, when "one man alone was not allowed to go single."[1] These and other stories paint a picture of the chaos and fear felt by members of the Ewe community. Such was the level of social upheaval that people were advised to travel in groups lest they be stolen or kidnapped. Parents were afraid for their children and sought all possible means to protect them. "Whenever they know the [European] ship was coming, they had to protect their children, they had to keep them inside."[2] An account from ninety-plus-year-old Lucy Geraldo corroborates the same: "When there is a commotion and you go there, you would never return. The Europeans would take you away. My mother said that her grandma [Agoshi] was eating at home and went outside to see the commotion and she never returned. They searched and searched. Finally, they heard about her in Vodza."[3] The young people of that time grew up in a state of ever-present fear of the unknown. This fear was associated with the arrival of European and other foreign ships.

Even where people chose to settle was affected by the ever-present concern for security, over and beyond economic considerations.[4] This sense of insecurity is also evident in the oral account of Kofi Geraldo, descendant of Geraldo de Lima, the most famous slave trader of the area.[5] He spoke of his own family's fear of his being sold. His testimony goes a long way in giving insight into the state of chaos and fear that existed even in the coastal areas. Even a trader's family, years after the trade was over, had a fresh sense of fear associated with the preceding era. "The trade was over, but the stories were still fresh. He was telling me this story because we are now free. We are now free to stay with him."[6] This is particularly significant given the importance of kinship roles in these societies. If the family was under attack, the very core of the society was under attack.

"Coastal people were afraid," said Chief James Ocloo of Keta, speaking of the aftermath of the incident at Atorkor in which the drummers were kidnapped.[7] This incident showed clearly that no one was immune to the vagaries of the trade. It suggests the unthinkable—that relatives of the chief of Atorkor were also taken away.[8] We may imagine that any prior agreements or working relationships would have been threatened as a result. Furthermore, any previous sense of mutual regard would have been seen as hollow. The coastal people always thought that they enjoyed a level of immunity. They had always felt that this "slave business," as they called it, concerned only the peoples of the interior. The Atorkor incident changed all that. It solidified the everyday fears that had been felt by the general population and affirmed in the minds of the Ewe people the principle that anyone, even those who engaged in the trade, could be vulnerable to it.

We know that on the other side of Atlantic in Diaspora communities this fear was all too real. As late as the 1930s when Dr. Martin Luther King was growing up, his sister recounts in her book on their childhood years that they were warned by their parents to be careful of where they went. "Because of those [segregation] laws," she said of Atlanta, Georgia, "my family rarely went to the picture shows or visited Grant Park with its famous Cyclorama. In fact to this very day I don't recall ever seeing my father on a streetcar. Because of those laws and the indignity that went with them, Daddy preferred keeping M. L., A. D. and me close to home where we would be protected."[9] Their parents and grandparents were only doing what other parents had been doing for generations throughout slavery and beyond—protecting their children by keeping them close where they could keep them out of the gaze of whites and thus from possible harm.

In terms of the social impact of the slave trade and slavery in general, we do not yet know how this fear affected then and now the psyches of Africans on the continent and in the Diaspora. This is a major gap in our fragmented history. Did subsequent generations overly shelter their children and grandchildren in an effort to protect them, and what effect did this have on their worldview as well as their capacity to take advantage of the world's resources and opportunities? Ironically, it was the situations in which there was full exposure to the horrors and injustices of racism that spurred many black leaders, including Martin Luther King Jr., W. E. B. DuBois, and Ida B. Wells, to fight beyond the narrow boundaries that been set for them.

With Martin Luther King Jr., it was the incident in which his white childhood friend across the street on Auburn Avenue in Atlanta was no longer allowed to play with him. When his mother tried her best to explain to him what was behind his first real experience with racism, the *Whites Only* signs, and the countless slights and injustices meted out to blacks, it was then that he reportedly uttered, "One day, Mother Dear, I am going to turn this world upside down."[10] For Ida B. Wells, it was racism on a streetcar and the lynching of a friend in the South that propelled her to become what at that time was quite revolutionary—a black female activist advocating antilynching laws. But what of the majority of blacks on both sides of the Atlantic? Did the historical encounters with "the Veil," as DuBois called it, or the glass ceiling, as it is called today, serve to pigeonhole black potential and possibilities in narrow spheres not unlike the set boundaries of the plantation? Did encounters with the horrors of the slave trade and slavery and their legacies instill fear that still lingers along the contours of historical and collective memory? These are questions yet to be answered.

Another important measure of the slave trade's impact on African society was the increase in the use of domestic slaves.[11] This certainly holds true for the Anlo coast and is strongly corroborated by the oral sources. Absent political controls on the growth of slave traffic, the inland trade grew steadily. "The trade started with Geraldo; he bought slaves to work—farming. About nine slaves—one woman and others men. The slave population in Keta was not so big. Some people needed help so got money to buy slaves."[12] Though this statement is not entirely accurate (we know that the trade did not start with Geraldo, although his name is synonymous with the rise in slave traffic in the area), it suggests that there was an evolution of the domestic trade in slaves that was spurred on by the international trade. At the same time, there is evidence that the practice of selling disobedient boys as slaves to local chiefs or others continued and flourished during the era. "The chiefs had slaves—not from the hinterland. When disobedient around the area, the chief would keep one of two."[13]

What emerges from the oral histories and other sources is a multifaceted picture of domestic slavery. Slaves were used for many purposes and in many different ways. Their own position in society depended on the family to whom they had been sold and the circumstances of their sale. In one situation they might best be regarded as dependents, in another as laborers, in still another as serfs. In fact, it can be said that even the term "domestic slavery" is limiting since it has been used to incorporate so many different variants.[14]

A good example is the story of the trader Anatsi of Woe. He was said to have acquired a tremendous amount of wealth due to his involvement in the transatlantic and domestic trades. In fact, his wealth was estimated by one oral source by the number of domestic slaves that he retained.[15] According to oral tradition, he had a system in which each cowrie on a string around his ceremonial stool represented each of his slaves. This stool, along with the original cowries, was presented as evidence of his wealth by his descendant in Woe. This account greatly supports Inikori's assertions that the rise in internal slavery was as much about social status as it was about economics: "As for those who held slaves for purposes of social status, the question to ask is why they preferred this form of showing off their material achievements.... The explanation for this behavior is to be found in the fact that opportunities for capital investment outside the slave trade were limited."[16] The same oral account goes on to reveal: "Those who had good character were sent as traders and he even allowed some to be involved in buying and selling slaves."[17] Another source discusses the use of slaves as laborers. "The people who were taken as captives [were] made to work in plantation farms and river creeks, not far from home—coconut plantations. Workers became adopted children, adopted Tamaklo names."[18]

Thus it is possible to see the multifaceted nature of African slavery along the Anlo coast.[19] This slavery contrasted greatly with the American system of chattel slavery, which at its height was highly structured, regulated, and restrictive. It is clear from these examples that slavery was at once a matter of business and family relationships. American slavery was a system that revolved around the economy, with all other issues being secondary or nonexistent. The laws and religious institutions of the land were designed to support this system, rendering mobility and kinship ties marginal. There were no outlets for slaves in their legal status as slaves to become independently wealthy. Buying one's freedom or being manumitted was the only way to break through the limitations of slavery, and still, freed blacks were often a most vulnerable group. They were subject to intense discrimination and they also lived with the ever-present threat of being sold back into slavery. As Herbert Gutman points out in several examples in *The Black Family in Slavery and in Freedom,* freed slaves by law often had to leave the state of their birth, leaving behind family and other loved ones. If American slavery was a closed system with few loopholes, African slavery along the Anlo coast—though its incidence increased as a result of the transatlantic trade—was an open one, allowing for a large variety of formations and transformations.

Governor Carstensen corroborates this in an 1845 entry: "It [African slavery] is a legal act based on the age-old customs of the country for the free negro to sell the villein negroes, belonging to him. The 'villeins' comprise all, subjected to the power of the paterfamilias. . . . other relatives and the 'house people' i.e. those who, without being relatives and whom we, *with invidious expressions,* call slaves imagining the relationship between the white plantation owner and his slaves beyond the sea, taking place between the 'master' and the 'servants.' "[20]

Notwithstanding the fact that domestic slavery in Africa was at once a matter of business *and* family and so was often much less harsh than its transatlantic counterpart, domestic slavery did have two very devastating effects. First, it attached to those who were directly affected a stigma, as discussed previously. Even several of the terms for *slave* are suggestive of this shame. In the Ewe language, *kluviwo* means "not originally from this family"; *wonutidzu* means "child of a slave" and is said to be a very painful insult. *Kluvi* also means slave, as does *tsovado,* which means "not originally from this family" or "a tree that has been cut and replanted. *Alomenu* or *alomevi* means "somebody that you toil or work hard to get." Other words for slaves include *adoko* or *kosi* (male and female respectively).[21]

Secondly, domestic slavery produced an as of yet understudied internal displacement within countries and regions in West and Central Africa. This is a subject that came out very clearly in the retelling of these oral histories. It was clear from several accounts that the memory of place—and thus of original identity—was not lost on many whose ancestors had been sold to other communities. It is as if an internal diaspora has since developed, but, once again, quietly and in the shadows. As a result of the many raids in the north by Babatu and Samori and other slave traders, the Konkomba people, for example, are dispersed in various places throughout Northern Ghana, including Sobaba and Salaga—the former the site of a major slave market.[22]

In other words, they now represent a small diaspora of sorts. They are not alone. Among the many groups that were raided heavily for slaves in northern Ghana, particularly in the late eighteenth and nineteenth centuries, were the Bumpurgu, the

Grunshi, the Frafras, the Builsas, the Kasenas, the Gonjas, the Namdams, the Dagartis, and the Sisselas, to name only a few. They, too, have members scattered throughout the region because of the displacement caused by raiding and trading. Some authors even go as far as to say that a fair number of the Akan of the central region (of whom the Asante people are the most famous) have ancestors originally from the north but do not dare say so on account of the shame attached to slavery in Akan society.[23] Had these movements been voluntary and not forced through the processes of the slave trade, the contemporary contestations about identity among the Akan and other groups might not exist in the same way.

Oral stories of Bono Manso, an Akan community in the central region, underscore the point. Bono Manso is almost equidistant between the northern region of Ghana and the Atlantic coast where slaves were traded. This is the place where the "sick and tired" were left with the local chief when they could no longer continue on the Long March to the Sea. As one storyteller recounts: "Where they are now, they are not from this place.... some of their neighbors tell them they should go back to their [own] place ... they couldn't go back. They do not know where to go back to." The same storyteller goes on to say, "You see, the effect is not just on the African Diaspora alone, but our people here. They rather took our wealth away."[24]

In the Ewe region as well there were such stories of internal displacement. One oral narrator spoke of his aunt of Mossi ancestry in Ewe country. She still had seven long marks on her face that identified her as being from the north, but no one ever talked about it. She had been given a local name and also a particular potion that several oral narrators characterized as being potent enough to prevent and discourage a domestic slave's return to his or her own home.[25]

No one was allowed to talk about it, and so the train of silence continued. On this level, the silence is more like the denial that often accompanies traumatic events like wars or other catastrophes. It is a silence born out of struggle—the struggle of the past and the simple will to survive the present in the best way possible. In my previous work with Vietnam veterans in the 1970s, this was exactly what I found. Veterans, particularly in the period before the National Vietnam Veterans Memorial ("the Wall") was built in 1982, often did not talk about the war and the horrors they experienced even with their own family members. A number of veterans, in fact, developed serious psychological problems as a result of this repression of a major part of their lives. At the time, I thought that this denial or silence was because this was the war that had not been won; this was the war after which there were few if any ticker tape parades; this was the war that was contested to its bitter end and is even now contested in and outside of the academy. But I was to find in a subsequent study of World War II veterans a similar though not as widespread phenomenon. Some veterans simply came home and kept that part of their lives in the shadows, so that even those closest to them had no idea of what they had gone through. It did not matter that this was a victorious war and that those who returned were largely welcomed and supported. Veterans still experienced the horror of war—losing comrades, watching people blown to pieces, and in some cases losing a limb themselves.[26]

I imagine this was somewhat akin to what has happened in Ghana and West and Central Africa in general, which experienced the bulk of the Atlantic slave trade. More than three centuries of slave trading meant numerous small and big conflicts and skirmishes as well as wars and raiding—all of which have taken their collective toll. Those who remained on the continent—that is, those who were not taken—were like veterans in a war-torn land, in some ways seeking to make peace with their trauma and in some ways seeking simply to put it behind them. This is one way of explaining why, according to the director of education at Cape Coast Castle (the former slave-trade dungeon), the people of the area are not interested in coming into the castle. In spite of the fact that the Smithsonian and other international donors have invested heavily in its refurbishment to attract visitors from all over the world and to preserve Ghana's historical heritage, many Cape Coast residents feel "they have nothing there. They have heard what happened there from their elders" and want little to do with the place. Even elders who live closer than a hundred meters from the site have not set foot in the castle and show little desire to.[27] These stories all add to the sense of fragmentation of historical memory and identity that is a direct result of the Atlantic slave trade.

One may also speculate whether part of the reason for this fragmentation stems from the phenomenon psychologists call survivor guilt. This issue of survivor guilt is connected to both effects of the slave trade—the shame factor and the internal displacement discussed above. In the article "The Guilt/Shame Debate Goes On," Lynn O'Connor and Jack Berry suggest that there is indeed a correlation between shame and guilt. "We believe that in many cases, shame is a defense against unconscious guilt." In other words, in their clinical studies, they found that patients who consistently expressed feelings of shame often did so to "keep themselves from feeling that they are better off than family members, siblings or other loved ones." It was because of their relatively privileged position that they harbored these feelings of shame.

Here, once again, a useful comparison can be made to Holocaust survivors. Some who have studied the effects of the Holocaust on survivors and their children have come to the same conclusion. "Imagine, a survivor who is now a psychoanalyst whose patients are children of survivors denying that their parents and their analyst had really suffered it!" says R. M. Chandler Burns in a panel discussion of psychoanalysts on the subject.[28] Apparently, for some children of survivors there was a shame attached to the Holocaust that they did not want to be party to. Yet at the same time, beneath this shame was guilt— the guilt associated with being a survivor of this monstrous crime against humanity.

That said, it is interesting to note that the Jewish community in general chooses to remember and to remember consistently in a public way this tragic event in their history. There is appropriately a great outpouring of literature on the subject (both nonfiction and fiction) as well as films (*Schindler's List* et al.). Museums and memorials in America and around the world and even an official day of remembrance on which the name of everyone who died as a result of the Holocaust is called also keep the memory of those who died alive.[29] Why do they choose to remember their holocaust when many black communities choose to forget? This is a question for which it is difficult to find a conclusive answer, but it may be that they find a sense of reclaimed dignity and agency in discussing a time of great powerlessness. In recalling their victimization, they do not again feel victimized but rather feel a sense of regained power in giving voice to their pain and suffering. Furthermore, it may be that to consciously remember is to take an active stance of resistance against such forces past and present. As the Survivors of the Shoah Visual History Foundation says in its mission statement, its purpose is "to overcome prejudice, intolerance and bigotry and the suffering they cause" through the educational use of the nearly 52,000 testimonies of survivors.

A good example comes from a book written by Holocaust survivor Jack Eisner. Haunted by what he calls the ghosts of the past, he asks in the beginning of the book that essential question: Why me? "This is the story of how I escaped from the Warsaw ghetto concentration camps, execution squads, the gallows and gas chambers. I am the one in a thousand who survived. Why me? Was I better than the 1/2 million Jews in Warsaw who did not? Why not Grandma, why not Halina, why not Hela, Lutek.... Artek the fighter, Markowski, the teacher ... and all the others? I can still see them all. They are in front of me now, talking to me."[30]

The oral accounts in this collection suggest that for some black communities just the act of survival after such horrific events has been their primary form of resistance. This, of course, was no mean feat. Giving voice to the tragic history of slavery has not been seen as a powerful tool to regain some of that which was lost. The interviews I conducted on my visit to northern Ghana—where much of the raiding for slaves took place —were very telling in this respect. In recalling the history and role of the Dagomba chiefs in raiding and trading along with the Asante, there was clearly much more evidence (and interest) in the stories of the raiders. There was little shame associated with the raiders yet much shame associated with the victims of their raids.[31] Historian Claude Meillassoux puts it even more starkly: "By a perversion of memory, the sumptuousness of the plundering kings and their *cabessaires* [appointed slave raiders] has left its mark on the area in its remembrance of the flourishing slave trade and the glories of the past, while the memory of their peasant victims has been effaced by their poverty."[32]

I would add here the ultimate irony of this cruel era was the fact that in many of these communities and regions (though there are notable exceptions, including and especially the more prosperous Asante community), it is difficult to differentiate economically between the former raiders and traders and their victims. Both sides seem equally mired in poverty, though the victims, it goes without saying, have borne the greater burden of this legacy—displacement and loss of land as well as the "shame" factor still associated with slavery in contemporary Ghana. They, too, like their counterparts in the Diaspora of the New World, also grapple with a fragmented sense of their history.

A fragmented sense of identity may also be at the heart of yet another major effect of the slave trade on African societies. In Africa, and certainly along the old Slave Coast, there was a drastic shift from a subsistence economy to one based on consumerism. Whereas members of the Ewe community, before interactions with Europeans and Americans in the trade, were content to farm and fish to meet their basic needs, the trade encouraged, and some say helped develop, a taste for consumer goods, in particular foreign goods. This we know. What we do not conclusively know is how these goods influenced their sense of identity. Did they cause them to see their own home-based products as inferior so they were willing to exchange slaves for things that came from abroad? This we do not know for sure, but we do know that there was a shift.

Some of the oral accounts are peppered with references to this growing influence of foreign items. Mama Dzagba, in her retelling of the incident of Atorkor and trading relations with white traders, speaks of them enticing the inhabitants with "German" biscuits, beef, and rice.

"The Europeans then invited the people on the beach to join them in the drumming and merrymaking on the ship. The people entered their boats and rowed over to the ship and danced and drummed with them. At the end of the dance, the Europeans offered the people of Atorkor some kind of large biscuits [believed to be German biscuits]. At the time of the incident, there was a slight famine in the region. When they were given the biscuits, they were also given beef and rice and other gifts and then they left the ship and went back to their homes."[33]

Given that the incident took place in 1856, it is interesting to note that by this time such goods would have been sufficient enticement when clearly other records of earlier times show that the Anlo were content enough in consuming what their land could produce. The best evidence for this comes from Bosman's early visits to the coast in 1698, when he noted that though the people were not rich, they had enough cattle and fish to feed the community.[34] Paul Isert, one hundred years later, claims the same. He describes the land as full of oxen and sheep and the lagoon and other rivers likewise full of ample amounts of fish, oysters, and crab.[35] As for agriculture, he says that the inhabitants had many garden plots replete with plantains, bananas, yams, and sugarcane. In fact, he suggests that produce was so plentiful it was casually regarded by the inhabitants, who cut down banana trees without regard to their value and who use the sugarcane primarily for cleaning their teeth. In the end, he describes the Anlos as a "well-to-do people" because of the many land and water resources that abound in the area.[36] But parts of Isert's narrative, even at this time, suggests a transformation in local tastes. After his description of the sufficiency of resources in the area, he says: "Usually there is no lack of European wares there, for just as they have the lagoon on the one side, they have the ocean on the other, and in exchange for slaves and provisions they can obtain anything from the ships that they are unwilling to buy at our lodge."[37]

Further in the narrative, when Isert tells of his return to the coast as a reformed abolitionist, he connects the trade to a pernicious growth in consumerism in even bolder language. Though it is clear that he has adopted a somewhat romantic view of Africa and Africans, his essential point is still well taken. "Great sins such as murder and thievery are completely unknown, except where the agents of Belial [slave trade agents] holds sway; where *the lure of European products* has now taken hold and alas! I fear, the greatest part of Africa is already contaminated."[38] These finished goods that Africans received (cloth, knives, brass bracelets, bowls, liquor, etc.) discouraged African production in certain areas.[39]

Though not enough is yet known regarding how the trade affected levels of production, specifically in Eweland, it is nevertheless clear that consumer products from Europe became more important commodities on the market in comparison to previous periods. This is important in part because of its relationship to consumer patterns in contemporary Africa (and also in the African Diaspora). Observers of contemporary Africa cannot help but see the overwhelming reliance on European imports, often at the expense of homegrown products.[40] Given world markets and the propensity of developed nations to "dump" their products on developing nations, this is not entirely the fault of African nations. Still, one sees a disturbing line of continuity between the era of the slave trade and contemporary Africa, whereby that which is made "abroad" has a higher value than items made on the continent itself. Even a quick perusal of the famous textiles that Africa is known for reveals many a "made in Holland" logo. This is, of course, part of a larger problem and debate regarding globalization, and there are undoubtedly many other factors involved, but it is certainly the case that this taste for foreign things started much earlier than the current period.

In Ghana and elsewhere in Africa, name brands from Europe and America have a certain cache—BMWs, Mercedes, Nikes, Samsonite luggage, and so on. For some of Africa's elite, these items may simply represent progress and hard-won options after centuries of historical struggle. But for others these brand names mean much more. Sometimes, as it is quietly said, they signify a move away from "the village." Ironically, in much the same way in the United States, some members of privileged African American communities value the same said items as a move away from "the ghetto." Even if it is necessary to go into debt to own these brand-name items, for some it is worth the trouble. Within this coded language—the much-feared "ghetto" and "village"—is a fragmented identity; an identity based on moving away from something as fast as one can and ironically moving toward consumer patterns that in no way benefit them or the community. These facts are borne out by the latest findings from *Target Market News,* a fifteen-year-old research and information company that specializes in black consumer marketing and media. Quoting the 2002 "Buying Power" report of the Department of Commerce, "black households had $631 billion in earned income in 2002, an increase of 4.8% over the $602 billion earned in 2001." At the same time, "while other ethnic groups are growing in population, black consumers are still out-spending all other groups in apparel, food, beverages, cars, and trucks, home furnishings, telephone service and travel.[41] Thus while growth in earnings is good news, as is the essential ability to choose how to spend one's money, outspending other groups is perhaps a dubious achievement. Could it be that these patterns of consumerism are somehow related to the legacy of slavery and the trade—from the Anlo Ewe community and other African communities to their Diaspora counterparts?

No, there was no rest in the land. These changes—the fear of being kidnapped or stolen from one's family and community, the growth of domestic servitude and the shame attached to it, and the shift from a subsistence economy to a consumer economy—certainly caused a certain amount of social upheaval and unrest. It was as if the foundations of their society were changing underneath their feet and changing at too rapid a pace. This social unrest was inevitably tied to political unrest in the Ewe region.

THE POLITICAL EFFECTS OF THE SLAVE TRADE: THE ENEMY WITHIN AND THE ENEMY WITHOUT

In many ways, the Atlantic slave trade had the most profound impact on the political life of the Anlo Ewe people. The trade, as it was carried out by European and American slave traders, helped to create political instability for Anlo rulers while being a stimulus to violence between the Anlos and their neighbors.

Intermittent warfare, once uncommon or relegated to minor skirmishes, became the rule of the day. The exchange of fire-arms for slaves became central to this vicious cycle of warfare. Most important, "slave business," inasmuch as it privileged in-dependent traders and their pursuits, stifled homegrown demo-cratic values and structures. European and African traders alike were unaccountable to the people, and it is this lack of account-ability that undermined Ewe society.

These effects of the slave trade bring to mind the image of the typical slave fort, where slaves were kept in small, dark, and windowless dungeons, separated by gender. On the balcony of Cape Coast Castle in Ghana, for example, there are two sets of old wrought-iron cannons pointing in two different directions. One set faces the enemy within—would-be indigenous African insurgents who would disrupt their trade. The other set faces the enemy without—foreign interlopers on the Atlantic Ocean who could at any time engage in battle not only for the slaves but for other cargo and ammunition kept in the castle. Likewise, the devastating political effects of the slave trade came from within and without.

The Enemy Within

As we addressed previously, there is a popular perception among some in the general public that African chiefs sold "their" peo-ple to foreign slave traders. But as we have already established, not all the chiefs were traders and not all traders were chiefs. This is part of the complexity of an era that lasted almost four hundred years and underwent several transformations during that time.

It is because not all the chiefs were traders that the follow-ing story of a paramount chief who traded slaves is all the more remarkable and telling. The version of this account with the most corroborative evidence was told to me by the elder

Herbert Atsu Afeku of Srogbe. I had been referred to him by Togbui Dosu, one of the current chiefs of Atorkor, who was convinced that Mr. Afeku would know much about the history of the area. His grandfather was Togbui Nanevi Tsikata II, who was so well known in the area that there is a statue on the edge of town to commemorate his many achievements. But more than that, perhaps more than anyone in his family Mr. Afeku, retired from the medical field, had maintained a great interest in the oral traditions of the area once called the old Slave Coast and in particular of his own family histories.

When I met with Mr. Afeku at his comfortable house at the edge of the town of Srogbe (neighboring Atorkor) toward the end of my third major trip to Ghana in 2003, he was full of energy and very desirous to share not only stories that he could record by heart about his family but also written documents that he had kept over the years that spelled out his rich and complex family tree. In this conversation he spoke about the Anlos' first move to the area as well as the trade in domestic slaves, in which some of his relatives had also participated. But the most telling story was of the former paramount chief Togbui Adzanu. "Togbui Adzanu was the son of Togbui Akotsui—a Bate chief that was exiled—and he was the paramount chief that was exiled. He ruled from 1750–53. He was the sixth king after Sri I from Notsie, 1490–1557—who ruled for sixty-seven years. [What happened was that] he was flirting with fetish girls and was selling them. When elders heard, he was put in a big sack and dumped in the fetish forest. They reported it to the fetish leader [Nyigbla priest]. Because they were friends they set him free and he ran to Ketakoro in Togo."[42]

Another version of the same essential story was also told to Sandra Greene by Anlo elders and recorded in her book, *Gender, Ethnicity, and Social Change on the Upper Slave Coast: A History of the Anlo Ewe*. In this version, unbeknownst to the community the Nyigbla order gets involved in the Atlantic slave trade in the early 1800s. Anlo elders offered at least two possible ways in which this abuse of authority came to light: (1) because of a dispute between the *awomefia* (the paramount chief) and the Nyigbla priest about how to share the profits; and (2) the pending sale of a number of Nyigbla initiates *(zizidzelawo)* to slave traders in Whydah.[43]

This version shares much with the one in my oral history collection but also differs in significant ways. First, in both sets of accounts there is a clear and decisive punishment when such egregious actions on the part of religious and political authorities are discovered. There is a serious consequence to selling locals to slave traders for personal profit and gain. The Anlo Ewe community, as said before, had drawn a line between those they considered potential slaves (inhabitants in the interior) and those they considered free men and women (inhabitants on the coast.). This action went beyond those boundaries and thus broke an unsaid rule. In Greene's version, however, there are some important differences. First, there is a different date (the early 1800s versus the 1750s). The paramount chief is executed and it is the priest who is banished. In my version from the interview with Mr. Afeku, the paramount chief in question is actually named, and it is further significant that his name—Togbui Adzanu—was said to be erased from the record because of his actions.

Nonetheless, what this story shows is how homegrown democratic structures were drastically undermined during the era of the slave trade. What we know of the traditional political structure of Anlo society is that it was loosely organized into about 120 polities that had important democratic features. They shared a common language and at different times in their history enjoyed mutually beneficial trading relationships. Their early settlements were villages or towns of small kinship groups. Chiefs emerged who were generally founders of the villages.[44]

Structurally, the chief was the constitutional head; his position was generally hereditary within a lineage or clan but also elective. Most important, his power was not unchecked. He was obliged to consult with a body of elders about every important matter in the village. He could not, for example, decide on matters of war without their consent and, in general, the consent of the people. Chiefs had to be responsive since they led with the knowledge that they could be destooled if they took positions contrary to the will of the people.[45]

Eventually, each polity began to include a number of towns. Anlo, for example, is said to have included thirty-six towns, which represent different territorial divisions.[46] Above this structure of local chieftaincies is the paramount chief, or awomefia. The position of paramount chief of Anlo is hereditary. Chiefs are chosen from either the Adzovia clan or the Bate clan. Still within the clans, succession is elective and patrilineal.[47] The awomefia was essentially the highest political office in Anlo. He presided over important matters brought to him by the local chiefs and external matters that affected the state. Finally, he had the ultimate say in matters of law and order. Cases of very serious offenses were brought before him and he meted out sentences, including capital punishment. Like the local chiefs, the awomefia was guided by various councils of elders. These included the clan council and the council of war chiefs (or the divisional chiefs).[48]

In such a structure there was little room for the paramount chief and chiefs in general to go over the heads of the people. Furthermore, it was expected that chiefs would do everything in their power to protect the people—as opposed to selling them, thus separating them forever from their clan and kin. This is what makes the story of Togbui Adzanu stand out. It speaks to the corruption of the political system during the Atlantic slave trade. What is also interesting, however, is the community reaction. Slaves were not from the coastal region. They were from the interior. Anyone caught selling slaves from the coast would have to be accountable for such deeds and that included the paramount chief. His punishment: exile and banishment—essentially akin to the fate that he had meted to those young women. He, too, would now be separated from his clan and kindred.

Not only was the political system undermined but also the legal system, called *Nyiko,* which the paramount chief traditionally oversaw. The Nyiko custom worked as both a deterrent to crime and a punishment of serious crimes. According to one elder: "If you are disobedient and a native of the place; if you have bad manners, a thief going after other people's wives, they take you there and kill you in the forest. The executors will take you in the middle of the night and knock you on the head.... The name Nyiko means you must accept the rules of the land. When you are doing bad things, you are going against the rules of the land."[49]

Other oral narrators spoke about the Nyiko drums that were played on such occasions. "The Agave drums will say, 'We went in the night and came back in the night. Children should obey their parents.' This would be played three times; then the Ashigbi drums would answer: 'Your voice is my voice,' also beaten three times."[50] What is significant about this method of punishment was the fact that these were not arbitrary decisions taken by the local chiefs or the paramount chief. At the same time, as asserted by the awomefia at the time of this study, Tog-bui Adeladza, "Nyiko was never performed without the knowledge of the awomefia." There had to be a report given first to the local chief, then to the awomefia and his council of elders. Only then would a decision be taken.

"There was complete arbitration; whoever brought the message would sit in council with the elders, who put a lot of questions to them. He will find out further what he (the offender) did. That person will either confirm or deny this. If confirmed, the person was expected to bring him to the elders."[51]

Finally, once a punishment of death was decided upon, "The one who would be killed, he won't go alone. A leader would be in front, others behind. The killers will be laying in ambush. Then they kill him and the others go away." According to other versions of this custom, the culprit is taken to a place in the capital called Toko Atolia, or the Fifth Landing Stage. Here, the offender is either choked or buried alive.[52] And so, there was not only a trial but also a number of checks and balances on every level. This practice was quite similar to the legal system detailed in Chinua Achebe's fictional account of the Ibo before colonial rule in *Things Fall Apart*.

Nyiko also functioned as a deterrent to crime. The sound of the drums beaten at night was understood by the whole community, even the children. Parents used these opportunities to caution their children about the consequences of going against the rules of the land. The drums were but one concrete signal to young people of the importance of obedience. Another was the cloth of the person who was executed which, according to custom, was removed and spread on the forest road.[53] The whole community would then know who had committed the offense and would be sufficiently cautioned about antisocial behavior. Offenses that were considered very serious included theft, pregnancy outside of wedlock, and adultery.[54] Such symbols reaffirmed the place of the chiefs and the elders in society as the arbiters of justice. In many ways, the Nyiko system could be likened to the death penalty in the United States, which, in the states where it is legal, must be approved by the highest courts.

Yet in spite of this complex structure with its adequate checks and balances, several oral history accounts confirm that the Nyiko custom was eventually used as a means of selling slaves. According to one source, "When the Danes built the fort, there was no more Nyiko. [Offenders] were directly sold to the Danes."[55] Given the importance of this custom, its subsequent corruption brings into focus the effect it must have had on the community at large. Joseph Miller in *Way of Death* recounts a similar practice that took place in Central Africa. "The court of Kasanje, beyond its role as broker in the trade to Lunda, gained fame as the judicial center where a great and terrible ndua poison oracle condemned defendants to slavery and exile. Plaintiffs came from Kongo, from elsewhere in the Kwango valley, and even from the Portuguese ruled highlands to the West to bring suits against neighbors and debtors.... The new owners of the condemned found ready buyers for them in the Kasanje market near the king's court."[56]

In the end, this corruption of the justice system was simply part of a larger breakdown in Anlo polities as a result of increased entanglement with the Atlantic system.

The Enemy Without

Much has been written about the role of firearms brought to the continent by Europeans that were exchanged for slaves and the vicious cycle of wars that this encouraged. Furthermore, much attention has been given to the rise of powers such as the Asante and Dahomey, who were often participants and in part beneficiaries of such warfare.[57] As said before, this concentration on the activities of the larger states in West Africa does not adequately give us a sense of the involvement of smaller states. Such a focus also obscures other issues of governance and the role that European traders played vis-à-vis such governance. For example, the Dutch and the English in the seventeenth and eighteenth centuries not only understood the importance of the increased importation of firearms to their pursuits, they actively armed one group of Africans against the other for the purpose of obtaining captives.[58]

The same dynamic took place in the coastal areas from Senegambia to north of the River Congo at the end of the eighteenth century (the state of Bonny). European government legislation exceptionally permitted the export of guns and powder to Africa during wartime because both were essential to the African trade.[59] At the same time, gun manufacturers in England were constantly being pressured to produce more guns. As a result a total of 1,615,309 guns were imported into Africa from England alone. The bulk of these firearms were exchanged for slaves.[60] P. E. Isert's contemporary account of his journey to Eweland also corroborates the fact that guns were the most important item of exchange at the time of his stay in Africa (1780s):

> However, there must always be included muskets, gunpowder and knives in payment for each slave or the trader will not sell them to us. Indeed at Christiansbourg and at Friedensburg [forts], where one deals mainly with Assianthees [Asante], one is often forced to pay for the slaves with guns and powder exclusively because there is no demand for any of the other goods, apart from a fine fabric or silk cloth. The reason for this is that they themselves are nearly always at war with an even mightier nation, the Dunkos, who live north of them. For some time now these Dunkos have been using guns, for which the Assianthees, who sell them, demand a very high price.[61]

There is no question that the vicious cycle of guns for slaves permeated the Upper Slave Coast. There is also no question that warfare among the polities was the rule of the day, particularly in the seventeenth and eighteenth centuries. The Anlos fought with their neighbors for many different reasons. Often disputes were about salt and fishing rights in the Volta River, but some were about slave-trading activities. In the seventeenth century, for example, the Ge, another coastal polity, attempted to conquer the Anlo. The Anlo retaliated, with Akwamu assistance. At this juncture, the Akwamu and the Ge were in an intense competition for control over the coast regarding a range of trading activities, including cattle, salt, beads, and slaves.[62]

What was interesting about such relationships, however, was the fact that these groups warred with each other or cooperated with each other as circumstances demanded. Perhaps it is for that reason that the oral histories recount, in what is certainly an overstatement, that before the Europeans their fights with outside groups were *"fights, not wars."*[63] Some authors attribute the development of heavy fighting to other political developments such as the "intrusion of the Akwamu into Krepi country and the organization of a strong and aggressive Akan state in Akwapim." Still, before this period in the mid-eighteenth century, it appears that conflicts in the area were more akin to "petty bickering with their neighbors about fishing rights in the Volta."[64]

Whatever the case, what is likely and what is known is that European presence and intervention in this territory greatly served as an additional contentious factor among these groups. It is clear that the actions of European nations were a direct stimulus of interethnic warfare on the coast in that they armed various groups when it suited their purposes. This only served to fan the flames of preexisting conflicts and to create new ones where they would not otherwise have existed.[65]

A good example is the hostility that existed between the Anlo and their neighbors, the Adas, which eventually culminated in the Sagbadre War of 1784. Important information regarding these hostilities can be found in the contemporary account of P. E. Isert, who was a chief surgeon to the Danish establishments on the Guinea coast during this period. He was both witness and participant in this war. Isert confirms that the

Danes allied with the Adas as well as the Akyem, Akwapem, and Anexo against the Anlos.[66] Regarding the cause of the war, he says:

> From time immemorial, the Adas, or the Blacks who live on this, the west side of Rio Volta and also on the islands in the river, have been enemies of the Blacks living on the east side of the river. Their frequent disputes were mostly because of disagreements about the fishing boundaries. Since both nations live in the Volta, it is natural that both should have rights to fishing, yet they could never agree how far out in the river the one or the other nation should engage in fishing.... And they also quarrel out of pure envy—when one nation was prospering more than the other, this gave cause for war. These wars started with small skirmishes until the parties became so exasperated with each other that war became general.[67]

Though Isert does not specifically identify Danish interests as playing a role in the war, he does note that victory for the Danes, the Adas, and their allies was good for business. In fact, he says, business was never better, with an estimated 300,000 captives sent across the Atlantic to be sold. Victory also reinforced the prestige of the Danes in the area.[68] What is particularly interesting about this account is Isert's identification of the Adas and their allies as "*our* Adas and *our* lagoon blacks." For example, he says, "Our Adas and Lagoon blacks now performed a masterpiece of bravery. With guns held in their mouths and with their other implements on their heads they waded through the ditch at one place where the Augnas [Anlos] were not expecting them."[69]

In the end, though the Anlos fought bravely, they were apparently overwhelmed by European artillery. The envoys from Anloga, the capital of Eweland, confirmed as much during the peace treaty negotiations: "We cannot possibly resist the weapons of the Whites, therefore we take our hats off and beg for our lives. This persistent and long lasting war has exhausted our strength and our goods. We are suffering hardship, since our children are either dead or wounded. We agree to all the conditions you have presented to us."[70]

This statement was significant because it was coming from a defiant foe. The Anlos were already well known for their defiance and bravery. Isert says at one quiet moment in the battle, "Thus things remained for a while, until the young men among the Augnas [Anlos] could not endure the peace any longer. They swore that it was a disgrace to let themselves be subjugated, so to speak, by the White Man. So they made a camp near the river and attempted to waylay our Blacks, as well as to free Blacks and capture them."[71] Later Isert calls the people of Woe "our bitterest enemy." He goes on to say that "the Way [Woe] blacks are the worst rogues among the entire admirable Augna nation. Their body-build probably contributes to their godless actions."[72]

Given their spirit of defiance and known prowess in past pursuits, it is not surprising that the Anlos were understandably crestfallen when they lost the war. They had particular difficulty with the fact that one of the peacetime conditions that they were obliged to agree to was the establishment of a new fort in the area, Fort Prinzenstein. Even the people of Keta—who were alternately allies and enemies in the war—did not receive the Danish victory very well: "The Quittas who would have preferred anything to permitting the whites to build a fort there, looked on askance, clearly despondent [yet] not daring to allow their displeasure to be noticed since we still had with us a mighty army with sword in hand."[73]

Thus we see the role of both guns and European intervention in the affairs of local polities. We see one group weakened by alliances between local groups and the Europeans. Most important, we witness an attempt by the latter to take full advantage of historical hostilities that existed among various groups, with the end result being a cornucopia of captives as well as the establishment of a new trading base.

It is in this light that the question that is often associated with the gun-slave circle theory should be reasked: Did Africans go to war to procure slaves? There are many views on the subject. Some authors have traditionally drawn an unjustified dichotomy between political enslavement and economic enslavement, yet both conditions are in a dialectic, as demonstrated by the above example.[74] Some African polities may have at different points in their history gone to war for slaves, but it stands to reason that given their historical relationship with their neighbors, there would always be other issues—economic and political—that might cause conflicts. Furthermore, the above narrative beckons us to ask the other side of the question: Did Europeans in Africa arm African groups and/or go to war themselves for slaves? The Sagbadre War is one clear example that they did. Their primary purpose in Africa was an economic one, and at this time slaves were the most profitable commodity on the world market. The same cannot be said for Africans and in this case the Ewes. They had many different reasons for entering into conflicts and alliances with their neighbors. These reasons extended beyond, though sometimes included, the Atlantic slave trade.

In Anlo Ewe territory, there was violence associated with the trade, but there were other ways in which the Anlo political structure was adversely affected. These included: (1) the diminishment of a system of accountability because of the rise of individual traders who were not accountable to anyone; (2) the diminishing authority of the chiefs, including the paramount chief; and (3) the continual intervention of Europeans in local affairs.

One major impact on Anlo polities brought out by the oral histories was the rise of the individual at the expense of broader political structures.[75] Individual traders who became wealthy as a result of slave traffic in some ways rivaled the authority of the chiefs in the nineteenth century.[76] Historical sources certainly confirm that this was the case along the Anlo coast. There was decidedly more power in the hands of individuals in the nineteenth century than there had ever been before. In Anlo, as elsewhere along the coast, these individuals were generally Afro-European traders, Brazilians, or those who had strong connections to Europeans. The best example of the latter is the trader Geraldo de Lima, who upon the death of his former employer, Cosar Cequira Geraldo de Lima, took his name and continued his business.[77]

The notion of the rise of the individual versus the group is extremely significant for many reasons. First, in a society that stressed kinship and other communal ties, the change was substantial. The key factor, however, was that this rise in power of a few individuals vis-à-vis the chiefs did much to erode the system of political accountability. Previously, collective mobility was achieved by the aforementioned system of paramount chief, local chiefs, and their councils of elders. All these parties were ultimately answerable to the people. The chief was said to be "a first amongst equals, to be installed or destooled if need be according to custom and usage."[78] Accordingly, the elders and the chiefs were encouraged to be accountable and responsive. If the chiefs were technically accountable to the general populace, to whom were the wealthy traders of this new era accountable? This lack of accountability is particularly evident in the case of Geraldo de Lima, who used both Anlo and European authorities to his own benefit.[79] Even though he became adopted into the Adzovia clan (one of the leading Anlo clans), his actions were not suggestive of any particular loyalty or accountability to any one group.

European contemporary accounts confirm the same. Governor Carstensen, in his mid-nineteenth-century diary, describes the freedom that these rogue traders enjoyed. There are countless references to the inability of the Danes to control these traders in spite of numerous palavers with chiefs and paramount chiefs. In fact, it is for this reason that he continually makes the case to his superiors that the forts and castles be restored to their original strength. For example, he says in his entry of May 13, 1845:

> The slave trade, however, found the country beyond the Volta too narrow. Gradually, among the negroes themselves, grew up a lot of petty slave trade agents and commissioners who roamed the country in all directions to bring numerous heads to the market. Thus it came about that a great number of consignments could take place right from the fort of Elmina. Usually, the slaves are brought to Vay [Woe], where a store room is found.... Dutch Accra has for a long time been the residence for several slave trade agents, especially immigrated Brazilian negroes who have correspondents in Vay and Popo.[80]

These individual traders were not accountable to any authority, political or otherwise, on the coast. One reason for this lack of accountability could be the structure of Anlo polities. The fact that in Anlo there has never existed a supreme centralized body that itself regulated trade may have contributed to this rise of individual power bases. We know from the history of the early trade in the kingdom of Benin that the oba as the chief political officer was able to regulate the slave trade in part because all traders were required to join specialized trading institutions under his authority. Unlike other smaller states along the Guinea coast, these traders, as members of such institutions, were not free to act in any way they desired. Each association had a different trading route. The oba maintained a delicate balance among these associations in two ways: first, by being a member of all of them and second, by allowing relatively free trade but with a protectionist policy.[81]

By contrast, the lack of accountability on the Ewe coast rendered the position of paramount chief vulnerable and unstable. Governor Carstensen confirms this instability in an 1846 entry: "The repair of the fort [Fort Prinzenstein] is welcome to the Augna [Anlo] chief. This man is mentioned as a well meaning ruler. Still, because of his inability, he lacks the necessary influence on the inhabitants of the country, especially its rich men, ie. slave traders and their so very grasping adherents: in the repair and reorganisation of the fort so that in this place palabres [palavers, or talks] can be decided, guilty people arrested and punished, in the presents which in fairness will fall on him, the Augna chief sees his own advantage."[82]

The Danish governor Carstensen here mistakenly identifies the inability of the paramount chief to control traders as the problem. In fact, it was perhaps not so much a question of personal ability as the fact that Anlo polities remained loosely organized in structure in spite of the onslaught of new challenges brought on by the slave trade. Such a structure made it difficult for those chiefs not involved in the slave trade to challenge rogue traders, who were wealthy and had their own adherents. In the end, this diminished the authority of the paramount chief.

Finally, while a direct line of continuity cannot be drawn between the era of the slave trade to the present with respect to the transformation of the political landscape, it is important to note that there are some correlations that can be made between yesterday and today. First, there a fair number of chieftaincy succession problems in Ghana at present in part due to the tension between those who are traditional heirs and those who have achieved success in business and/or education.[83] This tension is being played out in the many customary courts across the nation. In some cases, though by no means all, the legacy of slavery looms large. As the Didahene, Nana Owusu Kwaa Dida of

Kumasi, said in our meeting: "Regarding someone's nationality, we do not go into it at all, except if you are applying for a stool [i.e., a chieftaincy]. When we are trying a case here, we only take cases up to five generations."[84]

THE PERSISTENCE OF SLAVERY
IN GHANA AND AFRICA

And so, these debates persist, even if only in the shadows of national debates. The "shame" attached to servile status is a live memory. But this memory is not publicly acknowledged, nor is the continued presence of various forms of servitude in Ghana or elsewhere on the continent. In the Ewe states of Tongu and Anlo, for example, the institution of *trokosi* persists in some quarters. Trokosi is a form of female religious servitude in which a young woman is forced to serve a local religious order or shrine in atonement for some debt incurred or offense committed by her family. It is an institution left over from the eighteenth and nineteenth centuries that persists in spite of bills passed to ban the practice as well as the advocacy of international organizations such as International Needs Ghana, which has liberated hundreds of trokosi.[85] In 1996–97 the practice was brought to the attention of the general Ghanaian public, though one of my oral narrators, Mr. Kpodo, brought it to my attention as early as 1993. "Regarding Fiashidi. It is one of the complicated spirits in our society, and the people are trying to avoid it. If you see a fine woman and you make advances without asking the priest, you will have to produce a woman to replace that woman."[86] Fiashidi is said to be the process by which a virgin in dedicated to a shrine because her family has committed a particular offense. If, for example, there are a series of abnormal deaths in a family, a virgin may be sent to appease the god.[87]

Furthermore, though in 1996–97 there were intense debates on the issue, at the time of this writing, however, in 2003, there seemed little sense of public outrage about the continuation of this or any form of servitude in Ghana. At the same time, an undetermined number of women are enslaved, as this practice is reported to also exist in Togo, Benin, and Nigeria.[88]

Fortunately, some Africans themselves, including former slaves such as Julie Dogbadzi, who now works for the organization International Needs, are beginning to speak out about this awful practice. "The priest caught me and got angry. He asked three other men to hold me down and tie me to a table. They put ropes on my feet, legs and hands, and I was beaten mercilessly. I thought I was going to lose the baby."[89]

Ms. Dora Galley tells a similar story, which highlights the aspect of sexual exploitation of these young women and reveals a particularly gendered form of abuse. "I was forced to have sex with the priest as one of the rituals in the shrine, but luckily I didn't get pregnant." Ms. Patience Akope, who spent fifteen years as a servant to one of these priests, is even more vehement in her remarks: "The practice of trokosi is a crime and it should be stopped completely. Human beings are not animals to be sacrificed. The government should move quickly to arrest and jail those who are still perpetuating this evil and dehumanizing practice of keeping and abusing young innocent girls in the shrine."[90] Others, too, like assistant professor of education Anthony Owusu-Ansah in the online journal, the *African Symposium,* are attempting to break the silence and to make connections between liberating female trokosi and African development: "The government of Ghana should also find ways of implementing the laws of the land to save the girls. Ghana needs her very capable women in the quest toward attaining a better standard of living for her people. The country certainly advances at great peril, if women in this corner of the country are not empowered to strive for the same attainable goals as men but are left at the mercy and whims of the gods and lords of the land."[91]

Still, for some, the debate rages on as to whether banning this practice is an infringement of religious and cultural freedom. It should be clear, however, that where religious practice (or any other practice) infringes upon basic human rights and in fact encourages abuses, such practices should be eliminated. But that this is not so clear is, I believe, in part because of the murky legacy of slavery in Ghana and elsewhere in Africa. A practice like trokosi survives not only because of die-hard "traditions" but because of the climate of silence on the issue of slavery. It must be said that though we have evidence in the cases of the Nyigbla and the Yewe religious orders of priests selling female initiates to slave traders, there is no direct link between trokosi today and this past. Yet, as we have shown in this chapter, Atlantic operations greatly increased and influenced the maintenance and growth of domestic slavery. In trokosi, we see that this legacy lives on. It is a legacy that has not yet been reconciled in Ghana's past, and as a consequence it is not reconciled in its present. This stands as one very devastating effect of this period.

CHAPTER 7

Subversion of the Sacred

The Effects of the Atlantic Slave Trade
on Anlo Ewe Religious Organizations

This was a very secret cult and many people did not know
what happened. Most of the children were sold into slavery.
G. Kpodo, Woe

For many, the Middle Passage journey of the Atlantic slave trade
is understood in physical terms—shackles; whips; large numbers
of African slaves packed like sardines in too-small holds; air
thick with the smell of urine, blood, and tears; and the dead
strewn in the midst of the living. My thoughts on the Middle
Passage, however, have often been dominated by another image
—one expressed in spiritual rather than physical terms. What, I
would imagine, would Africans who in traditional societies acknowledged the sacred in every sphere of life and particularly at
the point of death do in the face of such sacrilege? For people
who upheld such strong and abiding beliefs in the power of the
ancestors and in the reincarnation of ancestral spirits, *not* to able
to bury their dead according to the proper rites and most im-
portantly in the proper place must have been as devastating as
the loss of their freedom. To witness the sick dying in the night
below deck of a slave ship only to be thrown overboard by slave
traders in the next morning, as was routinely done, must have
engendered an unbearable grief that defies description.

Even today, with more and more Ghanaians moving to the major city centers and Ghanaian society lunging deeper into a more urbanized culture, when someone dies, there is little debate about where he or she should be buried. Such is the sacred tie to hometowns or villages. Even if in life these individuals had not lived in or even visited these areas in many years, it is understood they will be buried there, close to their ancestors.

Ideas of the sacred have always mattered in most if not all ethnic communities in Ghana and all over West Africa. These are not theoretical questions but ones connected to everyday life and living. Given this fact, it was all the more egregious that traditional religious organizations of the old Slave Coast—specifically the Nyigbla and Yewe orders—became involved in the activities of the slave trade in the mid-nineteenth century. Such behavior represented the subversion of sacred values in the community. This involvement, however, given this environment and its respect for the sacred, was not taken lightly particularly by the female members of the community. Collusion on the part of the traders and religious priests was met with what can only be called a quiet yet formidable resistance from Anlo Ewe mothers, who took a stand by pointedly withdrawing their children from participation in these organizations, which in some cases led to their decline.

At the same time, the Yewe and Nyigbla religious organizations were not the only religious influences on the Slave Coast. By the mid-nineteenth century, these groups had to contend with some new arrivals, who would leave a lasting mark on the area. These were the Bremen missionaries from northern Germany who established a church and a school in 1854. The record shows that these missionaries not only competed with these traditional religions for adherents, they also turned their mission station into a refuge for slaves. Over a period of almost ten years, they "ransomed" children who were taken as slaves by slave traders. But notwithstanding some of these more laudable activities, the witness of these missionaries was marred by key subversions of their own sacred values. In this era of the Atlantic slave trade they, too, like other religious organizations, fell prey to the exigencies of the time. This was one very devastating effect of the Atlantic slave trade. It appears that this era was unrelenting in its threat to the important belief systems of the day. While "ransoming" African slaves, these missionaries at the same time did not take a stronger and bolder stand against the institution of slavery in general, nor did they confront white and black traders alike about the continuation of this evil practice. Furthermore, their joint business and evangelistic efforts raised questions as to whether they helped pave the way for colonial exploitation of the then Gold Coast.

Before looking at Ewe religious institutions and their subversion during the slave trade, it may be helpful to place these traditional groups in the greater context of religion in Africa. The religious picture in Africa is multifaceted. It has deep roots —the length and breadth of which have not always been easy for outsiders to understand. Even today in many parts of Ghana (and West Africa in general), since the 1980s, there has been a great increase in interest in Christian Pentecostalism. In addition to the increasing popularity of existing Pentecostal churches, new churches were founded, such as Dr. Mensa Otabil's International Central Gospel Church, Bishop Duncan William's Christian Action Faith Ministries and Rev. Sam K. Ankrah's International Bible Worship Centre.[1] At the same time, Islam and traditional religions continue to grow side by side.

Even the casual observer of the contemporary scene in Ghana would be hard pressed not to notice the many public references to religion and faith in general. "Thy Will Be Done" beauty parlors can be found next to "Jesus Cares" auto shops. "God is great" (an Islamic reference) adorns many a local taxi or minibus. These and other sometimes scriptural references can be seen interspersed with more secular and humorous ones, such as the water truck emblazoned "Fear Woman."

Kenyan scholar Ali Mazrui calls this religious tradition a "triple heritage."[2] Early Christian roots in Ethiopia from the first century AD and the introduction of Islam in roughly 700 AD are only two important markers of this rich history. Before and after these markers, the presence of thousands of indigenous or what is often called "traditional" religions has rendered Africa very complex in terms of religious expression. European (and later American and West Indian) missionaries of the modern era from the fifteenth century onward did not introduce religion to Africans who had no religion. Contrary to some of their recorded statements, many of the ethnic groups they encountered in West and Central Africa had deeply felt beliefs that were woven into the very fabric of their societies. Moreover, European and later American and West Indian missionaries were not the first to introduce Christianity to the continent as Ethiopia then, as now, had already won many converts.

The fact that religion was not separated from everyday life may have been precisely the reason that many of these foreigners mistakenly assumed that Africans either had no religious life or worshipped pieces of wood and stone. Life itself was given meaning by religious practice and in fact, there was no formal distinction between the spiritual and the material.[3] Furthermore, I contend that it is because religion was so important to African communities that some of the most durable African survivals in the New World are in the area of religion as well as oral communication (music, oral narratives, etc.). Many communities in the African Diaspora have held tightly to various elements of African religions. Santeria of Cuba, Vodun of Haiti, and much of the religious expression in Bahia in Brazil, for example, are fused with elements of this African past. In addition,

African American church traditions have long been influenced by African religious expression.[4]

Finally, another key element of West African traditional religion is that it has historically been inclusive—ever open to change and adaptation. At the same time, closely related to this lack of exclusivity is often an element of secrecy. Where Christianity and Islam have sought to spread their message and reveal their tenets to the world at large, traditional religion in West Africa has maintained a strong element of secrecy. As such, a systematic set of creeds and sacred scriptures is often absent, or at least unavailable to the general public.[5] The lack of this dogma allows for a certain freedom but also leaves itself open to potential abuse. Mary Nooter and other contributors to the book *Secrecy: African Art That Conceals and Reveals,* show the connection between secrecy and power in many African communities. Nooter's work among the Luba of Zaire and Quarcoopome's work among the Dangme illustrates this phenomenon. According to a Dangme elder, "What I know, that you ought to know, but do not know, is what makes me powerful."[6] Ewe oral traditions in the form of proverbs go even further, admonishing those who have knowledge not to boast of it. "Nunya la ave-mexevie, ame deka melene o," translates as "Knowledge is like the forest bird, one person cannot catch it."[7]

Traditional religion among the Anlo Ewe community follows closely in this West African tradition. In particular, two significant religious organizations—the Yewe and Nyigbla—share many of the above-mentioned characteristics. Yewe and Nyigbla are themselves part of a large and varied religious system. First, Anlos recognize one Supreme God called Mawu, which means "God does not kill" and/or "God cannot be killed," "the bountiful, the kind, the good One," or "This is the One who surpasses all."[8] The Supreme God is He who gives life and provides all that is necessary for sustaining life. Mawu simultaneously represents benevolence, sustenance, and immortality. He has no beginning and no end. Mawu is considered elusive and invisible, associated as he is with some faraway place in the sky.[9] One Anlo informant in a 1965 study corroborates: "Mawu is too big to be put into a small room and worshipped in that place. In all Anloland, it is only Christians who do this. How can we put into a room a Being we can never see and who is like the wind blowing everywhere? The deities we are able to house because they reveal themselves to us to see them and are locally connected with us just as other nations have theirs."[10] Mbiti prefers to downplay the supposed elusive nature of the Supreme God, preferring to emphasize that God in these communities is perceived as both near—in the many proverbs, greetings, and sayings of daily life—and far, in his transcendence over human matters.[11]

Perhaps because of this notion of Mawu's transcendence, there exists a plethora of *trowo* or *vodu* in Anlo traditional life. These trowo are more earthly spiritual agents that are worshipped regularly to enhance day-to-day existence. They act as intermediaries that temporarily inhabit objects or natural phenomena.[12] Taking care of the physical needs of the deity, such as feeding and bathing, thus is very important. Such care and worship, however, is not what has previously been called "fetishism" —"the literal worship of wood and stone."[13]

Likewise, the ancestors play a very important role in traditional Anlo life, as they do in many parts of West Africa. When an elder dies, he or she is understood to enter another "spiritual plane." "Death does not rob life of meaning; on the contrary, it gives greater depth of meaning to life by prolonging it on the spiritual plane."[14] The ancestors then continue on in the daily life of the people as guides and protectors and as tangible connections to life after death. It is for this reason the ancestors are referred to as "the living dead."[15] It is only in this context that the overwhelming significance of funerals can be understood.[16] And so Anlo reverence for their ancestors and the hereafter clearly shows their belief that life on earth is only a small part of a greater continuum. Anlo traditional culture sees life as much more than a short existence on earth.

THE NYIGBLA AND YEWE RELIGIOUS GROUPS: ORIGIN, STRUCTURE, AND UNDERLYING PRINCIPLES

In the midst of this multifaceted religious picture are various traditional religious groups that exemplify many of the principles discussed above. Nyigbla is the most famous national tro of Anlo and the oldest of the two religious sects. Traditionally, it was a tro of warfare imported from Gbugbla (a town near Accra, the capital of Ghana). Tradition has it that it was brought from Gbugbla at a time when there was much intertribal warfare along the Ewe coast.[17] According to German missionary Spieth, the Anlo had heard of the great powers of this tro and sent messengers to investigate. The reports being favorable, they brought it back to Anlo territory and have since held it in high regard. This was an early example of the principle of inclusion and adaptation of a new god in the West African tradition.

Though it is regarded as a communal religion, there is evidence in former times of a distinct initiation process. *Zizi fo asi* was the ritual by which young women were initiated into the order. Young women were said to become possessed. At this time they would be taken into the forest, where they would learn the secrets of the order. This initiation process took anywhere from six to twelve months, during which time some initiates were said to have died.[18] Moreover, another important feature of the religion was and is the "outdooring" (literally bringing the priest/god out of doors) of the Nyigbla priest every year, at which time three sections of the town—Lashibi, Agave, and Woeawo—are obliged to donate a cow. The entire community is involved in this annual event.[19]

It is further believed that during times of war Nyigbla rides on horseback in front of the warriors with a bow and arrow. According to some sources, originally there was intense competition between the Nyigbla priest and the paramount chief. Eventually, the two came together and performed various ceremonies in concert. As such, today the paramount chief serves as both chief and Nyigbla high priest.[20] This represents one of the underlying principles of Anlo traditional religion—the connection of religious and secular spheres.

On important occasions the awomefia (the paramount chief) wears the dress of Nyigbla, a loose white gown.[21] At the annual Hogbetsotso festival he is brought in on a stretcher, lifted by elders and covered with a cloth. This concealment signifies the reverence and deference that must be accorded him as well as the awesome secrecy that must surround him. It also sets him apart from the populace in that he is the only man who can dress in the traditional religious dress of the god Nyigbla. In fact, before the turn of the century the paramount chief alone had the right to wear European clothes or to mount a horse in the capital Anloga. According to Spieth, commenting on the nineteenth century, "a heavy penalty is inflicted for wearing European clothes. The high priest himself is set above all kings. Whoever meets him must turn around and throw himself down and may only proceed after that."[22] Currently such taboos are not upheld, as many in Anlo territory wear interchangeably European or African clothing. Other taboos, such as those against the killing of certain species of snakes dedicated to Nyigbla (called *Anyagbo*), are also held in less regard at this time.[23]

This was not always the case. Such was the tenacity with which Anlos held onto the Nyigbla religion that European missionaries from Bremen, Germany, famously said regarding Anlo territory, "it was a hard soil for preaching."[24] They were repeatedly forced to stay on the coast because it was said that the Nyigbla god did not desire them to set foot in the interior, where their presence might undermine its power.[25] Eventually, they were granted permission to go further inland and were thus more successful in their efforts in areas like Ho. Still, the missionaries referred to the Anlos as "the wildest tribe and most trouble to the white men" in their flouting of evangelical efforts in the area.[26] Though much has changed since that time, there is still a national acknowledgment among the Anlo of the religious and political significance of Nyigbla, even though it is essentially a god of war whose powers are less necessary in times of peace. It is as one informant said, "the religion for the whole people."[27]

The Yewe order, on the other hand, has assumed more significance in contemporary Anlo culture. The Yewe organization is dedicated to the worship of the thunder pantheon, of which Hebiesco is the most prominent figure. Yewe is sometimes said to mean, "it is a profound trick." This is most certainly a reference to their secret rites.[28] Yewe, like the trowo, are intermediaries between man and the Supreme God. Yewe is considered a protector against harm, and one of the central tenets exhorts members not to do anyone harm.[29]

Yewe became a force in the nineteenth century, although there are differing accounts regarding its origin. According to one oral source, Gilbert K. Kpodo of Woe, two traders, Doe and Afedima, brought the Yewe god from Dahomey.[30] The implication was that these traders brought Yewe back to enhance their trade. In this way it became a status symbol of their newfound wealth. They and others were attracted to Yewe because it was a means to show one's wealth and status. "They keep changing clothes; they wanted to show themselves as wealthy," said one oral source. Yewe was thus used as a source of power. Oral sources concur that traders saw Yewe as a means of increasing their wealth and enhancing their efforts.[31]

Some of the oral traditions suggest that before the 1847 Danish bombardment of Keta, Yewe was just another religious cult of minor importance. Others suggest that the earliest shrine was established by Togbui Honi and his wife, Boe, in the late 1700s. The Yewe gods were reputed to have assisted her with her problem of barrenness.[32] Whatever the actual origin, the Yewe god was certainly "the stranger god," like Nyigbla, brought from elsewhere to assist the people and to be a vehicle of enhancement of power in the community: a panacea for individual and community problems at a critical juncture in the history of Anlo territory.[33]

As such, Yewe is acquired and is often owned by individuals or families. This acquisition takes place after, for example, a discovery of siliceous stones *sokpe* or *agozee* (a small pot with cowries).[34] After this discovery, a *Midao*, or priest, is invited to establish Yewe for the one who has discovered it. This person becomes known as the owner of the cult, or *Hubano*, and is henceforward assisted by the priest in initiating new members. Traditionally and to this day, at the center of the cult is a secret lodge or compound. In this compound are the complex organizations of a secret society, complete with its own language, dances, prayers, food taboos, rules and regulations for initiates and nonmembers.[35] There is a strict wall of secrecy built up around the compound and all activity within its walls. Cult houses have white, blue, and red flags above the entrance, and there is a special password that must be uttered in order to enter.[36] A Yewe song confirms, "The child is looking up but what is down he cannot see."[37]

Initiates are instructed in its ways for a period of months, during which they are kept separate from their families and the rest of the community. In this way the sect is similar to a modern-day convent or monastery. During this time, initiates undergo a complex training process that can last up to three years. At the end of this period there is a great ceremony, much like a Christian baptism. The initiate is given a new name and marks are added to his or her chest, back, arms, and cheeks as a symbol of cult membership. "During the dancing ceremony, the graduates, especially the women, change their cloths as many times as they can. They display their dancing skills and try to outclass each other."[38]

Notwithstanding the shroud of secrecy, elements of the cult are selectively introduced to the outside world as a way of attracting new members. An array of different charms, as well as the above-mentioned dance and drumming styles, are the primary means by which this takes place. One informant, an experienced master drummer and instructor at the University of Ghana, talked about how drummers are forbidden to play certain types of dance music. Only Yewe members may play these styles, which they perform in elaborate dress at special public outings outside their compound.[39]

At these outings, nonmembers are often entranced by the unusual rhythmic music styles as well as the display of "wealth" as shown by their elaborate cloths.[40] In fact, the attraction to these styles is said to be so great that many informants suggested that it is as if the Yewe gods were entrancing new worshippers into their cult. One informant claimed that this had been the case with his sister, who at a very young age was beckoned by the appealing sounds of the drums into the Yewe compound. Now an elderly woman, she had remained a Yewe cult member, and in fact, it was expected that the cycle would continue with the next generation of her family. "Now this is what happens: if she dies as a cult member, a member of the family becomes a reincarnation of the dead person. My father had a sister and she died and my mother gave birth and they asked the Oracle about the birth. It was said that the new baby is my father's sister, so as she grew older, she [my sister] had to join the cult."[41]

This was typical of many of the stories about the Yewe cult told in Anlo territory. For nonmembers, who frequently are among the spectators of these public performances, there is a deep sense of mystery and awe about the cult. And so we see that even within this secret structure there is an element of inclusiveness. There is a willingness and openness to attract new members.

One reading of the sources suggests that historically part of the reason for this attraction is the apparent freedom that the Yewe cult has offered its members, particularly in the mid-nineteenth century. For example, women who did not want to submit to marriages arranged by their parents sought out the Yewe compound, where they could have more of a say in their choice of partners.[42] Furthermore, those who wanted to put some distance between themselves and a problematic past (accused thieves, for example) sought out Yewe because of its long-standing tradition that the initiate becomes a new person with a new name when he or she becomes a member.[43] In fact, there is a strict taboo about anyone calling the new member by his old name, thereby further establishing his new identity.[44]

Yewe offered members freedom and protection in Anlo traditional culture. The Yewe group, like most aspects of religious life in Anlo, appears to provide many different avenues for entrance and participation. Though there is a prescribed structure and specific prayers, rituals, and taboos, the cult allows a rebirth, and with that, a sense of freedom cherished by its membership.

YEWE, NYIGBLA, AND THE ATLANTIC SLAVE TRADE

Oral sources show that at some point in the history of both religious organizations, there was an intersection between their activities and the operations of the slave trade. This involvement had two distinct components that were necessarily at variance with each other. On one hand, the groups, Yewe in particular, represented a very concrete form of protection from capture and slavery. In this way they were beneficial to the general population. On the other hand, cult leaders at specific periods in the nineteenth century, in opposition to the public good, used the cults to further their own economic interests in cooperation with slave traders. As a result, Yewe and Nyigbla cult practices in the nineteenth century were corrupted.

There is ample evidence that the Yewe sect was viewed during this time as a refuge. During a period of great uncertainty, when parents feared their children would be kidnapped and when there was a general state of chaos, community members saw the Yewe sect as both a physical and spiritual means of protection.[45] The injunctions against those who dared to harm a Yewe cult member most certainly would have added an almost untouchable quality to cult lodges and the members themselves. Furthermore, as often criminals and/or debtors were likely candidates for sale on the Atlantic market, they, too, sought refuge in the confines of the cult. As one source said, a bad person could run to the cult and pledge allegiance as a means of protection. Once a member, the person would wear a piece of black cloth to indicate to slave catchers that he or she was not for sale.[46] Thieves or debtors were then known for joining to elude creditors as well as slave traders.[47]

On the other end of the spectrum, some sources suggest that the rise of the Yewe group in the nineteenth century is connected to the case of corruption involving the Nygibla priest and awomefia that was discussed in the previous chapter. Both leaders reportedly used the period of seclusion as a means of abducting innocent young women and selling them to European slave traders. This incident was said to have taken place in the 1750s.[48] This induction process took place in the forest, and it was said that some of these women "died" before coming out from the forest. This incident was discovered only because there was a dispute between the awomefia and the Nyigbla order regarding the profits. It was later discovered that these women were not dead but in fact had been sold into slavery. As a result, the awomefia was exiled, as was the priest, and the Nyigbla order lost a great amount of respect and popularity.[49]

The Yewe cult rose to prominence in the midst of these tragic events. Initially, it, too, was connected to the trade in that an influential Afro-European by the name of Quist used the Yewe group and compound as a means of acquiring more wealth. He established his shrine in the mid-nineteenth century and gained prominence in the domestic trading area at a time when the Europeans were attempting to abolish the slave trade. Eventually, he and others of the Yewe order began to use the compound as a way station for slaves—replicating the same ill-fated error of Nyigbla.[50] They, too, were able to use the seclusion process as a way to sell initiates into slavery. They were aided by the existence of a long-standing injunction that if an initiate died, Yewe cult leaders were not obligated to inform the family until the end of the training period—and even then no questions were allowed. In essence, the inherently secret nature of the cult was used as a cover for this corrupt activity. What began as a means of enhancing both spiritual and earthly powers became corrupted by its interaction with the slave trade.[51]

Eventually, according to one oral source, mothers stopped letting their children go to the compound since they feared hearing at some point in the future that their child had died. Other oral sources went so far as to say that "most people who joined the Yewe cult were sold into slavery."[52] The same is said of Nyigbla; one source says that to this day children in Anlo area are afraid of kevigatowo—carriers of big baskets traditionally made of bulrushes. These baskets were said to be the means by which slave catchers caught and sold children into slavery.[53]

SUBVERSION OF COMMUNITY
VALUES AND AN ABUSE OF POWER

At the beginning of this chapter we looked at a number of significant features of traditional African religions. Many of these were present in the practices of the Yewe and Nyigbla religious organizations. Given the all-encompassing role of religion in community life, in many ways these characteristics represent important community values or ideals. Ewe oral traditions in the form of proverbs also provide substantial evidence of these community values. As Professor Dzobo says regarding his two-volume collection of Ewe proverbs, "The more I study the Ewe proverbs, the more I become convinced that they form a collection of 'The Holy Sayings of Africa.' They represent how the Ewe-speaking community not only sees the world but also the modes of conduct that they expect should guide personal and social behavior."[54] As such, they are foundational to the society. Many of these values, when taken by themselves and in isolation of the trade (a time of great social upheaval), may be regarded as strengths. During the era of slave traffic, however, these same strengths became severe liabilities. This is, then, the context within which we may consider Yewe and Nyigbla's involvement in the slave trade. The subversion of these religious cults and thus of community values represented one of the most devastating effects of the slave trade on the area.

First, it should be said that the following discussion on values is not meant to advocate a kind of African essentialism. This discussion, rather, is consistent with recent work by Mary Nooter in *Secrecy: African Art That Conceals and Reveals,* who attests to the universality of the value of secrecy in all societies, for example, but still sees that such a value manifests itself differently in Africa than it does in the West. It is also similar to an analysis attempted by Patrick Manning, who in *Slavery and African Life* correctly asserts the difficulty of reconstructing

African thought in any great detail during this period. Nonetheless, he makes such an attempt in part by the use of anthropological sources. Likewise, the discussion here will also draw on useful anthropological work when appropriate.[55]

First, we consider the importance of the sacred in Anlo traditional life. In Dzobo's collection of proverbs, the concept of God (Mawu) and the sacred in general is prevalent. This is the case since many of the proverbs were intended to instruct the young and others in the moral teachings of the community. For example, "Mawu metsaa didri (apasa) si o." The literal translation is: "God does not trade in dishonesty." Another goes as follows: "Mawue nya tagbatsu na la asikekpo," meaning God drives away flies from the tailless animal. This proverb, like many others, speaks of the trust of the people in the power of God to care for the helpless and the poor. Like the following, it is an expression of hope. "Mawue wo xexeame, ne egble la, ame kae adzrae do?" This means "It is God who has made the world, if it has gone wrong, who would repair it?"[56]

Thus these proverbs are further corroboration of the sacred in Ewe life. So important was this value that parents would consent to the virtual loss of their child to either cult for such substantial periods of time so that they would be properly schooled in the sacred rites of the order. This initiation process served to prepare members to adopt a lifestyle in conformity with Yewe's injunctions. Yewe was not a god to be served only on a particular day or in one particular place. Notwithstanding the importance of the cult houses, there was indeed a very private and personal nature to the cult.[57] Yewe affected what you ate, what you wore, and with whom you consorted. All that represented the sacred, and its manifestations were to be observed on an everyday basis.

Alongside this prevalence of the sacred, there was a deeply utilitarian aspect to both religions. With Yewe, for example, though there are debates about its exact origin, one element features in all accounts: that Yewe was brought to the Anlo coast to solve a particular problem or to fill a particular need. Whether, as some sources say, that problem was the barrenness of the wife of its discoverer, Togbui Honi, or whether it was adopted by important traders simply to enhance their wealth, the *usefulness* of Yewe has always been an important feature. Certainly, stories abound of wealthy traders who adopted Yewe to increase their fishing ventures. Yewe, then, filled many needs in the society—spiritual as well as material. The same can be said of Nyigbla, particularly in the early decades when it was considered central to successful efforts at war between the Anlos and their neighbors.

The problem arose when the delicate balance between the sacred and the utilitarian aspects of both religions was affected by prolonged contact with the Atlantic system. The ensuing corruption had the result of emphasizing the utilitarian aspect at the expense of the sacred. The balance, which had previously tipped in favor of the sacred, was no more. For example, the Yewe injunction "Do no harm" now became secondary to the economic needs of cult leaders. This was one very substantial effect of the slave trade on this area.

To some extent, we can compare the collusion of the religious cults to the more systemic use of Christianity in slave-trading efforts. From the beginning of the European encounter with the African continent, economic prospects for Africa were tied to notions of a religious crusade.[58] Prince Henry the Navigator, who made contact with the Gold Coast in 1471, expressly hoped to divert the profits of the gold trade to Portugal as well as to convert "the heathen." There was always a sense of twin objectives. Furthermore, Christianity was often used to justify slave traffic, as evidenced by statements of traders like Barbot, who rationalized his part in the horrible business by claiming that Africans would then be able to receive the ultimate salvation.[59] In fact, two synods of the Reformed Church in France in

1637 failed to come to the determination of the incongruity of slavery and Christianity. In the end they, along with others, concluded that "slavery had always been the right of nations (*jus gentium*) and was not condemned in the Word of God."[60] Finally, most of the slave forts in Ghana had chapels next to the dungeons where slaves were kept like sardines awaiting slave ships. The forts, like the ships, had chaplains, part of whose job it was to give their blessings to the sale in human beings.[61] In a similar vein, though to a lesser extent, the interests of Yewe and Nyigbla colluded with the interests of slave traders.

The most significant difference here that whereas in the case of Europe, there existed a more systemic support of Christianity for the slave trade (up until abolition sentiments were stirred), in the case of the Anlo traditional cults, the corruption involved individual cult leaders and were not a consistent part of the cults' dogma. These events were idiosyncratic. This is a significant distinction borne out by the fact that these incidents of collusion took place in *secret*. When, as in the case of the Nyigbla incident, it was discovered that the paramount chief and the priest were involved in such activities, sanctions quickly followed. This showed that these activities were not the norm and would not be accepted by members and nonmembers alike. The public showed their own disapproval for a while by not sending their sons and daughters to the cult houses as they had done before. This community disapproval was an act of defiance in response to a perceived breach of public trust. Furthermore, understanding the significance of religion in the lives of this community, this defiance also meant that they were temporarily without the assistance of their most valuable resource.

This discussion highlights another important feature of the religious cults that was also subverted—secrecy. Secrecy played a great role in both cults. There were strict rules about cult members sharing information with nonmembers. In the case of Yewe, even those who left the cult and converted to Christianity were expected to keep Yewe's secrets.[62] Many often did through fear of punishment or retribution, though others chose to offer testimony of what took place behind cult doors. The benefit of this characteristic secrecy was that it bound Yewe members together as a community. They had a distinct identity vis-à-vis nonmembers of which they could be proud.[63] Secrecy also lent an air of awesome respect to the god itself and by association to those who worshipped it. Ironically, at the same time it is this very secret nature of the cults that invited abuse. During the time of the trade it worked to the advantage of corrupt cult and political leaders. Furthermore, along with the secrecy went a certain lack of accountability.[64] The fact that the families of Yewe initiates who had died during the initiation process were not allowed to ask questions regarding the circumstances of death meant that Yewe cult leaders wielded a certain kind of power over these families. This power, operating as it did behind the closed doors of the cult houses or in the depths of the forest, was not accountable to the general public. Such a situation was an invitation for individuals to abuse that power when faced with the pressures and temptations of slave-trading activities. In a society that prided itself on the promotion of communal interests over those of the individual, this was even more problematic.

This abuse of power was very significant in this kind of preliterate society where members of the order had no access to the special knowledge of the god, Yewe, except through the priest. Because there was no written dogma available, members were even more dependent on the priest to be trustworthy in all his dealings. It is easy to see in such a context how these young women could have been easily tricked into being sold across the Atlantic.

Finally, another important feature of Anlo traditional religions—and thus of Anlo communities in general—was also to be turned on its head in the era of the slave trade: the long-term view of life. Every element of the Anlo's religious life strongly suggests this view. Life extended backward and forward along a very complex spectrum. The preeminent role of ancestors and the belief in reincarnation also attest to this long-term thinking. It is no wonder that funerals are so central and that no expense is spared to give a relative a proper burial. This, after all, is the celebration of new life in the hereafter *(Tsiefe)*. Life, for the Anlos, was thus significant from many angles. To assert this is not to downplay the role of the present but to place it in a much greater context.

The respect for old age also bears testimony to this value. The proverb "The palm wine is never taller than the calabash" means that in traditional society wisdom comes from age. This wisdom is passed on from elders to children, and thus children cannot assume they are wiser than their parents. Another proverb says the same thing even more succinctly. "Deka nye xoxo na alafa" translates as "One is older than one hundred." Here again, age and experience—and thus the long view—are valued greatly.[65]

Notwithstanding the existence of human greed, how was this value, in even this limited respect, subverted for short-term gain? How did individuals in this society put short-term interests (profits from the slave trade) before long-term ones? We may never know the full answer to this question, but certainly it is true that the widespread and consistent existence of slave-trading activities prompted from outside the continent did much to encourage such a contradiction within it. It may not be enough to say, as some have asserted, that "every man has his price."[66] This price existed in an Anlo cultural context that valued the long-term view.

Elsewhere in West Africa there are other examples of the corruption of indigenous institutions. The Aro of southeastern Nigeria were known to be great slave traders in the region. At the center of their thriving trading efforts was the Oracle of

Chukwu. Oral accounts and other records show that the Oracle was originally an important religious and legal institution for the Aro and their neighbors. People from all around would come to the Oracle to seek guidance, settle disputes, or request the punishment of an offender.[67] The Oracle was considered the ultimate spiritual force in the land. It was even thought capable of causing death and misfortune. At the same time it was considered the "highest court of appeal." In an environment where diviners and oracles were routinely sought in times of distress, the Aros had many choices. The Oracle of Chukwu assumed prominence because of its efficacy.[68]

Perhaps because of its centrality to the people, it was inevitable that it would become involved in one of their primary activities at that time—slave trading. There is indeed evidence that, in addition to tribal wars, kidnapping, and raids, the Oracle did become a vehicle for the appropriation of slaves during the trade. People destined for slavery were "sacrificed" to the Oracle—while they were in reality being traded to Europeans. In fact, Bonny became one of the most well-known slave markets in part as a result of these activities.[69] The corruption of the Oracle, however, was but one tragic moment in a long tradition of an institution that made a difference in the lives of the Aro people. Its religious and judicial functions existed before the trade and continued after its abolition—such that even the British were later unsuccessful at suppressing it.

It is in the same vein that we may consider the circumstances surrounding the Yewe and Nyigbla cults. The collusion of cult leaders with slave traders was a tragic moment in the history of these religions. The whole community witnessed a subversion of the sacred for individual short-term gain. Idiosyncratic rather than systemic, such incidents were a reflection of the pressures and temptations presented by the Atlantic system. Clearly, contradictions existed prior to the advent of the trade, but at this one horrible moment in time these contradictions were woefully thrown off balance. The one saving grace was the revulsion of the community which, when such dastardly acts were discovered, resisted both the trade and corrupt religious leaders by refusing to send their children to the cults. Still, the end result was that serious blows were levied against traditional institutions, and the Anlos witnessed a subversion of what they have held dear for centuries—the notion of the sacred. They also witnessed a terrible abuse of power by leaders they respected. These were both very devastating effects of the Atlantic slave trade.

CHRISTIAN MISSIONARIES AND THE ATLANTIC SLAVE TRADE

As mentioned before, missionaries from Bremen, Germany set up a mission station in Keta in 1854. They were preceded in Ghana by their sister organization, the Basel Mission, whose missionaries arrived in Osu (in the present-day capital of Accra) on December 18, 1828. Several of the original missionaries died; hence the well-known phrase that Africa was "the white man's grave," but by 1832 the Rev. Andreas Riis came to Ghana and was instrumental in planting a mission station at Akropong. Eventually, the Basel mission had stations at Osu, Aburi, Abokobi, Ada, Kyebi, Nsaba, Abetifi, Anum, Gyadam, Krobo-Odumase, Akuse, Begoro, Winneba, Nsuta, and Kumasi.

Both the Bremen and the Basel missions were not churches as such but groups of fervent Christians from a number of Protestant denominations in Germany, Denmark, Switzerland, Alsace, Sweden, Holland, and Russia, as well as black West Indian missionaries from the Moravian Brothers Church in Jamaica. They were international groups who were rigorously trained in a very selective process.[70] They were known as Pietists —or, in Europe, Puritans—and they emphasized the view that God speaks to all of us, thus highlighting the importance of daily prayer. They had pointedly moved away from the concept of the state-sponsored Roman Catholic Church and instead put a lot of emphasis on self-reliance. For this reason they set up business and trading ventures alongside their mission stations.

They also strongly believed in the "inner life" of the Christian, which they emphasized more than outward behavior such as going to church or behaving well. They believed that God sees the hearts of all men, and true knowledge comes from God and the Bible, not from science.[71] The Bible was considered the ultimate authority on all things, and they believed that layperson and pastor alike could access God equally.[72] The pastor had no special relationship with God that the layperson could not also have. This was very different from traditional Roman Catholic traditions as well as from other Protestant denominations. In this sense, their dogma placed much less emphasis on church hierarchy and much more on equal access to God.

The Bremen missionaries first set up a base in Peki, but due to circumstances beyond their control (largely local pressures), under the leadership of Rev. Wolf, they moved to Keta in the heart of Eweland and established a mission there in 1854.[73] Later they established mission stations at Anyako (1857), Waya (1856), and Ho (1859). Their motto, as emblazoned on the daily journals called *Montsblatt* that they kept and sent back to their headquarters in Bremen, was: "Come over and help us"—a reference to Acts 16:9 in the Bible where St. Paul had a vision of a man from Macedonia calling him to preach the Gospel in his land. Likewise, these missionaries from Europe fervently believed that their mission was part of the great commission in Matthew 28 to share the Gospel far and near.

The Bremen missionaries arrived at an ominous time. The Anlos were making great profits from the slave trade and, according to church records, they opposed the antislavery attitude of the missionaries.[74] At the same time, as mentioned previously, the Bremen missionaries found that the Anlos would not be converted to Christianity from their local religions easily; accordingly, this was as much a source of tension between the two groups as anything else.

These two issues merged in the practice of ransoming slaves. The Bremen missionaries established a school and over a ten-year period (1854–64) bought and freed over 150 children. Very few of them became the Christian nucleus in the area as the missionaries had hoped, but such were the auspicious beginnings of the mission station at Keta. At first, in fact, there was a stigma attached to the schools, and by extension the schoolchildren, since all had been slaves.[75] At the same time, the mission school was attractive to some children who were taken with the uniforms that students had to wear. Missionaries reported that children in the area would approach them and say, "Let me put on the trousers"—evidence of their interest in the outward appearance of these strangers in their midst.[76] In this regard, one Inspector Zahn, upon his visit in 1874, lamented: "It is really sad that these young folk are so little aware of the blessing bestowed upon them."[77]

One may wonder, however, what it was about the witness of these missionaries, whose dogma stressed the inner life of the Christian versus the outer life, that caused would-be converts who watched them day by day to in most cases eventually embrace merely the outer trappings of Christianity. What was it about the way they set up their *kpodzi,* or Christian villages (which were usually established on a hill with a school and small houses for nuclear families) that gave that impression to their Ewe neighbors?[78]

Still, for young people who were enslaved on the coast, the mission station was primarily known as a place of refuge. Bremen missionaries went so far as to make appeals to Germany for money to be used as ransom for the children. In fact, the donated sums were were listed in their daily journals, *Montsblatt.*[79] Later Bremen missionaries would be associated with other ventures such as the creation of an Ewe dictionary by D. Westermann and the translation of the Bible into Ewe. These examples represent some of the positive aspects of the missionary presence in Africa, especially when linked with the fact that many missionaries lost their lives in the process of these efforts. The missionary gravesites in Osu (for the Basel Mission) and Keta for the Bremen missionaries are testimonies to this fact. These examples also point to the complexity of the missionary experience in Africa. One thing is clear: The missionary experience in Africa cannot be neatly categorized. It varied greatly depending on time period, locale, and the beliefs of the missionary groups in question.

Notwithstanding these positive elements mentioned above, the missionary presence in Eweland, as elsewhere in Africa, was often highly contested and not without its contradictions. The association of Bremen missionaries from the beginning in what could be called early colonial business ventures made some question the sincerity of their religious mission. Even Rev. Lorenz Wolf was conscious of this connection in his remarks regarding the first Bremen missionaries, who had sailed from Hamburg in 1847 to the coast of Ghana. "I had the impression that there was a war afoot, and these boats went out to conquer as indeed they do: on the war of conquest through trade and we go with them. When we saw the open sea we greeted it with the hymn: 'A safe stronghold our God is still.'" This link was to be further solidified when the British colonial government in 1874 gave 475-pound educational grants to the Bremen, Basel and Wesleyan missions to establish educational and religious programs in the country.[80]

In fact, the link between missionaries and business existed from the beginning. The company F. M. Vietor and Sons built a trading ship called the *Dahomey,* which both brought missionaries and their needed supplies from Bremen to the coast of Africa and engaged in trade in African raw materials of cotton, kola, skins, and coffee.[81] The man in charge of this Vietor enterprise, Christian Rottman was also the accountant for the Bremen mission: business and evangelism were already hand in hand.

This is a key contradiction that would not be missed by African activists and writers at a later date. Ghanaian author and activist Casely Hayford, in his famous book, *Ethiopia Unbound,* makes a stinging critique on missionaries in Ghana. He is particularly strident in his remarks about the missionary presence in Sekondi in southwestern Ghana. Describing a scene involving an African choirmaster—who looks out of place and time in his morning coat and patent leather shoes (complete with a handkerchief to periodically clean them)—and a young man who struggles with the English in an English hymn, he says: "And this the sum total of a half a century of missionary zeal and effort. Could it be for this that the simple good hearted fathers of our races had suffered and died. They prayed for light themselves and for their children's children. But instead of light, say ye Gods, does not darkness brood over the land?"[82]

Chinua Achebe and other authors also question what they might call the "darker side" of missionary history in Africa. As Achebe says in *Hopes and Impediments,* missionaries prepared the ground for the colonial powers to take over.[83] In the Ewe case, it would appear, they came hand in hand. Furthermore, and particularly pertinent to this work, even their response to the rampant and persistent business of slavery on the coast was not without ambivalence. Mission records show that missionaries, in part because of their business ventures, used local "boys" in ways akin to domestic slavery. They depended on these boys to help them experiment in the planting of wheat, to build their homes, to teach them the language, and to prepare herbal remedies to ward off disease. They needed to draw on the local labor pool for assistance in developing their mission station, but on such a "hard soil" they found themselves able to depend only on the children they had ransomed. Child labor was one thing, but the question of whether these children were ever paid for their efforts was perhaps another thorny and unknown issue. This contradiction comes up time and time again in their monthly journals.

THE SLAVE-TRADE ERA: A THREAT TO CHRISTIAN AND TRADITIONAL RELIGIOUS BELIEFS

Thus through this period we see a clash of cultures between the Ewes and the German Pietist missionaries, but we also see that they shared something very significant in common: a subversion of the values of their respective religions. Christian Pietist dogma and practice in Eweland and the values of local traditional religions versus their practices were at odds at this crucial point in their history—the era of the slave trade. It may be that the nature of the slave-trade era was such that it greatly tested the most deeply felt beliefs of both sides. At such a critical time, it presented a formidable challenge—if not outright threat—to those beliefs. Could adherents on either side still hold fast to what they believed in their heart of hearts was right, or would they be swept up with the exigencies of the times?

In the end, just as the values of the Ewe religious groups became casualties in this period, so did the values of the Christian missionaries. A subversion of the sacred also took place in their midst. These men and women who were so fervent about the Gospel found themselves in compromising situations where their very ideals were as murky as muddy water and their spiritual credentials questionable. The association with business ventures that prefigured colonial economic pursuits—where raw materials were continually taken out of the continent to be processed abroad—set a dangerous precedent. As Nkrumah says in *Africa Must Unite,* for all the good they did in setting up the earliest formal educational institutions in Ghana, they also engaged in some questionable activities: "While missionaries implored the colonial subject to lay up 'His treasures in Heaven where neither moth nor rust doth corrupt' the traders and administrators acquired the minerals and land. There was no intention of processing locally the discovered raw materials. These were intended to feed the metropolitan mills and plants, to be exported back to colonies later in the form of finished commodities."[84]

In other words, their business was not only evangelism. As late as 1963, at the time Nkrumah was writing, they dominated the textbook market.[85] Perhaps the value that they compromised most, however, was the question of equality before God. What differentiated the Pietist Christian from other Christians at home in Europe, in their view, was their belief that everyone had equal access to God. God saw the hearts of all people and so no one, be they black or white, had any additional entrée to God. Bible reading, introspection, and prayer were open to all and would increase and enhance the relationship one had with God. Yet in their dealings with the local people, in particular the children—in some cases the very ones they had ransomed—they revealed long-standing European biases of the civilized European versus the uncivilized African.[86] They subverted their own ideals about equality before God. This attitude "racialized" the Bible, according special privileges and status to white Christians as opposed to black. The very Bible doctrine of Acts 17 that God "hath made the world and all things therein...and hath made of one blood, all nations of men for to dwell on all the face of the earth" was subverted to suit the biases of the day. Other biblical references that suggest that all are equal in the sight of God were also ignored.

Finally, perhaps the greatest subversion was an important omission on their part: the lack of any mention in their records of their attempts to convert the white slave traders who were operating on the coast. While they stridently opposed all forms of traditional life that were at odds with the Bible—puberty

rites, payment of bride wealth, polygamy, and other practices
—most missionaries did not explicitly oppose practices exported from their own home countries. As Lucy Mair says, they
were silent on the issues of mechanical warfare and the use of
weapons of mass destruction.[87] Still, what is most striking is the
fact that they did not see the white traders living and working
on the coast who worked in and out of the slave fort in their
midst as candidates for salvation. There was an urgency for the
African population to be converted, but white slave traders such
as Don Jose Mora and others of Spanish or Portuguese origin
were not seen as targets for their evangelism. Why, one must
wonder, were they not earmarked for evangelism, when these
individuals shared a common European ancestry and likely
shared at least a nominal Christian heritage? Why were they not
singled out for conversion when it was their actions (in conjunction with their African counterparts) that prolonged this
evil trade in human beings? Surely this was a stronghold that
needed to be pulled down. This is a major question that remains
to be answered.

And so, this period of the slave trade posed a grave threat to religious practices on the Slave Coast—traditional and Christian.
Great and serious contradictions between ideals and practice
were evident, contradictions that had a devastating effect on the
people and the land. Furthermore, we see that the breakdown of
traditional structures took place long before the actual and
official advent of the colonial era. In fact, this breakdown likely
helped to usher in other more destructive forces of the incoming colonial administration. These have to be among some of
the saddest consequences of this era.

Still, in this time of crisis—physical and spiritual crisis, if
you will—we can look back and find at least two notes of resistance. One was the resistance and resilience of African women
and mothers who stood up to their local priests and voted with

their feet. Once news came that their children were disappearing, they chose to keep them home rather than send them to these religious sects. It was a brave move in the context of a community that simply assumed that these young women would be sent for religious instruction to one sect or another. Likewise, not all Ewes and not all Africans in general who were exposed to some of the contradictions of the missionaries accepted their views wholesale. We know, for example, that eventually, Africans themselves fought for the incorporation of some of their cultural practices into the church, such as drumming. Believing as they did that the Bible did not outlaw such activities, as long as they did not contradict the main aspects of the Gospel, some fought to retain their cultural identities, and most of all, their own understanding of the Christian experience. And so we see two notes of resistance—not the kind with guns and other weapons—but nonetheless effective and important examples of African agency.

CHAPTER 8

Reparations as Rememory and Redress

Sethe: "It's so hard for me to believe in [time]. Some things go. Pass on. Some things just stay. I used to think it was my rememory. . . . But it's not. Places, places are still there. If a house burns down, it's gone, but the place—the picture of it—stays, and not just in my rememory, but out there, in the world."

Denver: "If it's still there, waiting, that must mean that nothing ever dies."

Sethe: "Nothing ever does."

Toni Morrison, Beloved

Toni Morrison's *Beloved* so richly captures the essence of the African American experience during and after slavery, particularly with respect to the concept of "rememory." Broadly speaking, rememory refers to the ways in which past events greatly affect the present and the future. In her novel the past in question involves a child named Beloved who was killed by her mother, Sethe, in an effort to spare her from the indignity that was slavery. But Sethe and other characters in the book can never fully free themselves from their past. Morrison appears to be saying that whether or not we consciously *choose* to recognize its importance, our past is still living and breathing within us in the present. This is one lens through which we can look at the issue of the effects of the Atlantic slave trade and slavery on people of African descent. Furthermore, no debate on the effects of slavery is complete without an examination of the issue of reparations. In this concluding chapter, we will review a brief history of the reparations movement. Finally, we will look at the implications for the current debate in light of the insights of the oral history collection of this book.

In my view, there are two possible ways to look at the current reparations movement: (1) reparations as rememory—or recovery of the memory of the past in a variety of ways, from the setting up of a national and international instrument to teach and learn about the history of the period to slave memorial sites and other methods of memorialization; and (2) reparations as redress of past wrongs, to be specifically addressed by countries and continents on both sides of the Atlantic. Before looking through these prisms, it may be helpful to retrace our steps and go back to one of the major findings of the preceding chapters —the silence of the African past.

As we have shown in the Ewe example (and with reference to other places in Africa), there is a great degree of silence on the issue of slavery. An ethnic group like the Anlo Ewe, who have meticulously recorded many events in their history including the great migration from Notsie (an area in northeastern Nigeria) to their present location along the southeastern coast of Ghana, have developed a collective amnesia regarding this troubling past. Many Ewes, like several other groups in West and Central Africa, have an uncanny ability to remember and retain for posterity the names and histories of their ancestors, yet they have retained few stories about the era of the Atlantic slave trade. Though it was common for the people I interviewed to share with me details of their lineage—complete with full names and towns of origin—it was not common for them to have retained details of an era that lasted almost 350 years. The result is an overwhelming silence that has covered this period.

What is equally striking, however, is a similar silence that covers the history of the African Diaspora on the issue of slavery, including and especially on this issue of reparations. Still, there are several important historical markers that break this silence in the New World. Under Special Field Order no. 15, issued in 1865, newly emancipated slaves were to receive "forty acres and a mule." A number of freedmen had already received their forty acres at the time Congress passed the bill. But this promise was not to be kept; President Andrew Jackson soon thereafter vetoed the bill.[1] At the same time it cannot be underscored enough that while there was no restitution for slaves, Lincoln during the Civil War supported a plan to compensate slave owners for their loss of property. In fact, though the slave-owning classes of the South did not receive compensation for emancipated slaves, those of the District of Columbia reportedly were compensated through the work of the Board of Commissioners for the Emancipation in the District of Columbia.[2]

And so while there was a silence on questions of restitution for blacks, there was action for whites, who had already been the primary beneficiaries during the era of slavery. It is apparent that during this period of emancipation and its aftermath, there was little commitment to truly advancing parity and equality between blacks and whites. Historian Eric Williams affirms that the same was true in the Caribbean, in that the British gave emancipation to black slaves primarily for their own economic goals, and parity and equality for the ex-slaves was never a strong overriding issue. Furthermore, the British compensated the white Caribbean landowners to the tune of $20 million for their loss of property, while giving no similar restitution to those who had lost home and heritage—and often life and limb—over 250 years of slavery.[3]

And so we see that this silence in the Western Hemisphere was near total for the ex-slaves. There was no one to advocate their cause effectively. They had, of course, advocates in Wilberforce, the Quakers, and the black abolitionists, but none were able to convince the various spheres of power and influence to compensate the Negro for those centuries of pain.[4] In the 1890s a black woman by the name of Callie House did attempt to set up a pension scheme for older ex-slaves, but her efforts were soon thwarted by the U.S. government. According to historian Mary Frances Berry, her organization, the National Ex-Slave Mutual Relief Fund, "working through meetings, literature and traveling agents, the organization successfully developed membership across the South as well as Oklahoma, Kansas, Indiana, Ohio and New York."[5]

The call for reparations was not heard or presented on a large public scale until Queen Mother Moore, a longtime champion of reparations, delivered a petition to the United Nations demanding reparations for slavery in 1962. A year later Martin Luther King, in his book *Why We Can't Wait,* advocated the same.[6] Still, it is fair to say that this was not a major part of King's agenda or his platform, at least not in a explicit sense. His efforts were largely relegated to equal rights for blacks in public spaces and on public transportation and the fight for the right to vote. Toward the end of his short life he did advocate for the economic rights of the poor through his Poor Peoples Campaign, but this was an issue that was not restricted to relations between blacks and whites. In the end he may have raised the issue of reparations as a justice issue, but it was the fulfillment of equal rights and civil rights that dominated his agenda.

Activist James Foreman in and around 1970, however, made a more explicit call for reparations at Riverside Church. Specifically, he called on American churches and synagogues to pay $500 million "as a beginning of the reparations due us as a people who have been exploited and degraded, brutalized, killed and persecuted." Foreman was roundly criticized in the white press and once again, as Robinson says, "the American white community had turned a deaf ear almost uniformly."[7]

And so we see that this silence cannot be uncoupled from

the role of mainstream forces in maintaining the silence. As Carole Boyce Davies and other authors in her book *Moving beyond
Boundaries* suggest, it is possible to differentiate between being
silent and being silenced.[8] It is as if even to raise the question is
in and of itself heretical. Congressman John Conyers of Michi-
gan has also met with the same silence in Congress 120 years
after Thaddeus Stevens made his bid on behalf of ex-slaves.
Conyers in 1989 submitted a bill asking for a commission simply to study the issue of slavery and possible restitution. This bill
has since been stuck in the House Judiciary Committee and, at
press time, appears to have little chance of getting out.

On a similar front in an international context, South Africa,
coming out of the period of the gross injustices of the apartheid
era, has attempted to confront its past and provide some sort of
restorative justice to the victims of apartheid. The Truth and
Reconciliation Commission, headed by Archbishop Desmond
Tutu, was one means by which South Africa was breaking the
silence of the past. Alongside the transfer to power of Nelson
Mandela in 1994, the impaneling of the TRC stood as one important attempt by this nation to address these issues. Though
many have debated the form, purpose, and outcome of the
commission, its existence has been deemed a step in the right
direction in terms of expanding the debate, raising serious questions, and addressing injustices of the past. The stated intentions
of the panel were: (1) to uncover truth and to provide amnesty to
perpetuators of certain crimes to that effect; (2) to bring about
reparations; (3) to provide a kind of restorative justice; and (4) to
create a way to memorialize officially this key period of South
Africa's history. Finally, the goal of the panel was to publicly acknowledge the trauma of victims.[9] The period the panel chose
as a focus was 1960–94, with the intent to examine "gross vio-
lations of human rights." Unlike the Truth Commission of
Chile, which compensated survivors of human rights abuses and

the families of victims, South Africa's Truth Commission made recommendations in this regard but was eventually informed that the government was short on funds.[10]

Critics say that whereas one can acknowledge that the TRC met its goals of memorializing and publicly acknowledging the trauma of apartheid's victims, the record on reparations is not as strong. Still, the very fact that the TRC was set up and the generally positive response it received, particularly outside of South Africa, give credence to the importance of debate and a public airing of injustices on a mass scale. It presented a model to the world as one way in which such issues could be addressed, and as such it is an important marker in the historical debate around reparations.[11]

The call for reparations went out elsewhere on the continent of Africa in 1990 and 1991. The then Organisation of African States (precursor to today's African Union) convened meetings to address the issue of reparations for slavery in conjunction with the call for the forgiveness of African debt. By 1997 the presidents of the member states of the OAU had formally appointed twelve eminent persons, including Kenyan historian Ali Mazrui, to study and make recommendations regarding this issue.[12]

Finally, the U.N. launched the World Conference against Racism in August 2001, after years of preparation. This was a convening of grassroots organizations, government officials, and others in Durban, South Africa to discuss the issue of racial injustice done from a historical and contemporary perspective. Early on the issue of reparations was raised, and similar attempts to silence the debate arose as in times past. The calls from representatives from Nigeria and Zimbabwe (and other African nations) and the U.S. African American Congressional Caucus for an official apology as well as reparations were largely shot down.[13]

In addition to the advocates discussed above, there have been other organizations and individuals who have made the call for reparations on a public scale. The following is by no means an exhaustive list: the organization N'COBRA (the National Coalition of Blacks for Reparations in America), a grassroots coalition based in Washington, D.C.; the Jamaican Reparations movement, spearheaded by Barbara Makeda Blake Hannah, and others; and, of particular interest, three major lawsuits (although there are many more).

The first lawsuit is a class action suit to be brought by Harvard law professor Charles J. Ogletree Jr., Johnnie Cochran, and others of the Reparations Coordinating Committee against the government and institutions like Harvard, Yale, and Brown University in pursuit of reparations. According to Ogletree and the rest of the committee, whose members are working on a pro bono basis, they are not seeking monies for individuals but would like to establish a huge charity fund that would benefit the poorest in the black community—a kind of Marshall Plan for black America.[14]

The second is a suit brought in 2002 by Daedria Farmer-Paellmann, whose research showed the links between U.S. corporations and the slave trade. The lawsuit, filed on behalf of 35 million African Americans, asks for financial payments from companies like Aetna Life Insurance and others who, according to Paellmann, made profits through insuring slave ships and other business based on unpaid and exploited labor of slaves. Aetna's response: "We do not believe a court would permit a lawsuit over events which—however regrettable—occurred hundreds of years ago. These issues in no way reflect Aetna today." FleetBoston is also named in the suit because it is the modern-day successor to Providence Bank, which was founded by the Rhode Island slave trader John Brown.[15] This suit has recently been dismissed by U.S. District Judge Charles Norgle on the basis that no clear link was reportedly established between the companies in question and the plaintiffs.[16] The case has been left in such a way, however, that plaintiffs are free to file an amended complaint.

The third suit is similar and is being brought by Jamaican lawyer Michael Lome against the British government and its representatives in Jamaica. Finding no success within the Jamaican judicial system, Lome is reportedly looking into other avenues to bring his suit for reparations on behalf of all Jamaicans of African descent.[17]

REPARATIONS AS REDRESS

Having concluded this brief review of the history of the movement to the present, we may now ask the question: What can be said about the historical argument for reparations in light of the oral histories of this collection? As a historian, I am neither a politician nor a lawyer, but the conclusions drawn from these narratives beg the question of reparations. At the same time, it is significant first to note that in my interviews the actual word "reparations" was hardly mentioned. There was, however, a deep acknowledgement on the part of many that various communities had indeed been greatly affected by the slave trade, and that in fact, today they were a shadow of what they were in the past. Some talked about the need for development monies to be brought to bear, possibly in the form of reparations, but in general no one was overtly pressing the case—perhaps, as we have said before, because of the historical silence on the issue. In fact, the caretaker of the renovated Fort Prinzenstein in Keta recalled an interesting story of some Danish visitors who came to take the tour not long ago. Apparently, they were interested in talking to the inhabitants of Eweland about the possibility of reparations for specific families. According to the caretaker, no one responded affirmatively; no one wanted to acknowledge their connection to this awful history, though they knew there was indeed a connection.[18]

But it *is* possible, given our findings about the real and dev-astating impact of the slave trade on the Ewe community as well as on other communities in Africa, to affirm that some sort of redress is warranted. That there is a debt to be paid, there can be little doubt. Some 250 years of free labor in North America and almost 350 in South America and the West Indies is evidence enough that there is an outstanding debt. Furthermore, justice systems in today's democracies are based on "an [historical] ideal of corrective justice that recognizes a legal duty com-pelling wrongdoers to remedy wrongfully-caused losses and to surrender wrongfully obtained gains."[19]

But who should pay that debt? Should not those who profited a little and a lot be the ones who should shoulder that responsibility? That North America and Europe controlled five of the six legs of the slave trade and thus were the greatest beneficiaries of free labor—the very foundation of Western cap-italist society—has already been established. That these same nations attempted in part to restore the "property" and thus compensate those who had exploited African labor has also been established. Clearly, there is a role for them to play here. Some expressions of regret have been given by U.S. government officials and even the pope and the Church of England in 1997.[20] It should be noted, however, that the governments of Europe and North America have never, to date, offered any official apologies for their comprehensive role in the slave trade and the institution of slavery. Furthermore, what remains to be seen are concrete ways of addressing the disparities between white and black communities worldwide. It is here that proposals such as that of Charles Ogletree Jr. and the Reparations Coordinating Committee may be taken into consideration: reparations as re-dress not for individuals but for the building up of communities that can be shown to be living with the legacy of slavery and the slave trade. At the same time, voluntary admissions and accep-tance of responsibility are highly recommended, if not preferred, to legal action, though legal and legislative efforts should not be ruled out.

But what of Africa? African nations, and in particular the African Union, could also continue to consider the matter carefully in light of African agency in the Atlantic slave trade. The case for the Ewes has been laid out here, but the case for other groups must also be made. It is here that African nations could take leadership on this issue and offer first their own apologies on behalf of those who participated—as has already been done by some nations—and then make concrete suggestions as to compensation. Compensation here does not need to be focused on financial compensation. Apologies are an important first step because the acknowledgement of wrongdoing clears the air and ushers in a climate of change. In some quarters of the African American, Caribbean, and South American communities, the idea of dual citizenship and other benefits from direct connections with the continent is very attractive. Ghana's government, for example, is at present considering some of these initiatives, as is the African Union as a body.[21]

Furthermore, for those who say that slavery was a long time ago and the African Union and its members need to concentrate on development in Africa, I contend that there is no development without learning the lessons of slavery. The attitudes we bring to the very best development plans and programs can and should be informed by the lessons of slavery, in particular the question of how we treat the most vulnerable members of our communities.

Finally, there are those who would say: What has Africa to apologize for? It has been ravaged by foreigners for over five hundred years. It has been exploited ceaselessly from every angle —its land, its people, its resources. But apologies for wrongdoing on both sides may be critical to the restoration process. It is for this reason that the many U.N. conferences on race, gender, and the environment—in particular the one on race in Durban,

South Africa—have stressed the need for apologies for crimes against humanity. Furthermore, even a limited apology expressed toward the injured party carries great moral authority.[22]

As discussed earlier, it is important to look at the choices of Africans during critical periods of the slave trade. The nineteenth century for the old Slave Coast was a "sell or be sold" era. The slave business, promoted as it was by persistent European and American forces as well as African middlemen, had largely marginalized all other types of economic activity in the area. Within this context of such prescribed choices and under substantial pressure for slaves from slave traders, Africans had few choices. Nonetheless, they had agency; they had choices and some, particularly those of a certain class, exercised them to their own benefit. An apology from African nations and even specific groups whose involvement is on the record would go a long way toward establishing a high moral ground upon which to ask likewise for apologies from Europe and America as well as restitution.

Along these lines, it can also be said that a greater commitment must be made within Africa's borders to eradicate modern African slavery in all its forms. The age-old appeal to tradition cannot and should not be an excuse for the toleration of slavery within Africa's borders—not when the research here and elsewhere is clear on the devastating impact of the Atlantic slave trade to the continent. From north to south, from east to west, African nations could take leadership on this issue of African slavery instead of remaining silent or in the reactionary mode to U.S. and European NGOs and others who have been protesting against modern African slavery. Denials in the face of substantial evidence and testimonials to the contrary will not suffice and will not bolster any call for restitution. How can one call for restitution for a past evil practice if that practice is still tolerated and, in some quarters, promoted today? What moral standing is there for the African nation that tolerates slavery within its borders under the guise of "tradition," but yet joins in the present international call for reparations for slavery? It stands to reason that if slavery was an evil practice yesterday, it is an evil practice today. If it was a crime against humanity yesterday, it is a crime against humanity today.

Attempts to eradicate internal slavery *must* thus be part of the overall restitution proposal. Ideas regarding citizenship proposals for people of African descent in the Americas might also be considered. But perhaps the most important issue, second only to apologies, is the underscoring of the need for political accountability of African leaders. What is clear and evident from the Ewe case study is that when political accountability breaks down, the greater is the capacity of destructive forces—internal and external to a society—to bring about a devastating impact on that society. A lack of political accountability, in other words, opens the door to chaos and to individual gain at the expense of communal advancement. The breakdown of accountability between chiefs and their subjects in the nineteenth-century Slave Coast has a direct correlation to the breakdown of traditional structures in Ewe society. It also rendered Ewe society vulnerable to colonial domination.

This pattern is still in evidence as long as there exists even one African country that has not wholeheartedly embraced democratic structures and has persisted in propping up despotic leaders whose interests are private gain, not the public good. This vicious cycle did not start in the modern era. Though it was greatly exacerbated by the European colonial enterprise, history shows that it has earlier antecedents. It is here that a greater effort to bolster enlightened leadership on the continent as well as to renounce African despots is sorely needed. This can and should come as much from African institutions as from without. This is one legacy of the slave-trade era that should be put to rest by the unrelenting call for the promotion of the public good over individual gain in African societies and nations.

With such a restitution program in hand, Africa and the people of African descent in the Diaspora can claim the debt that is owed them.

Finally, the idea of reparations within the continent of Africa, specifically within certain countries themselves, might be studied. As we have seen in the example of Ghana, the North suffered greatly at the hands of middlemen in the South. Today the underpopulation and other social effects that are connected to the slave-trade era (in conjunction with the colonial era) are there to be seen. It is as if even within Ghana itself, *a civil rights movement* is in order to assist in creating a greater balance of economic, political, and social power between North and South. Finally, Ghana is not the only country in Africa where relations are strained between two particular regions in part because of the legacy of the slave trade. Redress here is also worthy of consideration.

REPARATIONS AS REMEMORY

But the concept of reparations is also fundamentally about the restoration of historical memory. The antidote to the silence of the past is a loud, clear voice in the present and future. This voice can manifest itself in many forms, including memorial sites, curriculum revision, and the like. As a start, any attempt to further deconstruct this history of slavery and the slave trade and its effects is a worthy effort. An establishment of a National and International Truth and Reconciliation panel to address this issue would be a step in the right direction. It would open up the space for much-needed debate and a conversation that is yet to fully take place. Much like the TRC of South Africa, participation could be voluntary.

Dr. Ruth Simmons, president of Brown University and a great-granddaughter of slaves, has recently proposed her own panel of scholars and others to study this issue. The Committee on Slavery and Justice will spend two years studying whether Brown, which has well-known historical ties to the trade through its benefactors, should pay reparations for slavery. Efforts like these go a long way to bridging gaps and providing knowledge about an era upon which much light is still to be shed. What is particularly interesting and noteworthy about this example is that it is a voluntary effort. While legal and legislative means are being exhausted, voluntary efforts should be encouraged. This in the end goes even further toward healing the wounds of the past.

Memorialization in the form of a National Slavery Museum is already in the works. The museum is scheduled to open its doors in Fredericksburg, Virginia in 2007.[23] These and other ways of consistently remembering this period (not just on holidays or in a particular month) will keep slavery in the national consciousness: not as a weapon but as a means of remembering so that we do not repeat the crimes of the past. If we forget, will it not be easy to disregard the same patterns when they shapeshift in the present? Will it not be easy to neglect the needs of the most vulnerable among us who are living with this legacy, and furthermore, those who are caught up in this legacy by virtue of it being a part of the fabric of American society? Immigrants who are new to North America, for example, even if they are not of African descent, are not exempt from the racial rubrics of America's past. Often, the most vulnerable among them, particular immigrants of color, find themselves subject to the same kinds of institutional and attitudinal barriers based on race that North America has yet to overcome.[24]

Perhaps the most fascinating enterprise yet to be attempted would be the collection of oral historical material all over the continent of Africa with respect to the slave trade as well as the same in various locales in the African Diaspora. This oral record would stand as a living testimony to the triumph of the African voice over the evils of the past. It is my hope that such an endeavor will indeed take hold and take root. And so, in the end, reparations is not simply about money; it is about redress from both sides of the Atlantic, a continuing dialogue and, most important, the recovery of memory or, as Toni Morrison so aptly put it, "rememory." In the end, beyond the silence and the shame, may this tragic period of history be remembered for the purpose of honoring those who did not survive it and addressing the problems and the challenges faced by those who did.

ACKNOWLEDGMENTS

There is a well-known African proverb that goes: "It takes a village to raise a child." It may also be that it takes a village to write a book—in this case, many villages all over the world. I am deeply indebted to many people. First, I would like to thank the members of my 1998 dissertation committee—my supervisor, Dr. Mary Frances Berry; Dr. Lee Cassanelli; and Dr. Sandra Greene—for their assistance and support over the years. Second, I am grateful to the Tsikata family, including Fui, Victor, Matthew, Enoyam, Emily, Doe, and Dotse, as well as my very able and willing translators, Mr. Kofi Geraldo and Mrs. Edith Vuvor. Several professors and others at the University of Ghana provided me with important information and resources to complete this project. While it is not possible to mention them all here, I would like to acknowledge a few: Dr. G. K. Nukunya, Dr. Brempong Osei Tutu, Dr. Kofi Anyidoho, Dr. E. Y. Egblewogbe, Dr. T. Manuh, Dr. Kwesi J. Anquandah, Dr. D. E. K. Amenumey, Dr. Kwabena J. H. Nketia, Johnson Kwadzo Kenneh (master drummer), and Dr. Kwame Arhin. I am particularly grateful to those whose unpublished dissertations or other work proved invaluable as resources for this study, including Dr. C. R. Gaba, Dr. D. K. Fiawoo and Joseph Yegbe.

The oral accounts of elders and others along the Anlo Ewe coast have been central to this study. An attempt has been made here to record the voices of what some have called the human libraries of Africa. This project would not have been possible without the openness and hospitality that was shown to me along the coast, in Accra and elsewhere in Ghana. I am indebted to all the interviewees who helped me with this work but would like to thank particularly Paramount Chief Togbui Adeladza II, Joe Aidam, Mama Dzagba, and G. Kpodo, who did not live to see publication of this book but without whose assistance it might not have been possible.

I also want to say that this work in no way could be a definitive collection of the oral history record of the Anlo Ewe group or other groups in Ghana. There are undoubtedly many other versions of some of these stories (and so many other interviews to be done one day), as is the nature of storytelling in Ghana. This book represents my views and the views of those who so kindly granted me interviews but does not diminish the views of others.

I also would like to thank the following individuals: the chiefs and Queen Mother of Bono Manso, Mamponghene Daasebre Osei Bonsu; Dr. Kathryn Geurts; James O'Neill; my editor, Gayatri Patnaik; my copyeditor, Robin DuBlanc; Rev. Mische, Dr. Rainer Alsheimer; Dr. Evelyn Brooks Higginbotham; Richard Newman; Chris and Charity Scott; Shirley Toland; Dan Bascelli; Bonita Tidwell; Dr. Joyce King; Dr. Beverly Daniel Tatum; Debra Egan; Ann Martin; Dr. Beverly Guy-Sheftall; Dr. Bahati Kuumba; Dr. Mike Gomez; Dr. Michael West; Dr. Ato Quayson; Dr. Alfred Hornung; Dr. Mina Donkoh; Dr. Romi Tribble; Dr. Henry Louis Gates Jr.; Denise Riley; Dr. Robin Kelley; Dr. Sandra Barnes; Dr. Jay Iselin; Dr. Lynn Lees; Mr. Klevor Abo; and Mrs. Theresa Gadzepo.

I am grateful to the following institutions for their support: the Fulbright Scholar Program and the Council of International Educational Exchange, Spelman College, the Rutgers Black Atlantic Fellowship (Dr. Deborah Gray White and Dr. Mia Bay), the University of Gutenberg at Mainz, the Mellon Foundation, the Assemblies of God Church on the Legon campus, the U.S. embassy in Ghana, the North German Missionary Society in Bremen, Times Square Church, Big Bethel AME Church, Harvard University's W. E. B DuBois Fellowship program, and the Institute of African Studies of the University of Ghana.

Finally, I extend my heartfelt thanks to my friends and family for their unfailing support.

Chapter 1

1. Important work has been done by Barry; Isichei; Harris; Law, *The Slave Coast of West Africa;* Miller, *Way of Death;* Harms; Wright; and Greene, *Gender, Ethnicity and Social Change on the Upper Slave Coast.* Also see Engerman and Inikori, which highlights many of the major issues in this debate. Also see Lovejoy, *Transformations in Slavery* and "The Impact of the Atlantic Slave Trade on Africa."

2. The Federal Writers Project of the Works Progress Administration, Library of Congress Manuscript Division, http://memory.loc.gov/ammem/wpaintro/wpahome.html and Equiano.

3. See the work of Lovejoy and Gomez for similar models.

4. Both Lovejoy and Manning have looked closely at this era in terms of a transformation thesis.

5. Alessandro Portelli, "What Makes Oral History Different," in Perks and Tomson, 72–73.

6. Conversations with Daphne Bailey, July 2002.

7. Interviews 38 and 39.

8. Interview 37.

9. Interview 39.

10. Interview 37.

11. Anquandah, 14.

12. See the works of Braithwaite and M.G. Smith.

13. Christopher.

14. Quoted in Breed.

15. Ibid.

16. Davies and Ogundipe-Leslie, 8.

17. Interviews 40 and 41.

18. Awoonor, *The Breast of the Earth,* 122–23.

19. Manning.

20. Perbi, 1–3.

21. Meeting with Nana Nketia, Ghana Museums and Monuments Board chairman, January 6, 2003.

22. See Miers and Kopytoff.

23. Conversation with scholar Richard Newman, Harvard University's W.E.B. DuBois Center for African American Studies, November 2000.

24. Interview 35.

25. *Reporter: The Anti Slavery International* (London) (January 2003): 5. See also their Web site, http://www.antislavery.org/ on slavery in Sudan.

26. Ibid.

27. Akyeampong, 221 and see chapter on social effects for more.

28. *Chronicle,* February 13, 2003. See also "Lack of Legislation in Child Trafficking: 5,000 Cry for Help," *Daily Graphic,* March 21, 2003.

29. Van Dantzig, introduction.

30. Anquandah, 11.

31. Ibid.

32. Ato Ashun, *West Africa,* March 23, 2003, 26.

33. Interview 27 with caretaker of the fort, James Ocloo, regarding St. Croix and St. Thomas natives visiting and saying they are from Keta.

34. Osei Tutu.

35. Interview 24. The lease was withdrawn some years later for reasons that are not entirely clear.

36. Rita Marley Foundation, Ghana, http://www.bobmarley-foundation .com/ghana2003.html.

37. Elia and see also Meriweather.

38. Davies and Ogundipe-Leslie, 7.

39. The others are the slave market at Bono Manso, Ewe paramount chief

Adzanu and his participation in the slave trade, the story of the Danish Lt. Svedstrup stationed at Fort Prinzenstein, and the slave narrative *Memoirs of Boyrereau Brinch.*

40. Nora.

41. Rathbone. See also McGowan. It should be noted here that I did not include but easily could have the many examples of slave resistance in Brazil and elsewhere in South America.

42. Morrison, 36.

43. Hesse. Hesse here is alluding to Toni Morrison in Beloved, 274.

44. Trouillot, 146–47.

Chapter 2

1. Amenumey, *Hogbeza,* 6.

2. Greene, "The Anlo Ewe: Their Economy, Society, and External Relations in the Eighteenth Century," 24, 40.

3. Ibid., 36; Amenumey, *Hogbeza,* 6.

4. Greene, "The Anlo Ewe: Their Economy, Society, and External Relations in the Eighteenth Century," 14–15.

5. Yegbe, 3–4.

6. Yegbe, 36; Amenumey, "Geraldo de Lima," 66.

7. Conversations with translator, Mrs. Edith Vuvor of Dzelukofe.

8. Interviews 1 and 5.

9. Yegbe, 69.

10. The elders often referenced the Danes, Americans, and Europeans interchangeably to signify white traders.

11. Interview 5.

12. Ibid.

13. Chief Tamaklo was a rich trader and plantation owner who was somewhat of a controversial figure in the nineteenth century, in part because in his role as a prominent chief in the area, he argued that the Anlos should attempt to work with the ever-encroaching colonial government. It appears that he was very politically minded—adopting Christianity, for example, as

much for political reasons as out of faith. Conversation with Sandra Greene, April 20, 1998 and Interview 7. In any event, this particular part of the account has not been confirmed independently.

14. Interview 1.

15. Interview 11.

16. An extensive review of CO 96 of the Public Records Office in London (specifically 1850–60 records) as well as newspaper accounts from the mid-nineteenth century viewed at British Library Newspapers in London provided no confirmation of a famine.

17. Interview 23. The details of this dispute are unclear. Togbui Adeladza revealed as much as he knew about the affair but was not aware of further details.

18. Excerpts from the Treaty of Washington, quoted in Thomas, 316–17.

19. National Archives, Washington, D.C.: M89, African Squadron logbooks.

20. Thomas, 240.

21. National Archives, Washington, D.C.: M89, roll 108, entries 30, 39, letter to Commodore Crabbe from Secretary of the Navy, January 27, 1855.

22. PRO, FO 313/27/p. 34, Havana mixed court commission records.

23. Lloyd, 169.

24. Interview 15. Also see Aimes and Knight.

25. Awoonor, *The Breast of the Earth,* 12.

26. Conversations with Klevor Abo of Woe (Spring 1998), who recorded the song as sung by his aunt, Theresa Gadzekpo of Vodza. It is not conclusive that this song, as noted by Mrs. Gadzekpo and Kofi Awoonor's informants in *Breast of the Earth,* refers to the Atorkor incident. It may be that it refers to the slave trade in general. The references to Afedima, who was a famous female trader from Woe who also traded slaves, may refer to a voyage that she reportedly took to England from which she brought back the first *yevudor*—European fishing net. According to Greene, *Gender, Ethnicity and Social Change on the Upper Slave Coast,* 80 and 165, this voyage took place sometime between 1850 and 1874. The Atorkor incident took place in 1856.

27. Mammattah, 1.

28. Yegbe, 69. Since Scotland was united with Great Britain as of 1707

and this incident took place in the mid-nineteenth century, it is possible that the interchangeable references to English or Scottish traders are not contradictory.

29. Shaw, introduction and 3.

30. Vansina, 14–24. This is consistent with Vansina's definitions of oral traditions.

31. Amenumey, "A Political History of the Ewe Unification Problem," 8–11 and also his *Ewe Unification Movement.*

32. Greene, *Gender, Ethnicity, and Social Change on the Upper Slave Coast,* 144–51.

33. James, *Nkrumah and the Ghana Revolution,* 104, 177; Opoku Agyeman; Nkrumah, *I Speak of Freedom.*

34. In 1997, for example, he received Minister Louis Farrakhan on his visit to Ghana and also made a high-profile visit to Jamaica.

35. This information was gathered from my own meetings with the Historical Preservation Committee of the National Museum of Ghana in 1993 on the subject of restoration of the slave forts and castles. Also see Shillington, 32–33.

36. Interview 11.

37. Portelli, *The Death of Luigi Trastuli,* introduction.

38. Interview 1.

39. Elie Wiesel, quoted in Naomi Rosh White, "Making Absences: Holocaust Testimony and History," in Perks and Tomson, 173.

40. Primo Levi, quoted in ibid., 176.

41. Irina Sherbakova, "The Gulag in Memory," in Perks and Tomson; Freud (1920), in Perks and Tomson, 193.

42. Aluwahlia, 193, referencing Freud (1920).

43. Portelli, "What Makes Oral History Different," in Perks and Tomson.

44. Lloyd, 167, 121.

45. Ibid., 121.

46. National Archives, Washington, D.C.: M89, roll 108, letter to Commodore Crabbe, January 27, 1855.

47. Lloyd, 168.

48. PRO, FO 313/29/p. 172, Havana mixed court commission records.

49. DuBois, *Suppression of the African Slave Trade,* 110–12, 165; Lloyd, 168.

50. Cruickshank, 307.

51. Ibid., 331.

52. Interview 23.

53. Interview 4.

54. Perbi, 3.

Chapter 3

1. Kopytoff, introduction.

2. See Miers and Kopytoff.

3. Interviews 25 and 28.

4. Interview 25.

5. Nkrumah was so serious about Pan-Africanism that he married an Egyptian woman as a symbol of the unity between Sub-Saharan Africa and North Africa.

6. The African Union, http://www.africa-union.org/.

7. Thornton, 104; emphasis added.

8. Ryder, 45.

9. See the Primary Source organization, which documents these statistics, http://www.primarysource.org/default.htm.

10. Eric Williams, *From Columbus to Castro,* 136–43.

11. Yegbe, 36.

12. Egblewogbe, *Games and Songs as Education Media,* 52.

13. Aduamah, 7.

14. Ibid, no. 3, p. 1.

15. Interview 10.

16. G. K. Nukunya, in Miers and Roberts, 243–44.

17. Interview 28.

18. The following discussion is consistent with the transformation thesis of Manning and Lovejoy, *Transformations in Slavery.*

19. Bosman, 330.

20. Ibid., 333. See also Law, *The Slave Coast of West Africa,* 144–48, for the relatively small volume of early trade.

21. Bosman, 334.

22. Ibid., 331

23. Interview 20; Greene, *The Anlo Ewe: Their Economy, Society, and External Relations in the Eighteenth Century,* 64.

24. Wilks, "Akwamu," 16.

25. Ibid., 30.

26. Ibid., 32.

27. Yegbe, 11.

28. Wilks, "Akwamu," 34.

29. Greene, *Gender, Ethnicity, and Social Change,* 37.

30. I reach this conclusion based on my personal tour of the fort and a review of pictures of all three forts.

31. John Newton, quoted in Hart, 1:31.

32. Reindorf, 152. The exact quote from Reindorf is: "It was a disease imported by Europeans and which had disastrously affected the country for 357 years."

33. See Rodney, *How Europe Underdeveloped Africa.*

34. Evidence of Chief Akolatse before the Crowther Commission, in Crowther, appendix 3.

35. This period coincides with Manning's date for the last phase of the trade, 1830–60, which is consistent with his discussion of the transformations of the trade. See Manning, 140.

36. Interviews 3 and 20.

37. Amenumey, "Geraldo de Lima," 66.

38. Interview 9.

39. Greene, *Gender, Ethnicity, and Social Change on the Upper Slave Coast,* 165.

40. See chapter 7 on religion for more.

41. Greene, *Gender, Ethnicity, and Social Change on the Upper Slave Coast,* 74–75.

42. Ibid., 73–74.

43. Carstensen, 5.

44. Yegbe, 19.

45. Ibid.; see also Reindorf, 146–48.

46. See also Yegbe, 29–38. Another such individual was the Portuguese trader Baeta, a resident of Atorkor, who also had local connections through marriage. Like Mora, he was forced to continually move his base of operations to avoid capture.

47. Interview 10.

48. Ibid.

49. Interview 2.

50. Amenumey, "Geraldo de Lima," 65.

51. Greene, *Gender, Ethnicity, and Social Change on the Upper Slave Coast,* 127.

52. Turner.

53. Greene, *Gender, Ethnicity, and Social Change on the Upper Slave Coast,* 128; Amenumey, "Geraldo de Lima," 67.

54. Amenumey, "Geraldo de Lima," 67.

55. See Interview 20 as an example.

56. Interview 18.

57. See *Greene, Gender, Ethnicity, and Social Change on the Upper Slave Coast,* 133–34, for detailed discussion.

58. Interview 4.

59. Interview 11.

60. Interview 18. It is not clear why he was in prison, but it is likely that he was imprisoned by the British, who were trying to curtail his trading efforts.

61. Ibid.

62. Ibid., 243.

63. Amenumey, "Geraldo de Lima," 68.

64. Ibid., 75–77.

65. Falconbridge, in Dow, 139.

66. Johnson, in Anstey and Hair, 27–28.

67. Interview 11.

68. Interview 22. Kpego and Kajani are murky characters in the historical record; not much is known about their origin or their base of operations.

69. Interview 23.

70. Interview 22.

71. See Der for more.

72. Interview 33; Der, 11–14.

73. "The History of the Kagbanya People (Gonja) People," Gonja Association of North America, http://www.geocities.com/Athens/4495/history1.htm.

74. Interview 21.

75. Interview 28.

76. Johnson, 41.

77. See Arhin, 11; LaTorre, 435–36. This view is held by Reynolds in *Trade and Economic Change,* which contradicts the earlier views of Ward.

78. Wilks, *The Asante in the Nineteenth Century,* 176.

79. Ibid., 675.

80. Arhin, 10. See also Wilks, "Asante Policy towards Hausa Trade in the Nineteenth Century," 124–33, for a different view of the role of traders. He maintains that there was a high level of organization of state trading from 1750 to1764, which became more entrenched from 1801 to 1824. This was part of what he calls the "bureaucratisation" of administrative function in the Asante empire.

81. Bowdich, 336.

82. Gouldsbury (1876), in Johnson, 39.

83. "An Exhibition on the Trans-Atlantic Slave Trade and Ghana," Ghana Museums Board, 6; "The Slave Routes of Northern Ghana," Chicago-Ghana Tourism Initiative, http//www.ghanaslaveroutes.org.

84. Tour of Bono Manso slave market and Interview 33.

85. Wilks, *The Asante in the Nineteenth Century,* 681.

86. Wilks, "Akwamu," 83.

87. Wilks, *The Asante in the Nineteenth Century,* 57.

88. Ibid.; *Greene, Gender, Ethnicity, and Social Change on the Upper Slave Coast,* 129.

89. PRO: CO 96/35; Wilks, *The Asante in the Nineteenth Century,* 223–24.

90. Claridge, 548–51.

91. Horton, 78–89; letter to the *African Times,* September 22, 1866.

92. Wilks, *The Asante in the Nineteenth Century,* 225.

93. Johnson, 37, 57.

94. See Inikori, *Forced Migration* for more.

95. Bowdich, 325.

96. Davis, 38–40.

97. *Brazil House Rehabilitation Project,* 5–8; meeting with Wolowski, December 2004.

98. Evidence of Chief Akolatse before the Crowther Commission, in Crowther, appendix 3.

Chapter 4

1. Dubois, *A Biography of Sylvia Dubois.*

2. Ibid., 3; also see Higginbotham, 267–310, for more on this discussion and queries about the timing of the incident.

3. James, *A History of Negro Revolt,* 21. See also Genovese.

4. U.N. Web site: http://www.unis.unvienna.org/unis/activities/against_slavery.html.

5. James, *A History of Negro Revolt,* 21.

6. Hart, 2:334–35.

7. Ibid., 337.

8. Richard Hart, public lectures at the Harriet Tubman Museum in London, Summer 1997.

9. Bosman, 365. See also Harris (1987), 87–88, regarding African resistance to the trade.

10. Gomez, 206; and see also Rathbone.

11. Greene, *Gender, Ethnicity, and Social Change on the Upper Slave Coast,* 112–13. In the oral collection of historian Sandra Greene, there is a more general reference to parents rather than simply mothers taking these decisions, though I am inclined to believe from my sources and others that the women in the family held sway over this decision.

12. Davies and Ogundipe-Leslie, 8. See also Henry Louis Gates Jr., in Larison and Lobdell.

13. Albert, 1.

14. Foster, introduction to Albert, xxx.

15. Albert, 3.

16. Ibid., 4.

17. Schwartz, 1.

18. Albert, 33.

19. Ibid., 34.

20. Ibid., 35–36.

21. Prince; "Documenting the American South," http://docsouth.unc.edu/, University of North Carolina at Chapel Hill, Academic Affairs Library, 17.

22. Thomas Pringle, preface to Prince.

23. Ibid., xxxii.

24. Goss and Barnes.

25. Prince, 24.

26. Ibid., 19, 24.

27. Gomez, 208; emphasis added.

28. Brinch; "Documenting the American South," http://docsouth.unc.edu/, University of North Carolina at Chapel Hill, Academic Affairs Library, 3–4.

29. Brinch, 21.

30. Ibid., 71.

31. Ibid., 81–84; emphasis added.

32. Brinch, 169.

33. Oldfield; Brown; Prince, 19.

Chapter 5

1. See the work of Ghanaian poet and scholar Kofi Anyidoho for more on traditional Ewe storytelling.

2. Gomez, 199–209.

3. Good examples are in Interview 18 and Interview 10.

4. See Eltis et al. This is a collection of the records of 27, 233 slave ships, but it is estimated that there were thousands more.

5. Equiano, http://www.brycchancarey.com/equiano/index.htm. In recent years, some academics, including S. E. Ogude and Vincent Caretta, have challenged the authenticity of this much-studied narrative. These findings, however, are still highly debated in the academy, and so for our purposes here we shall accept the long-standing tradition and use of this narrative as an important source on the history of the slave trade. See "Where Was Olaudah Equiano Born?" http://www.brycchancarey.com/equiano/nativity .htm. See also the narrative of Boyrereau Brinch for a similar perception of whites.

6. Isichei, 37.

7. Ibid., 39.

8. See also Harris (1987), 84, for similar discussion.

9. Gomer Williams, 466

10. These sources include records from the Gold Coast: *Governor Carstensen's Diary* (1842), Brodie Cruikshank's *Eighteen Years on the Gold Coast of Africa* (1853), Carl Reindorf's *History of the Gold Coast and the Asante* (1895), and English colonial records (1850–60). Much information has also been gathered from Gomer Williams's *History of Liverpool Privateers and Letters of Marque, with an Account of the Liverpool Slave Trade* (1897), Aimes's *History of the Slave Trade in Cuba,* (1907), Claridge's *A History of the Gold Coast and Ashanti* (1915), autobiographies of slave ship captains in the nineteenth century, and documents from the Havana Mixed Trade Commission (1840–60).

11. Falconbridge, in Dow, 136.

12. Ibid.

13. Brooks, *Yankee Traders,* 112.

14. Lloyd, 167.

15. Aimes, 87.

16. Ibid., 88–92.

17. PRO, FO 313/24/p. 212.

18. Aimes, 95; PRO, FO 313/23/ p. 7.

19. Law, *The Slave Coast of West Africa,* 147–48.

20. Davies, 11–17, 240–50, 266–67. Relations with the Dutch in the late seventeenth century were particularly contentious. The cause of the conflicts was not limited to the issue of interlopers but also concerned disputes

over the rights to certain settlements on the Gold Coast such as Kommenda and Sekondi.

21. Ibid., 18.

22. Gomer Williams, 468. The Spanish sovereigns inaugurated a system of special contracts (assiento), which became of international significance, under which they bestowed from time to time the monopoly of the supply of Africans for their American possessions on foreign nations, corporations, or individuals, who in turn employed subcontractors (http://www.jahsonic. com/SlaveTrade.html).

23. W. E. Minchington, "The Slave Trade of Bristol with the British Mainland Colonies in North America, 1699–1770," in Anstey and Hair, 39.

24. Anstey and Hair, introduction and 7; D. P. Lamb, "Volume and Tonnage of the Liverpool Slave Trade, 1772–1807," in Anstey and Hair, 91.

25. David Richardson, "Profits in the Liverpool Slave Trade: The Accounts of William Davenport, 1757–1784," in Anstey and Hair, 67.

26. This aspect was fictionalized by Jane Austen in *Mansfield Park.*

27. Richardson, in Anstey and Hair, 68.

28. Mannix and Cowley, 73.

29. For example, Thomas Golightly (1732–1821), mayor of Liverpool in 1772–73, was listed among the company of merchants trading to Africa in 1807. These and other examples are documented in the Liverpool exhibit "Transatlantic Slavery," Merseyside Maritime Museum, Albert Dock, Liverpool, England.

30. Gomer Williams, 598.

31. Eric Williams, *Capitalism and Slavery,* 52, 58

32. Ibid., 63, 64.

33. Walvin, 313.

34. Liverpool exhibit.

35. Mannix and Cowley, 73.

36. Behrendt; B. K. Drake, "The Liverpool-Africa Voyage, c. 1790–1807: Commercial Problems," in Anstey and Hair, 104, 128.

37. Richardson, in Anstey and Hair, 67–68.

38. Behrendt, 86–93.

39. Manning, 151, 206.

40. Stammers, 35.

41. Hoyt, 97; Walvin, 45.

42. Walvin, 46.

43. Eric Williams, *Capitalism and Slavery,* 68.

44. Walvin, 30–31; Clarke.

45. Interview 6.

46. Richardson, in Anstey and Hair, 74.

47. Walvin, 16–21; *Slavery: An Introduction to the African Holocaust,* 104.

48. Weskett, viii.

49. Ibid.

50. Richardson, in Anstey and Hair, 74.

51. Aimes, 171.

52. Canot, 106.

53. Dow, 10.

54. Walvin, 53.

55. Behrendt, 99.

56. Dow, 14.

57. Spiegl.

58. Gomer Williams, 688.

59. Mannix and Cowley, 143.

60. Behrendt, 112; Hunter, 138.

61. Carstensen, 9.

62. Ibid., 4

63. Ibid., 44.

64. Dow, 10–11.

65. Interview 7.

66. Walvin, 32.

67. Carstensen, 11.

68. Fage, "A New Check List of the Forts and Castles of Ghana."

69. Walvin, 32–33.

70. Daaku, *Trade and Politics on the Gold Coast,* 30. See also Inikori, "The Impact of Firearms in West Africa." In this article, Inikori estimates the total import of guns during this period to be between 283,000 and 294,000 per annum, most of which went to major slave-exporting regions. See also chapter 6 on the political effects of the slave trade for more detailed discussion.

71. The Basel mission began work in Accra in the 1820s. The North German (Bremen) mission came in 1847. Their efforts included developing the first Ewe primer, grammar, and dictionary and a translation of the Bible. See also chapter 7 on religion for more.

72. Cruikshank; "Dutch Slave Dealing in Africa," 3–4.

73. Lloyd, 118.

74. Stammers, 40.

75. Walvin, 22.

76. Ibid., 57–58.

77. Walvin, 48; Equiano, 26.

78. Falconbridge, in Dow, 146, 148.

79. Ibid., 146.

80. Ibid.

81. Walvin.

82. Ibid., 52.

83. Liverpool exhibit.

84. Gomer Williams, 477.

85. Equiano, 27. See also same phenomenon in the apartheid era discussed by Archbishop Desmond Tutu in *No Future without Forgiveness* in terms of white security officers and their abusive treatment of their wives and children.

86. Nukunya, *Kinship and Marriage among the Anlo Ewe,* 23–25.

87. Lloyd, 173. The *Wanderer* made many slave voyages. In 1857 it sailed to the Congo and bought 750 boys and girls, aged thirteen to eighteen, then set sail for the Savannah River.

88. Ibid., 118.

89. Aimes, 202.

90. PRO, FO 313/23/ nos. 30, 48.

91. PRO, FO 313/29/p. 74.

92. Aimes, 209, 171.

93. Walvin.

94. Aimes, 111.

95. PRO, FO 313/26/ p. 171.

96. Williams, in Davidson, 73–75.

97. Ibid.

98. Martin Klein, 16–19.

99. See Rohrbach.

100. Interviews 35 and 36.

101. See Norregard and some of his sources: the *Guinea Journal* and *Letters Sent to General Customs Department and Commerce Collegium,* Copenhagen.

102. Norregard, 214; Akyeampong, 53. Also see evidence of the incident in Claridge, 457–58, Ward, 152–53, and in the novel by Alexander Svedstrup called *Erik Gudmand.*

103. Isichei, 26.

104. Norregard, 173–78.

105. Ibid., 173.

106. Eltis and Walvin, 6. See also Anstey.

107. See Engerman and Inikori.

Chapter 6

1. Interview 11.

2. Interview 9.

3. Interview 18.

4. Inikori, *Forced Migration,* 28.

5. See chapter 3 on African agency for a discussion of Geraldo de Lima.

6. Interview 2. See also Harris (1972), 89, for a similar discussion of impact.

7. Interview 4.

8. Interview 5.

9. Christine King Farris, 17.

10. Ibid., 26.

11. See Manning, 142.

12. Interview 4.

13. Interview 6.

14. Much work has been done on the diversity of African slavery by Miers and Kopytoff, among others. Often, distinctions have been drawn between African slavery and New World slavery. Inikori, in a recent essay, suggests that it might be more apt to compare African slavery to servile social categories in medieval Europe. See Inikori, "Slavery in Africa and the Transatlantic Slave Trade," in Jalloh and Maizlish.

15. Interview 10.

16. Inikori, *Forced Migration,* 45.

17. Interview 10.

18. Interview 7.

19. See Miers and Kopytoff for a discussion on the need to put African "slavery" in quotes because of this fact.

20. Carstensen, 28–29; emphasis added.

21. Interview 29. Some of these terms were verified in a conversation with Ms. Kafui Ofori, University of Ghana Language Center, June 2004.

22. See Emma Toonen, "Ghana: Mediating a Way out of Complex Ethnic Conflicts," http://www.ama.africatoday.com/konkomba.htm/. Early and more recent collections of oral histories confirm that they were indeed victims of many raids, particularly at the hands of slave traders in neighboring Dagomba communities. See also Cardinall, 232; Interview 32.

23. Der, 32.

24. Interview 33.

25. Interviews 28 and 29.

26. Rutgers Oral History Archives of World War II, http://fas-history .rutgers.edu/oralhistory/home.html.

27. Interview 25.

28. Burns. See also Haas, 104–5, 136–40, for detailed discussion on the ways in which some survivors have blocked out memories of the Holocaust and the effect this has had on their children.

29. Survivors of the Shoah Visual History Foundation started in 1994.

30. Eisner, 13.

31. Interview 32.

32. Meillassoux.

33. Interview 11.

34. Bosman, 331; and see chapter 3 on African agency. See also Law, *The Slave Coast of West Africa,* 220.

35. Isert, 75.

36. Ibid., 56–57.

37. Ibid., 57.

38. Ibid., 189; emphasis added.

39. Reynolds, *Stand the Storm,* 98. See also Rodney, *How Europe Underdeveloped Africa.*

40. See Ali Mazrui, *The Africans: A Triple Heritage,* film series produced by WETA and BBC.

41. "The Buying Power of Black America" report is based on an analysis of expenditures reported by three thousand black households for the Department of Commerce's Consumer Expenditure Survey.

42. Interview 29.

43. Greene, *Gender, Ethnicity, and Social Change on the Upper Slave Coast,* 112–13.

44. Amenumey, "A Political History of the Ewe Unification Problem."

45. Ibid., 12–14; Amenumey, *Hogbeza,* 17; and see Awoonor, *The Breast of the Earth.*

46. Amenumey, Hogbeza, 28.

47. Ibid., 15.

48. Ibid., 17.

49. Interview 6.

50. Interview 20.

51. Interview 23.

52. Interview 20; Amenumey, *Hogbeza,* 17.

53. Interview 6.

54. Interview 20.

55. Interview 6.

56. Miller, *Way of Death*, 223.

57. Reynolds, *Stand the Storm*, 99; Rodney, *How Europe Underdeveloped Africa*, 107–8.

58. Daaku, "The European Traders and the Coastal States."

59. Inikori, *Forced Migration*, 127.

60. Ibid., 129–35.

61. Selena Axelrod Winsnes, in Isert, 83–84.

62. Greene, *Gender, Ethnicity, and Social Change on the Upper Slave Coast*, 133.

63. Interview 4; emphasis added.

64. Ward, 129.

65. See Harris (1972), 83.

66. Isert, 61.

67. Ibid., 41.

68. Ibid., 27.

69. Ibid., 54.

70. Ibid., 73.

71. Ibid., 42.

72. Ibid., 56–57.

73. Ibid., 74; Greene, *Gender, Ethnicity, and Social Change on the Upper Slave Coast*, 83.

74. Inikori, *Forced Migration*, 50.

75. See Law, *The Slave Coast of West Africa*, for discussion of a similar phenomenon elsewhere on the coast. Also see Engerman and Inikori, 7.

76. Reynolds, *Stand the Storm*, 114.

77. See chapter 3 for detailed discussion of Geraldo's activities in the context of the activities of other traders.

78. Awoonor, *The Breast of the Earth*, 19.

79. Greene, *Gender, Ethnicity, and Social Change on the Upper Slave Coast*, 130.

80. Carstensen, 19.

81. Bradbury, 49.

82. Carstensen, 36.

83. Conversations with Professor Kwame Arhin in Accra and Kumasi, September and November 2004.

84. Interview 31.

85. Akyeampong, 221. See also the last chapter of his book.

86. Interview 9.

87. Conversation with Kafui Ofori, University of Ghana Language Center, June 2004.

88. Nirit Ben-Ari, "Liberating Girls From Trokosi," *African Recovery* (December 2001): 9.

89. Obenewa Amponsah, "The Trokosi: Religious Slavery in Ghana," http://www.anti-slavery.org/global/ghana/.

90. Ben-Ari, 9.

91. Regarding slavery and other forms of servitude in contemporary Africa, see also Derrick, 19–33; Mercer; Jok; Bales; and U.S. Congress.

Chapter 7

1. Meyer, 218.

2. Mazrui, *The Africans: A Triple Heritage.*

3. Mbiti, *African Religions and Philosophy,* 2; and Kofi Asare Opoku, "African Traditional Religion: An Enduring Heritage," in Olupona and Nyang, 67. The word "traditional" here and in the preceding works refers to religions indigenous to the continent as opposed to those that were promulgated by missionaries and others from outside the continent.

4. See also Blassingame; Walker.

5. Mbiti, *African Religions and Philosophy,* 3.

6. Nooter, 10; Nii Otokunor Quarcoopome, "Dangme Art and the Politics of Secrecy," in Nooter, 114.

7. Dzobo, 66.

8. Rivière, 15; Gaba, 47

9. Fiawoo, 88.

10. Gaba, 54

11. Mbiti,. Concepts of God in Africa, 12–18.

12. Gaba, 77.

13. Ibid., 337.

14. Opoku, 75.

15. Ibid.

16. I attended a number of funerals during my stay on the Ewe coast. The attendance of funerals was a community affair and in general a joyous occasion. Often there was a small booklet published for the occasion on the life of the deceased. Every significant detail would be mentioned, including a list of ancestors and surviving relatives. Often also in this biography were tributes from friends and relatives who asserted their belief that the deceased would now join the realm of the ancestors.

17. Fiawoo, 221

18. Greene, *Gender, Ethnicity, and Social Change on the Upper Slave Coast,* 112.

19. Greene, "The Anlo-Ewe: Their Economy, Society, and External Relations in the Eighteenth Century," 399n32.

20. Fiawoo, 222–23; Greene, "The Anlo Ewe: Their Economy, Society, and External Relations in the Eighteenth Century,: 278n5.

21. Interview 23.

22. J. Die Spieth, *Die Religion des Eweer,* 147, quoted in Debrunner, *A Church between Colonial Powers,* 62.

23. Fiawoo, 220–29.

24. Debrunner, *A Church between Colonial Powers,* 78.

25. Muller, *Geschichte der Ewe Mission,* 23, quoted in ibid.

26. Debrunner, *A Church between Colonial Powers,* 84.

27. Interview 11.

28. Torgby, i.

29. Ibid., 10.

30. Interview 9.

31. Interview 10; Fiawoo, 75.

32. Greene, *Gender, Ethnicity, and Social Change on the Upper Slave Coast,* 145; Torgby, iii.

33. Greene, *Gender, Ethnicity, and Social Change on the Upper Slave Coast,* 95.

34. Torgby, iv.

35. Fiawoo, 70; Interview 10.

36. Torgby, iv.

37. Interview 9.

38. Torgby, 3–7.

39. Interview 19.

40. Interview 11.

41. Interview 9.

42. Greene, *Gender, Ethnicity, and Social Change on the Upper Slave Coast*, 101.

43. Torgby, 1–2.

44. Greene, *Gender, Ethnicity, and Social Change on the Upper Slave Coast*, 154.

45. See chapter 6 for more regarding the social chaos that resulted from the trade.

46. Interview 9.

47. Torgby, 1.

48. See chapter 6 on the social and political effects of the slave trade; Greene, *Gender, Ethnicity, and Social Change on the Upper Slave Coast*, 112–13.

49. Interview 29.

50. Greene, *Gender, Ethnicity, and Social Change on the Upper Slave Coast*, 98.

51. Torgby, 3.

52. Interview 9.

53. Ibid. Kevigatowo—owners/carriers of bib baskets—are also more generally associated with fishermen.

54. Dzobo, vii–viii.

55. See Manning, 122–25; Nooter, 18–19. Also see Rodney, *How Europe Underdeveloped Africa*, 35–43 for a similar discussion of various principles or ideals that can be loosely associated with precolonial Africa. Also it should be noted that these were ideals as distinguished from practices.

56. Dzobo, 53–54.

57. Torgby, 2.

58. Debrunner, *A History of Christianity in Ghana*, 14.

59. Ibid., 48–49.

60. Ibid., 50.

61. Recently the pope and the Church of England have made formal apologies for their role in the trade, cited in an article in the *Daily Telegraph* (London), "Church Leaders: Let's Say Sorry for Our Evil History," March 16, 1997; see also Debrunner, *A History of Christianity in Ghana,* 152.

62. Greene, *Gender, Ethnicity, and Social Change on the Upper Slave Coast,* 114.

63. Ibid.

64. Interview 9.

65. Dzobo, 142, 144.

66. Manning, 33.

67. Dike, *The Aro of Southeastern Nigeria,* 131. See also Harris (1972), 90.

68. Dike, *The Aro of Southeastern Nigeria,* 130–33, 139; Dike, *Trade and Politics in the Niger Delta,* 39.

69. Dike, *Trade and Politics in the Niger Delta,* 40.

70. Debrunner, *A History of Christianity in Ghana,* 208.

71. Meyer, 32.

72. Ibid., 39.

73. Fred Agyemang, introduction.

74. Ibid., 72.

75. Debrunner, *A History of Christianity in Ghana,* 152–53.

76. Muller, 44–57.

77. Debrunner, *A Church between Colonial Powers,* 87.

78. Meyer, 8–11.

79. Debrunner, *A Church between Colonial Powers,* 85; *Montsblatt der Norddeutschen Mission gesellschaft* up to and after 1850.

80. Fred Agyemang, introduction.

81. Ibid.

82. Hayford, 74.

83. Achebe, *Hopes and Impediments.*

84. Nkrumah, *Africa Must Unite,* 22.

85. Ibid., 45.

86. Ibid., 29–30.

87. Lucy Mair (1934), in Nukunya, *Tradition and Change,* 126–27.

Chapter 8

1. Robinson, 203.

2. Hill. See also *Negro History Bulletin;* Robinson, 204.

3. Eric Williams, *From Columbus to Castro,* 332, 282–84.

4. Ibid.

5. Mary Frances Berry, as quoted in Dr. Conrad Worrill, "A Reparations Historical Overview," National Black Law Students Web site, http://nblsa.org/programs/reparations/2003-2004/worrill.html.

6. Martin Luther King Jr.

7. Robinson, 202.

8. Davies and Ogundipe-Leslie, 8.

9. James and van de Vijver, introduction and 43. See also TRC Web site: http://www.doj.gov.za/trc/index.html.

10. Rothberg, 11.

11. Tutu, 58–62.

12. West Africa, February 1991. See also Osabu-Kle, "The African Reparation Cry."

13. Chris McGreal, "Africans Back Down at UN Talks," *Guardian Unlimited,* September 9, 2001.

14. Matthew Tokson, *Dartmouth Review,* February 4, 2002.

15. CNN.COM http://www.cnn.com/2002/LAW/03/26/slavery.reparations/).

16. Lori Rotenberk, "Slavery Reparations Lawsuit Dismissed: Families Had Argued That Firms Benefited," *Globe,* January 27, 2004.

17. Barbara Blake Hannah, Jamaican Reparations Movement, Listserv correspondence, October 13, 2002.

18. Interview 27.

19. Schuck.

20. "Church Leaders: Let's Say Sorry for Our Evil History," *Daily Telegraph* (London), March 16, 1997.

21. Representatives of the African Union have reported that the union is independently considering a number of outreach proposals with respect to the African Diaspora (outside of the discussion and context of reparations). Preparatory meeting of Conference of African Intellectuals, Dakar, Senegal, May 3–5, 2004.

22. See Tutu; TRC Web site on black collaborators in the apartheid regime.

23. See Web site for more information: http://clk.about.com/?zi=1/XJ& sdn=racerelations&zu=http%3A%2F%2Fwww.usnationalslaverymuseum.org %2F.

24. See also Tatum.

Interviews

1. Togbui Awusa III, Atorkor, August 24, 1992
2. Kofi Geraldo, Keta, August 24, 1992
3. Mr.Charles Kwaku Adjololo, Keta, August 1992
4. James Ocloo I, Keta, September 26, 1993
5. Togbui Awusa III, Atorkor, September 27, 1993
6. Cornelius Kwaku Soglo, Srogbe, September 1993
7. Benedictus Tamakloe, Keta, September 29, 1993
8. Emmanuel Kpoxa, Accra, October 18, 1993
9. G. Kpodo, Woe, October 20, 1993
10. Srovi Kwame Doe, Anlo Ga, October 20, 1993
11. Mama Dzagba, Anlo Ga, October 23, 1993
12. Togbui Kposege III, Anyako, October 27, 1993
13. Srogbi Doe, Woe, October 28, 2003
14. Togbui Adeladza II, Anlo Ga, October 29, 1993
15. Emmanuel Sowornu, Anlo Ga, November 4, 1993
16. David Sowornu, Anlo Ga, November 4, 1993
17. Thomas Klu Agokli Kovia, Anlo Ga, November 5, 1993
18. Lucy Geraldo, Keta, October 1993
19. Johnson Kwadzo Kenneh, Legon, September 1993
20. Regent Joe Aidam, Anyako, October 1993
21. Koku Azamedzi, Anlo Ga, November 25, 1993
22. David Kofi Togobo, Adise Dobono, Moses Anyabo, Akrobotu Nunyano, Anyako, December 1993
23. Togbui Adeladza II, Anlo Ga, December 6, 1993
24. Dr. Robert Lee, Accra, February 5, 2003
25. Stephen Korsah, Cape Coast Castle, August 1, 2003
26. Dr. Esi Sutherland, Legon, August 8, 2003
27. James Ocloo II, Keta, August 14, 2003
28. Togbui Dosu Adaku VII, Atorkor, August 18, 2003

29. Herbert Atsu Afeku, Srogbe, November 8, 2003
30. Kwame Arhin, November 11, 2003
31. Nana Owusu Kwaa Dida, Kumasi, November 12, 2003
32. Al-Haaj Gonje, Yendi, November 14, 2003
33. Felicia Obuobie, Tamale, November 15, 2003
34. Hon. Seth Assah, Bono Manso, November 16, 2003
35. Kojo A. Jantuah, London, September 4, 2003
36. Mrs. Stella Jiagge, Accra, November 2003
37. Father Ramsay, Kingston, Jamaica, December 2001
38. Joyce Ramsay, St. Elizabeth, Jamaica, December 2001
39. Vernon Morgan, Middle Quarters, Jamaica, December 2001
40. Hazel McCloun, Kingston, Jamaica, December 2001
41. David Brown, Kingston, Jamaica, December 2001
42. David Stimpson, Kingston, Jamaica, December 24, 2001

Archival Sources

Ghana

Ghana National Archives, Accra

ADM 11/1/69
ADM 11
    1091
    1661
    1662
    1714
ADM 2/4
ADM 4/1/1: Ordinances relating to H.M. forts and settlements on the
    Gold Coast
Secretary for Native Affairs
    Shelf no. 7 11/1/1
Keta District
    No. 12 41/1/1–35
    41/2/1–12
Keta Native Affairs ADM 11/1113
    ADM 1/1/7

Anlo Traditional Council Archives, Anlo Ga

Anlo traditional and state minute books
Memorandum of the representatives of the fifteen clans, the customary

advisory Council of the Awomefia, submitted by the standing
committee for themselves and on behalf of the clans in Anlo traditional area to the chairman and members of the Agyeman Bada
Commission, August 24, 1978

England

Public Records Office (PRO), Kew Gardens

CO 96 Dispatches from the Gold Coast
CO 47 (no. 4883)
CO 21–40 (1850–56)
Havana mixed court commission records
FO 313/23–29, (1851–64): Correspondence
FO 67: Logbooks of captured slave ships

University College, London

Ogden Manuscript Collection
Letters about slavery and the slave trade, with particular reference
    to America. Sir Thomas Foxwell Buxton, 12 letters, 1827–44;
    Louis Alexis Chamerovzow, Secretary of British and Foreign
    Anti-Slavery Society, letters, 1855–66; Thomas Denman, 1st
    Baron Denman, letters, 1838–51, including several on the
    African Squadron
Four letters from the Young Men's Anti-Slavery Society

British Library Newspapers, London

Gold Coast Chronicles, vol. 4, no. 160–vol. 17, no. 334 (June 13, 1894–
    December 6, 1901)
Gold Coast Assize, nos. 2–5 (November 1883–February 1884)
Gold Coast Times (1874, 1875)
Gold Coast Independent, vol. 1, nos. 45, 46; vol. 2, no. 70–vol. 4, no. 1

United States

National Archives, Washington, D.C.

Letters received by the Secretary of the Navy from commanding
    officers of squadrons, African Squadron, 1843–61, polls 105–9,
    M89 (1851–59)
Rev. Charles Thomas's private papers

South Street Seaport Museum, New York City
    New York shipping and commercial lists, 1850–59
    U.S. naval records, 1850–59

Germany

Norddeustche Mission Archive, Bremen

    Review of monthly journals of the Bremen missionaries in Ghana,
        1840–70 *(Montsblatt der Norddeutschen Mission gesellschaft),* as
        well as their correspondence and photos from this period

Other Primary Sources

Aduamah, E. Y. *Ewe Traditions.* Legon: Institute of African Studies, Univer-
    sity of Ghana, n.d.
Albert, Octavia Rogers. *The House of Bondage, or, Charlotte Brooks and Other
    Slaves* (1890). New York: Oxford University Press, 1988.
Anderson, William J. *Life and Narrative of William J. Anderson: Twenty Four
    Years a Slave.* Chicago: Daily Tribune Book and Printing Office, 1857.
Barbot, Jean. *A Description of the Coasts of North and South Guinea.* London,
    1732.
Bosman, William. *A New and Accurate Description of the Guinea Coast.*
    Utrecht, 1705.
Bowdich, T. E. *Mission from Cape Coast Castle to Ashantee.* London, 1819.
Brinch, Boyerereau. *The Story of the Blind African Slave, or, Memoirs of Boy-
    rereau Brinch.* St. Albans, Vt: Harry Whitney, 1810.
Brown, Henry. *Narrative of Henry "Box" Brown Who Escaped from Slavery
    Enclosed in A Box 3 feet long and 2 wide; Written from a Statement of facts
    Made by Himself with remarks Upon the Remedy of Slavery.* In *African
    American Slave Narratives: An Anthology,* vol. 2., edited by Sterling
    Lecater Bland Jr. Westport, Conn.: Greenwood Press, 2001.
Canot, T. *The Adventures of an African Slaver on the Coast of Guinea* (1854).
    London: George Routledge, 1928.
Carstensen, Edward. *Govenor Carstensen's Diary, 1842–50.* Edited by Georg
    Norregard. Copenhagen: I. Kommission hos G.E.C. Gad, 1964.
Crow, Hugh. *Adventures of an African Slaver.* London: George Routledge &
    Sons Ltd., 1854.
———. *Memoirs of the Late Captain Hugh Crow of Liverpool.* London: Frank
    Cass, 1970.
Crowther, F. G. *The Crowther Report.* Secretary of Native Affairs, Gold Coast,
    1912.

Cruikshank, Brodie. *Eighteen Years on the Gold Coast of Africa.* Vol. 1. London: Frank Cass, 1966.

Dubois, Sylvia. *A Biography of Sylvia Dubois, the Slave Who Whipt her mistress and Ganed Her Fredom* (1883). Edited by C. W. Larison and Jared C. Lobdell. New York: Oxford University Press, 1988.

"Dutch Slave Dealing in Africa" (*Pall Mall Gazette,* December 22, 1868). In Douglas Coombs, *The Gold Coast, Britain, and the Netherlands, 1850–1874.* London: Oxford University Press, 1963.

Equiano, Olaudah. *Equiano's Travels: The Interesting Narrative of the Life of Olaudah Equiano or Gustavus Vassa the African* (1789). Abridged and edited by Paul Edwards. London: Heinemann, 1967.

Falconbridge, Alexander. *An Account of the Slave Trade on the Coast of Africa* (1788). New York, 1973.

Horton, Africanus B. *Letters on the Political Condition of the Gold Coast.* London: Frank Cass, 1870.

Hunter, John. *Observations on the Diseases of the Army in Jamaica and on the Best Means of Preserving Health of Europeans in That Climate.* London, 1788.

Isert, Paul. *Letters on West Africa and the Slave Trade* (1788). Translated and edited by Selena Axelrod Winsnes. New York: Oxford University Press, 1992.

Kemp, Dennis. *Nine Years on the Gold Coast.* London: Macmillan, 1898.

Marees, Pieter de. *Description and Account of the Gold Kingdom of Guinea* (1602). New York: Oxford University Press, 1987.

Muller, G. *Geschichte der Ewe Mission.* Bremen: Norddeutsche Missionsgesellschaft, 1904.

Newton, John. *Thoughts upon the African Slave Trade.* London, 1788.

Oswald, C. *Fifty Years' Mission Work at Keta.* Bremen: North German Mission Society, 1903.

Prince, Mary. *The History of Mary Prince, a West Indian Slave. Related by Herself.* London: F Wesley and A. H. Davis, 1831.

Reindorf, Carl. *History of the Gold Coast and the Asante.* Basel, 1895.

Rutgers Oral History Archives of World War II. http://fas-history.rutgers.edu/oralhistory/home.html.

Snelgrave, William. *A New Account of Some Parts of Guinea and the Slave Trade* (1734). London: F. Cass, 1971.

South African Truth and Reconciliation Web site. http://www.doj.gov.za/trc/index.html.

Survivors of the Shoah Visual History Foundation. www.shoahfoundation.org.

Thomas, Chas. *Adventures and Observations on the West Coast of Africa and Its Islands* (1860). New York: Negroes University Press, 1969.

Weskett, John. *A Complete Digest of the Law, Theory and Practice of Insurance.* London: Frys Couchment Collier, 1781.

Williams, Gomer. *History of the Liverpool Privateers and Letters of Marque, with an Account of the Liverpool Slave Trade.* London, 1897.

Secondary Sources

Books and Articles

Achebe, Chinua. *Hopes and Impediments.* New York: Doubleday, 1989.

———. *Things Fall Apart.* New York: Astor-Honor, 1959.

Agyeman, Fred. *We Presbyterians: Sixteenth Anniversary of the Presbyterian Church of Ghana.* 2nd ed. Accra: Waterville.

Agyeman, Opoku. *Nkrumah's Ghana and East Africa: Pan-Africanism and African Interstate Relations.* London: Associated University Presses, 1992.

Aimes, Hubert S. *A History of the Slave Trade in Cuba: 1511–1868.* New York: G. P. Putnam's Sons, 1907.

Ajayi, J. F., and Michael Crowder. *History of West Africa.* 2 vols. 3rd ed. London: Longman, 1985.

Akyeampong, Emmanuel. *Between the Sea and the Lagoon: An Eco-Social History of Southeastern Ghana, c 1850 to Present.* Athens: Ohio University Press / Oxford: James Currey, 2001.

Alter, Robert. *The Art of Biblical Narrative.* New York: Basic Books, 1981.

Aluwahlia, Pal. "Towards (Re)Conciliation: The Postcolonial Economy of Giving." In *Relocating Postcolonialism,* edited by Ato Quayson and David Goldberg. London: Blackwell, 2002.

Amenumey, D. E. K. *The Ewe in Pre-Colonial Times: A Political History with Special Emphasis on the Anlo, Ge, and Krepi.* Accra: Sedco, 1986.

———. *The Ewe Unification Movement.* Accra: Waterville, 1984.

———. "Geraldo de Lima: A Reappraisal." *Transactions of the Historical Society of Ghana* 9 (1968).

———. *Hogbeza.* Booklet published for annual Ewe festival called Hogbetstosto.

Amponsah, Obenewa. "The Trokosi: Religious Slavery in Ghana." http://www.anti-slavery.org/global/ghana/.

Anquandah, Kwesi J. *Castles and Forts of Ghana.* Accra: Ghana Museums Board / Paris: Atalante, 1999.

Anstey, Roger. *The Atlantic Slave Trade and British Abolition, 1760–1810.* Atlantic Highlands, N.J.: Humanities Press, 1975.

Anstey, Roger, and Peter Hair, eds. *Liverpool, the African Slave Trade, and the Abolition.* Bristol: Historic Society of Lancashire and Cheshire, 1976.

Arhin, Kwame. *West African Traders in the Nineteenth and Twentieth Centuries.* London: Longmans, Green, 1957.

Armah. Ayi, Kwei. *Fragments.* Boston: Houghton Mifflin, 1970.

————. *The Healers.* Nairobi: East African, 1978.

————. *Two Thousand Seasons.* Nairobi: East African, 1973.

Awoonor, Kofi. *The Breast of the Earth: A Survey of the History, Culture, and Literature of Africa South of the Sahara.* Garden City, N.J.: Anchor Press / Doubleday, 1976.

————. *Guardians of the Sacred Word: Ewe Poetry.* New York: Nok, 1974.

Bales, Kevin. *New Slavery.* Santa Barbara, Calif.: ABC-CLIO, 2000.

Barry, Boubacar. *Senegambia and the Atlantic Slave Trade.* New York: Cambridge University Press, 1998.

Behrendt, Stephen. "The Captains in the British Slave Trade from 1785–1807." *Transactions of the Historic Society for Lancashire and Cheshire* 140 (1991): 79–140.

Berry, Mary Frances. *Black Resistance, White Law: A History of Constitutional Racism in America.* New York: Penguin, 1994.

Blassingame, John. *The Slave Community.* London: Oxford University Press, 1972.

Bradbury, Ray. *Benin Studies.* London: Oxford University Press, 1973.

Braithwaite, Kamau. *The Development of Creole Society in Jamaica, 1770–1820.* Oxford: Clarendon Press, 1971.

Brazil House Rehabilitation Project: Proposal for the Tabon Official Hall and Documentation Centre. Accra: UNESCO, 2003.

Breed, Allen G. "Slave Quarter Accommodations: Prettying Up and Ugly Past." *Atlanta Voice,* April 6–12, 2002.

Brooks, George. *Landlords and Strangers: Ecology, Society, and Trade in West Africa, 1000–1630.* Boulder, Colo.: Westview Press, 1993.

————. *Yankee Traders, Old Coasters, and African Middlemen.* Boston: Boston University Press, 1970.

Burns, Chandler R. M. "Denial Takes Many Forms." Resources for Children of Holocaust Survivors Web site. http://www.judymeschel.com/coshby2s.htm.

Cardinall, A. W. *Tales Told in Togoland, to which is added the mythical and traditional history of the Dagomba by E. F. Tamakloe.* Oxford: Oxford University Press, 1931.

Chernoff, John. *African Rhythm and Sensibility.* Chicago: University of Chicago Press, 1979.

Christopher, Ed Kritzler. "Adventure Jamaica, Beyond the Resort." *Air Jamaica Skywritings* (December 2001).

Claridge, W. Walton. *A History of the Gold Coast and Ashanti.* 2 vols. London: Frank Cass, 1915.

Clarke, John Henrik. *Critical Lessons in Slavery and the Slave Trade.* Richmond: Native Son, 1996.

Cliff, Michelle. *No Telephone to Heaven.* New York: Dutton, 1987.

Cudjoe, S. D. "The Techniques of Ewe Drumming and the Social Importance of Drumming." *Phylon* 14, no. 3 (1953): 80–291.

Curtin, P. D. *The Atlantic Slave Trade: A Census.* Madison: University of Wisconsin Press, 1969.

———. *Economic Change in Precolonial Africa: Senegambia in the Era of the Slave Trade.* Madison: University of Wisconsin Press, 1975.

Daaku, Kwame. "The European Traders and the Coastal States, 1630–1720." *Transactions of the Historical Society of Ghana* 8 (1965).

———. *Trade and Politics on the Gold Coast, 1600–1720.* Oxford: Clarendon Press, 1970.

Danticat, Edwige. *Krik? Krak!* New York: Soho, 1995.

Davidson, Basil. *Black Mother: The Years of the African Slave Trade.* Boston: Atlantic-Little Brown, 1961.

Davies, Carole Boyce, and Molara Ogundipe-Leslie, eds. *Moving beyond Boundaries.* Vol. 1. New York: New York University Press, 1995.

Davies, K. G. *The Royal African Company.* Bristol: Lowe and Brydone, 1957.

Davis, Brion David. *The Problem of Slavery in Western Culture.* Ithaca, N.Y.: Cornell University Press, 1966.

Debrunner, Hans. *A Church between Colonial Powers.* London: Billings and Sons, 1965.

———. *A History of Christianity in Ghana.* Accra: Waterville, 1967.

Der, Benedict. *The Slave Trade in Northern Ghana.* Accra: Woeli, 1998.

Derrick, Jonathan. *Slavery in Africa Today.* London: George Allen and Unwin, 1975.

Dike, K. O., and Felicia Ekejiuba. *The Aro of Southeastern Nigeria, 1650–1980: A Study in Socio-Economic Formation and Transformation in Nigeria.* Ibadan: University Press, 1990.

———. *Trade and Politics in the Niger Delta, 1830–1885.* Oxford: Clarendon Press, 1959.

Donnan, Elizabeth. *Documents Illustrative of the History of the Slave Trade to America.* 4 vols. Washington, D.C.: Carnegie Institution, 1930–35.

Dow, George. *Slave Ships and Slaving.* Port Washington, N.Y.: Kennikat, 1969.

DuBois, W. E. B. *The Suppression of the African Slave Trade, 1638–1870.* Baton Rouge: Louisiana State University Press, 1969.

Dzagbe, Cudjoe. "The Du-Legba Cult among the Ewe of Ghana." *Basseler-Archiv* 19, no. 2 (1971).

Dzobo, N. K. *The Moral Guide of Ewe Proverbs: Guide to Conduct.* Vol. 2. Accra: Bureau of Ghana Languages, 1975.

Egblewogbe, E. Y. *Games and Songs as Education Media (A Case among the Ewes of Ghana).* N.p.: Ghana Publishing.

————. *Personal Names as a Parameter for the Study of Culture: The Case of the Ghanaian Ewe.* Accra: Tema, 1975.

Eisner, Jack. *The Survivor.* New York: William and Morrow, 1980.

Elia, Nada. *Trances, Dances, and Vociferations: Agency and Resistance in Africana's Women's Narratives.* New York: Garland, 2001.

Eltis, David. *Economic Growth and the Ending of the Atlantic Slave Trade.* New York: Oxford University Press, 1987.

Eltis, David, Stephen D. Behrendt, David Richardson, and Martin Klein, eds. *The Transatlantic Slave Trade, 1500–1867.* Cambridge: Cambridge University Press, 2000.

Eltis, David, and James Walvin, eds. *The Abolition of the Atlantic Slave Trade.* Madison: University of Wisconsin Press, 1981.

Engerman, Stanley, and Joseph Inikori. *The Atlantic Slave Trade: Effects on Economies, Societies, and Peoples in Africa, the Americas, and Europe.* Durham, N.C.: Duke University Press, 1992.

Fage, J. D. *A History of West Africa.* Cambridge: Cambridge University Press, 1972.

————. "A New Check List of the Forts and Castles of Ghana." In *Transactions of the Gold Coast and Togoland Historical Society.* Legon: Ghana Universities Press, 1959.

Foucault, Michel. *The Archeology of Knowledge.* Translated by A. M Sheridan Smith. New York: Harper and Row, 1972.

————. *Madness and Civilisation: A History of Insanity in the Age of Reason.* Translated by Richard Howard. New York: Random House, 1973.

Gemery, H. A., and J. S. Hogendorn, eds. *The Uncommon Market: Essays in the Economic History of the Atlantic Slave Trade.* New York: Academic Press, 1979.

Genovese, Eugene. *From Rebellion to Revolution: Afro-American Slave Revolts in the Making of the Modern World.* New York: Vintage, 1981.

Geurts, Kathryn Linn. *Culture and the Senses: Bodily Ways of Knowing in an African Community.* Berkeley: University of California Press, 2002.

Gilbert, Michelle. "Mystical Protection among the Ewe." *African Arts* 5, no. 4 (1982).

Gomez, Michael. *Exchanging Our Country Marks: The Transformation of African Identities in the Colonial and Antebellum South.* Chapel Hill: University of North Carolina Press, 1998.

Goss, Linda, and Marian E. Barnes, eds. *Talk That Talk: An Anthology of African American Storytelling.* New York: Simon and Schuster, 1989.

Greene, Sandra. *Gender, Ethnicity, and Social Change on the Upper Slave Coast: A History of the Anlo Ewe.* Portsmouth, N.H: Heinemann, 1996.

―――. "The Past and Present of an Anlo-Ewe Oral Tradition." *History in Africa* 12 (1985): 73–87.

―――. *Sacred Sites and the Colonial Encounter: A History of Meaning and Memory.* Bloomington: Indiana University Press, 2002.

Green-Pederson, Svend. "The Scope and Structure of the Danish Negro Slave Trade." *Scandinavian Economic History Review* 19, no. 2 (1971): 149–97.

Gutman, Herbert. *The Black Family in Slavery and in Freedom, 1750–1925.* New York: Pantheon, 1976.

Haas, Aaron. *The Aftermath.* New York: Cambridge University Press, 1995.

Halbwachs, Maurice. *Les cadres sociaux de la mémoire.* New York: Arno, 1975.

―――. *The Collective Memory.* Translated by Francis J. Ditter and Vida Yazdi Ditter. New York: Harper and Row, 1980.

―――. *La topographie legendaire des evangiles en Terre Sainte.* Edited by Fernand Dumont. 1941. Reprint, Paris: Presses Universitaires de France, 1971.

Harms, Robert. *River of Wealth, River of Sorrow: The Central Zaire Basin in the Era of the Slave Trade and the Ivory Trade, 1500–1891.* New Haven: Yale University Press, 1981.

Harris, Joseph. *Africans and Their History.* New York: New American Library, Penguin Books, 1972, 1987.

Hart, Richard. *Slaves Who Abolished Slavery.* Vols. 1–2. University of West Indies, Institute of Social and Economic Research, 1985.

Hayford, Casely. *Ethiopia Unbound.* London: C. M. Phillips, 1911.

Henige, David. *The Chronology of Oral Tradition: Quest for a Chimera.* Oxford: Clarendon Press, 1974.

―――. *Oral Historiography.* London: Longman, 1982.

Hernaes, Per. *Slaves, Danes, and African Coast Society: The Danish Slave Trade from West Africa and Afro-Danish Relations on the Eighteenth Century Gold Coast.* Trondheim: Department of History, University of Trondheim, 1995.

Hesse, Barnor. "Forgotten Like a Bad Dream." In *Relocating Postcolonialism,* edited by Ato Quayson and David Goldberg. London: Blackwell, 2002.

Higginbotham, A. Leon. *In the Matter of Color.* New York: Oxford University Press, 1978.

Hill, Walter B. Jr. "The Ex-Slave Pension Movement: Some Historical and Genealogical Notes." *Negro History Bulletin* 59, no. 4 (1996). Special issue on black genealogy; also available at http://www.afrigeneas.com/library/hillarticles.html.

Hobsbawm, Eric, and Terence Ranger, eds. *The Invention of Tradition.* Cambridge: Cambridge University Press, 1983.

Hopkins, A. G. *An Economic History of Africa.* New York: Columbia University Press, 1973.

Hoyt, Edwin. *African Slavery.* London: Abelard-Schuman, 1974.

Ijere, M. O. "Economic Value of Shrines." *Nigerian Outlook,* October 13, 1964.

Hutton, Patrick. *History as an Art of Memory.* Hanover, N.H.: University Press of New England, 1993.

Inikori, Joseph. *The Chaining of a Continent: Export Demand for Captives and the History of Africa South of the Sahara, 1450–1870.* Mona, Jamaica: Institute of Social and Economic Research, 1992.

———. *Forced Migration: The Impact of the Export Slave Trade on African Societies.* London: Hutchinson University Library, 1982.

———. "The Impact of Firearms in West Africa, 1750–1807: A Quantitative Analysis." *Journal of African History* 18 (1977): 339–68.

Isichei, Elizabeth. *Voices of the Poor in Africa.* Rochester, N.Y.: University of Rochester Press, 2002.

Jalloh, Alusine, and Stephen E. Maizlish, eds. *The African Diaspora.* Arlington: Texas A & M University Press, 1996.

James, C. L. R. *A History of Negro Revolt.* New York: Haskell House, 1938.

———. *Nkrumah and the Ghana Revolution.* London: Allison and Busby, 1977.

James, Wilmot, and Linda van de Vijver, eds. *After the TRC: Reflections on Truth and Reconciliation in South Africa.* Athens: Ohio University Press, 2001.

Johnson, Marion. "Ashanti East of the Volta." *Transactions of the Historical Society of Ghana* (1969).

Jok, Jok Madut. *War and Slavery in Sudan.* Philadelphia: University of Pennsylvania Press, 2001.

Kea, R. A. *Settlement, Trade, and Politics in Seventeenth Century Gold Coast.* Baltimore, Md.: Johns Hopkins University Press, 1982.

Kincaid, Jamaica. *A Small Place.* New York: Farrar, Straus and Giroux, 2000.

King, Christine Farris. *My Brother Martin: A Sister Remembers.* New York: Simon and Schuster, 2003.

King, Martin Luther Jr. *Why We Can't Wait.* New York: Harper and Row, 1964.

Klein, Herbert S. *The Middle Passage: Comparative Studies in the Atlantic Slave Trade.* Princeton, N.J.: Princeton University Press, 1978.

Klein, Martin. *Breaking the Chains.* Madison: University of Wisconsin Press, 1993.

Knight, Franklin. *Slave Society in Cuba during the Nineteenth Century.* Madison: University of Wisconsin Press, 1970.

Kopytoff, Igor, ed. *The African Frontier: The Reproduction of Traditional African Societies*. Bloomington: Indiana University Press, 1987.

Ladzekpo, Kobla S. "The Social Mechanics of Good Music: A Description of Dance Clubs among the Anlo Ewe Speaking People of Ghana." *African Music Society Journal* (Roodepoort, Transvaal) 5, no. 1 (1971): 6–22.

Law, Robin. *From Slave Trade to "Legitimate Commerce": The Commercial Transition in Nineteenth Century West Africa*. New York: Cambridge University Press, 1995.

———. *The Slave Coast of West Africa, 1550–1750: The Impact of the Atlantic Slave Trade on an African Society*. Oxford: Clarendon Press, 1991.

Little, Kenneth. *West African Urbanization: A Study of Voluntary Associations in Social Change*. London: Cambridge University Press.

Lloyd, Christopher. *The Navy and the Slave Trade: The Suppression of the African Slave Trade in the Nineteenth Century*. London: Cass, 1968.

Lovejoy, Paul. *The Ideology of Slavery in Africa*. Beverly Hills, Calif.: Sage, 1981.

———. "The Impact of the Atlantic Slave Trade on Africa: A Review of the Literature." *Journal of African History* 30 (1989): 365–94.

———. *Transformations in Slavery: A History of Slavery in Africa*. Cambridge: Cambridge University Press, 1983.

Mammattah, Charles M. K. *The Eves of West Africa: Oral Traditions*. Vol. 1. Accra: Advent Press, 1976.

Manning, Patrick. *Slavery and African Life: Occidental, Oriental and African Slave Trades*. Cambridge: Cambridge University Press, 1990.

Mannix, Daniel P., and Malcolm Cowley. *Black Cargoes: A History of the Atlantic Slave Trade, 1518–1865*. New York: Viking, 1962.

Manoukian, Madeline. *The Ewe Speaking People of Togoland and the Gold Coast*. London: International African Institute, 1952.

Mbiti, John. *African Religions and Philosophy*. London: Heinemann Educational, 1969.

———. *Concepts of God in Africa*. New York: Praeger, 1970.

McGowan, Winston. "African Resistance to the Atlantic Slave Trade in West Africa." *Slavery and Abolition* 11 (1990): 5–29.

Meillassoux, Claude. "The Slave Route Project." UNESCO slave route Web site.

Mercer, John. *Slavery in Mauritania Today*. Dorset, England: Human Rights Group Remous, 1982.

Meriweather, Louise. *Fragments of the Ark*. New York: Pocket Books, 1994.

Meyer, Brigit. *Translating the Devil: Religion and Modernity among the Ewe in Ghana*. Edinburgh: Edinburgh University Press, 1999.

Miers, Suzanne, and Igor Kopytoff. *Slavery in Africa: Historical and Anthropological Perspectives*. Madison: University of Wisconsin Press, 1977.

Miers, Suzanne, and Richard Roberts. *The End of Slavery in Africa.* Madison: University of Wisconsin Press, 1988.

Miller, Joseph, ed. *The African Past Speaks: Essays on Oral Tradition and History.* Folkestone, England: Dawson, 1980.

———. *Way of Death: Merchant Capitalism and the Angolan Slave Trade.* Madison: University of Wisconsin Press, 1988.

Morrison, Toni. *Beloved.* New York: Knopf, 1987.

Negro History Bulletin 59, no. 4 (1996). Special issue on black genealogy.

Nketia, Kwabena J. H. *Drumming in Akan Communities of Ghana.* Edinburgh: T. Nelson, 1963.

Nkrumah, Kwame. *Africa Must Unite.* London: Heinemann Educational, 1963.

———. *I Speak of Freedom.* London: Panaf, 1961.

Nooter, Mary, ed. *Secrecy: African Art That Conceals and Reveals.* New York: Museum of African Art, 1993.

Nora, Pierre. *Rethinking France: Les lieux de mémoire.* Translated by Mary Trouille. Chicago: Chicago University Press, 2001.

Norregard, Georg. *Danish Settlements in West Africa, 1685–1850.* Translated by S. Mamen. Boston: Boston University Press, 1966.

Nukunya, G. K. *Kinship and Marriage among the Anlo Ewe.* London: Athlone, 1969.

———. *Tradition and Change.* Accra: Ghana University Press, 1992.

O'Connor, Lynn, and Jack Berry. "The Guilt/Shame Debate Goes On: The Case of Harold Menu." *Behavior Online,* October 3, 1996. http://www.behavior.net/forums/archives/clinicalcase/1998/harold/2_5-10.htm

Oldfield, J. R. Transatlanticism, Slavery, and Race." *American Literary History* 14, no 1 (2002): 131–40.

Olupona, Jacob K., and Sulayman S. Nyang, eds. *Religious Plurality in Africa: Essays in Honour of John S. Mbiti.* Berlin: Mouton de Gruyter, 1993.

Ong, Walter J. *Orality and Literacy: The Technologizing of the Word.* London: Methuen, 1982.

Osabu-Kle, Daniel T. "The African Reparation Cry: Rationale, Estimate, Prospects, and Strategies." *Journal of Black Studies* 30 (January 2000).

Osei Tutu, Brempong. *Transactions of the Historical Society of Ghana,* no. 5 (2004).

Owusu-Ansah, Anthony. "Trokosi in Ghana: Cultural Relativism or Slavery." *African Symposium* 3, no. 4 (December 2003).

Padmore, George. *The International Public Opinion.* 1901–59.

Pemberton, John III, and Funso S. Afolayan. *Yoruba Sacred Kingship.* Washington, D.C.: Smithsonian Institute Press, 1996.

Portelli, Alessandro. *The Death of Luigi Trastuli and Other Stories: Form and*

Meaning in Oral History. Albany: State University of New York Press, 1991.

Quayson, Ato. *Strategic Transformations in Nigerian Writing: Oral History in the Work of Samuel Johnson, Wole Soyinke, and Ben Okri.* Oxford: James Currey, 1997.

Rathbone, Richard. "Some Thoughts on Resistance to Enslavement in West Africa." *Slavery and Abolition* 6, no. 3 (1985): 11–22.

Reynolds, Edward. *Stand the Storm: A History of the Atlantic Slave Trade.* London: Allison and Busby, 1985.

———. *Trade and Economic Change on the Gold Coast, 1807–1874.* London: Longman, 1974.

Rivière, Claude. *Union et procreation en Afrique: Rites de la vie chez les Eve de Togo.* Paris: L'armattan, 1990.

Robertson, Claire C., and Martin Klein, eds. *Women in Slavery in Africa.* Madison: University of Wisconsin Press, 1983.

Robertson, Randall. *The Debt: What America Owes Blacks.* New York: E. P. Dutton, 2000.

Rodney, Walter. *A History of the Upper Guinea Coast, 1545–1800.* London: Oxford University Press, 1970.

———. *How Europe Underdeveloped Africa.* London, 1972.

Rohrbach, Augusta. *Truth Stranger than Fiction: Race, Realism, and the U.S. Literary Marketplace.* New York: Palgrave Macmillan, 2002.

Rothberg, Robert J., ed. *Truth vs Justice: The Morality of Truth Commissions.* Princeton, N.J.: Princeton University Press, 2000.

Ryder, A. F. C. *Benin and the Europeans, 1485–1897.* New York: Humanities Press, 1969.

Schuck, Peter H. "Slavery and Reparations: A Misguided Movement." *Jurist,* December 9, 2002.

Schwartz, Marie Jenkins. *Born in Bondage: Growing Up Enslaved in the Antebellum South.* Cambridge: Harvard University Press, 2000.

Shaw, Rosalind. *Memories of the Slave Trade: Ritual and the Historical Imagination in Sierra Leone.* Chicago: University of Chicago Press, 2002.

Shillington, Kevin. *Ghana and the Rawlings Factor.* New York: St. Martin's, 1992.

Slavery: An Introduction to the African Holocaust. Liverpool: Grosvenor Printers Bootle, 1995.

Smith, Edwin. *African Ideas of God.* London: Edinburgh House, 1950.

Smith, M. G. *Caribbean Studies: A Symposium.* Seattle, 1960.

Spiegl, Fritz. *Slavers and Privateers.* Liverpool Packet, no. 5. Liverpool: Scouse Press.

Stammers, M. K. "Guineamen: Some Technical Aspects of Slave Ships." In

Transatlantic Slavery: Against Human Dignity, text for exhibition, Mersey-side, Maritime Museum, Albert Dock, Liverpool, England.

Tatum, Beverly Daniel. *Why Are All the Black Kids Sitting Together in the Cafeteria and Other Conversations about Race.* New York: Basic Books, 2003.

Thornton, John. *Africa and Africans in the Making of the Atlantic World, 1400–1680.* Cambridge: Cambridge University Press. 1992.

Tomson, Alistair, and Robert Perks. *Oral History Reader.* London: Routledge, 1998.

Trouillot, Michel-Rolph. *Silencing the Past: Power and the Production of History.* Boston: Beacon, 1995.

Tutu, Desmond. *No Future without Forgiveness.* New York: Doubleday, 1999.

U.S. Congress. Senate. Committee on Foreign Relations. *Slavery throughout the World: Hearing before the Committee on Foreign Relations.* 106th Cong., 2nd sess., September 28, 2001.

Van Dantzig, Albert. *Forts and Castles of Ghana.* Oxford: African Books Collective, 1999.

Vansina, Jan. *Oral Tradition as History.* London: James Currey, 1985.

Walker, Sheila, ed. *African Roots/American Cultures: Africa in the Creation of the Americas.* Lanham, Md.: Rowman and Littlefield, 2001.

Walvin, James. *Black Ivory: A History of British Slavery.* Washington, D.C.: Howard University Press, 1994.

Ward, W. E. F. *A History of Ghana.* London: Allen and Unwin, 1967.

———. *The Asante in the Nineteenth Century.* London: Cambridge University Press, 1975.

———. "Asante Policy towards Hausa Trade in the Nineteenth Century." In *Development of Indigenous Trade,* edited by Claude Meillassoux, 124–33. London: Oxford University Press, 1971.

Williams, Eric. *Capitalism and Slavery.* New York: Capricorn, 1966.

———. *From Columbus to Castro: The History of the Caribbean, 1492–1969.* London: Deutsch, 1970.

Worrill, Conrad. "A Reparations Historical Overview." National Black Law Students Web site, http://nblsa.org/programs/reparations/2003-2004/worrill.html.

Wright, Marcia. *Strategies of Slaves and Women: Life Stories from East/Central Africa.* New York: Lilian Barber, 1993.

Dissertations, Master's Theses, Unpublished Papers

Aligwekwe, I. E. "The Ewe and Togoland Problem: A Case Study in the Paradoxes and Problems of Political Transition in West Africa." Ph.D. diss., Ohio State University, 1960.

Amenumey, D. E. K. "The Ewe People and the Coming of European Rule, 1850–1914." Master's thesis, University of London, 1964.

———. "A Political History of the Ewe Unification Problem." Ph.D. diss., University of Manchester, 1972.

Anyidoho, Kofi. "Oral Poetics and Traditions of Verbal Art in Africa." Ph.D. diss., University of Texas, Austin, 1983.

Dillard, Mary. "The Legacy of the Transatlantic Slave Trade in Contemporary Ghana." Paper presented at the Institute of African Studies, Legon, Ghana, 1992.

Fiagbedzi, Nissio. "The Music of the Anlo: Its Historical Background, Cultural Matrix, and Style." Ph.D. diss., University of California, Los Angeles, 1977.

Fiawoo, D. K. "The Influence of Contemporary Social Changes on the Magico-Religious Concepts of Organization of the Southern Ewe Speaking People of Ghana." Ph.D. diss., Edinburgh University, 1959.

Gaba, Christian Robert. "Anlo Traditional Religion: A Study of the Anlo Traditional Believer's Conception of and Communion with the "Holy." Ph.D. diss., University of London, 1965.

Greene, Sandra. "The Anlo Ewe: Their Economy, Society, and External Relations in the Eighteenth Century." Ph.D. diss., Northwestern University, 1981.

Guerts, Kathryn. " 'I Shall Sleep in the Desert Land': An Analysis of Narrative Aspects of Ewe Song Texts at Funeral Celebrations." February 3, 1992. University of Pennsylvania.

Larson, Pier. "A History of Silence: Memory and Identity and Enslavement in Central Madagascar." Paper presented at the conference, "The Atlantic Slave Trade and African and African American Memory," University of Chicago, 1997.

LaTorre, Joseph. "Wealth Surpasses Everything: An Economic History of the Asante." Ph.D. diss., University of California, Berkeley, 1978.

Patten, Sonia Gustavson. "The Avuncular Family, Gender, Asymmetry, and Patriline: The Anlo Ewe of Southeastern Ghana." Ph.D. diss., University of Minnesota, 1990.

Perbi, Akosua. "Servitude and Chieftaincy in Ghana: The Historical Evidence." Paper presented at the International Conference on Chieftaincy in Africa: Culture, Governance and Development, Accra, University of Ghana, January 6–10, 2003.

Torgby, Richard Tetteh. "A Study of the Yewe Secret Society among the Ewe-Speaking People of Southern Ghana." Bachelor's essay, University of Ghana, 1977.

Turner, Jerry Michael. "Les Bresiliens: The Impact of Former Brazilian Slaves upon Dahomey." Ph.D. diss., Boston University, 1975.

Wilks, Ivor. "Akwamu, 1650–1750." Master's thesis, Cardiff University, 1958.

Yegbe, Joseph. "The Anlo and Their Neighbors, 1850–90." Ph.D. diss., University of Ghana, 1966.